Your Kingdom Come

1st printing December 1980
2nd printing September 1981

Your Kingdom Come

Mission Perspectives

Report on the World Conference
on Mission and Evangelism

Melbourne, Australia
12-25 May 1980

Commission on World Mission and Evangelism
World Council of Churches, Geneva

© 1980 World Council of Churches, 150, route de Ferney, 1211 Geneva 20, Switzerland.

ISBN: 2-8254-0663-5

Cover design: Paul May. Photo used: "Thy Kingdom Come", a woodcarving by Martin Loh Nyonka, presented to CWME by the Presbyterian Church in Cameroon.

Printed in Switzerland

Table of Contents

SECTION PLENARY PRESENTATIONS

Section III

Section IV

FOREWORD

Melbourne: Mission in the Eighties

Melbourne was a christological conference. The preparatory process, the introductory speeches, the worship life, the Bible studies and the report testify to the fact that whatever we say and do in mission is rooted in God's final revelation in Jesus Christ. To speak of God's reign is to speak of Jesus; to preach Christ is to proclaim the kingdom of God.

This does not mean that one can find in the Melbourne documents fully developed, systematic, christological doctrinal statements—and the conference has been strongly criticized for that. The reason lies in the fact that while the Christians present at Melbourne would not deny the full message given to us through the Bible and the churches' traditions on Christ, they implicitly or explicitly felt that one specific point of the christological tradition was to be highlighted in the moment of history in which they met. And that point is not the salvific atonement on the cross, nor the affirmation that in Christ all was created and will be summed up, nor reiteration of our hope in his second coming. These elements, and others, of our faith, are not dismissed (cf. II/5, III/4, 29, IV/3, 19, last phrase).* Rather Melbourne's reflection centred around a specific missionary aspect of Christology stressed in the presentation by Ernst Käsemann: the identity of the resurrected or elevated kyrios, Christ, the Lord, with the earthly Jesus, the Jew, the Nazarene, who lived as a simple Galilean man, suffered and was executed, dying on the cross.

The Melbourne Conference was a methodological conference at which an attempt was made to draw the implications of what it means to be sent in mission by the resurrected and ascended Lord as disciples of the crucified Jesus, having received the power of the Holy Spirit. This is certainly a most central element of the earliest confessions of faith of the Church and of the self-understanding of the first disciples and apostles. For a reflection on mission in the eighties, it seemed the most appropriate emphasis for a world conference. It can be criticized as partial; it is, however, clearly justifiable.

---

* Roman numerals refer to the Section Report and Arabic numerals indicate the paragraph.

Melbourne was an ecclesiological conference, not in the sense that it produced important statements on ecclesiology, but in the sense that, while recognizing the theological impossibility of limiting God's reigning activity to the churches' boundaries, the conference nevertheless affirmed that one must not separate God's kingdom from the central and specific role and being of the Church. This is a clear consequence of the choice mentioned above. If one cannot seriously speak of the kingdom of God without reference to the historical, crucified Jesus of Nazareth, then today those who clearly name the Name of Jesus and live in a community centred around his table, in historical continuity with him, have a central role to play, whether they are good or bad people. To refer to the Melbourne Conference without emphasizing the passages referring to the specific evangelistic task of the Church in word and deed (I/16, II/5, III/4-10, IV/19) and the missionary importance of the Eucharist (III/28-31, IV/27) is to miss its essential point. This should be borne in mind when reading the rest of this introduction.

Jesus of Nazareth, whom we believe to be the centre of God's kingdom and his Son, died outside the city gate (message, IV/20), at the "periphery". This striking picture proposed by Kosuke Koyama, is a real missionary interpretation of Jesus' life and action. Jesus is *par excellence* the one who breaks through walls built by humankind to limit God's sovereignty, grace, love and healing power. He incarnates what Paul calls "justification by grace" as opposed to "justification by law" through his being born, living and dying outside the places where righteous people normally are born and live and die. The only real King of the world was born outside of any king's palace, outside of the house of the wealthy in which there was no place for him. The Nazarene offered God's grace and kingdom to those who—because they had been excluded from community with God by the religious and political elite—could never hope to participate in the final banquet of the kingdom: the poor, the sick, the Samaritans, the sinners, the prostitutes, the impure. He incarnated the message by becoming impure (in terms of the law) through eating with impure people—sharing the meals with them. He was and brought Good News to the excluded, to those at the periphery, by pushing back to the edges of the inhabited world the limits of God's kingdom. There is no periphery in God's reign: the poor are promised the kingdom, the sinners are forgiven, women become part of the community, children are placed in the centre, the sick are healed, the impure have access to God.

More reflection is needed at this point, since this was one of the hottest points of debate at the conference. Under Latin American leadership especially, the "centre-periphery" language (not to be confused with the development theory bearing the same name) was interpreted in Section I mainly as referring to the materially rich and poor, Jesus being understood as having identified himself with the poor and excluding the rich who are seen as oppressors. I would argue that biblically speaking this restriction of the understanding of Jesus' ministry is not possible. Jesus went also to those who, while being at the periphery of Jewish society, were nevertheless rich and exploiters of the poor; for example, the tax-collectors (Mark 2:13-17, Luke 18:9-14). There are two criteria used dialectically in the Gospels by Jesus: the one contrasting the materially poor and rich; the other the righteous and the poor before God. Luke's version of the beatitudes tends to stress the first; Matthew's, the second. I would argue that the "centre-periphery" language encompasses both and lies behind them. Wherever people use religious, ideological, economic or other means to organize their lives as if they were their own gods and in order to exclude those "outside" from the material and spiritual fruits of God's benediction, they place themselves at the centre. That's where Jesus is not to be found. He has moved to those at the periphery. I see an important reason why two different versions of the beatitudes have been transmitted to us, not that all the groups will thus be allowed to pretend to have a right to the kingdom, to claim it. The struggling poor who are sure that God is on their side can easily fall into the category of the self-righteous Pharisee (as did the Zealots). The wealthy, middleclass, "good" Christian, with deep faith in Jesus, falls easily into the biblical category of rich. And at different moments of personal history, each of us hears the Good or Bad News differently: it is the specific charisma of pastors to discover how to testify to the kingdom of God according to hope and despair of particular individuals and groups. It is the specific charisma of a missionary church and of evangelists to discover in each cultural and economic situation what are the barriers, the limits, the walls that define who is at the centre and who at the periphery. It is the merit of pauline theology to have reformulated the centre-periphery language in a new missionary situation as the message of justification by faith and not by law, thus opening the kingdom of God to the Gentiles, who from the point of view of a strict interpretation of Jewish law were excluded and at the periphery (cf. Eph. 2:11ff).

While there was much hesitancy about the full implications of the biblical message of the kingdom as Good News to the poor (cf. I/5ff), the specific missionary choice made by the conference in the present world situation is definitely justified: in the world perspective and within many countries of the world, mission under the kingdom of God cannot be faithful today if it is not formulated as Good News to the materially poor (I/5, 8). This is today's most scandalous division and every attempt to soften that scandal must be denounced as non-Christian. As Emilio Castro repeatedly says: the frontier to be crossed today is not primarily to be defined in religious terms (people never reached by the Gospel), but in bluntly material terms: it is that which defines whose children will die, whose husband will be tortured, whose wife will be raped, whose home will be built on the garbage heap, whose life will be short. Melbourne has spoken on many of the classical mission themes discussed in previous IMC or CWME conferences, but it did so in terms of that specific choice. Therein lie its message and its importance. Therein lie its limitations.

a) Participation in God's mission in the world outside the church's boundaries is seen and understood primarily as joining the poor in their struggles for liberation and self-determination, for self-reliance (II/12, I/9ff). The judgement on a possible positive role played by political, economic or religious, cultural powers within the total plan of God for his creation also proceeds from the same criteria (IV/5-7).

The second most used criterion for discerning how to participate in the struggles of the world under the perspective of the kingdom as revealed in Jesus is that of human rights (including religious freedom). It should be noted—in the light of the third and fourth points discussed above—that this is another application of the "centre-periphery" language, and a primarily non-economic one. While it can be rightly argued that those who suffer most from deprivation of their basic human rights are the materially poor, the human rights criterion has to be seen as another main frontier for missionary activity. Following Jesus to the "periphery" of every society, breaking through religious, economic or ideological boundaries, means finding oneself also among those whose exclusion from the "centre" is manifested through the fact that their human rights are suppressed. As a missionary judgement on political events, it is a major and necessary corrective to a purely economic understanding of reality. It would be an exaggeration, however, to say that the conference dealt satisfactorily with this criterion in its own evaluation of political events in today's world seen as a whole.

b) Melbourne statements on non-Christian religions—a classical theme of missionary conferences—are not more than an agenda for further discussion, given the urgency of and universality of the renewal of "religion" in today's world. This is partly linked to the institutional fact that there is in the WCC another sub-unit dealing specifically with this question. The approach to the problem as it is described in II/21, however, is typical of the Melbourne Conference's style of work. Much more reflection is needed, specifically with regard to the relation between a "dialogical" attitude to "people" and the choice of struggling against structures of oppression and exclusion including those having as basis and justification an institutional religion. The same dialectical relation between dialogue and struggle needs to be found with regard to ideologies on the one hand and to people adhering to them on the other.

c) If the centre of God's reign is to be found at the periphery of every society, this raises challenging questions about the use of financial resources by
churches, as Section IV indicates in the paragraphs 14 and 26. The latter
paragraph contains nothing less than a programme for slow but steady
loosening of relationships between powerful churches and the financial
centres of society. In practically all societies of the world, to have much
money means to have links with the centre. To use it as proposed in the
Section IV report might easily close down important money sources and,
in the middle term, lead churches or mission societies to a simpler and
poorer lifestyle, thus moving a step towards what Section I proposes in its
final paragraph (20a). More work needs to be done on a description of the
necessary evangelistic dimension of the activities and programmes mentioned in IV/26. Crossing barriers and frontiers, co-operation in mission,
money flow, etc. are still seen too exclusively in development terms. We
need to define more clearly what we recognize as frontier-crossing
evangelistic projects and work.

d) Practically all sections of the Melbourne Conference tried to come to grips
with the consequences of Melbourne's message for the life and structure
of the Church itself since most of them mention the Christian base community as a signpost to what it means to be communities of the followers
of Jesus of Nazareth living with and among those at the periphery.

Out of this understanding of *communidades de base* as primary bearers of
mission for the eighties the following questions emerge:

First, there is the challenge to parishes and communities to deepen their
spiritual and material sharing and to open themselves to people living at the
periphery. Some conference sections have produced quite profound texts on
community life in relation to the gathering around the Lord's table as a sign
of the expected messianic meal (cf. III/6, 11ff, 19, 30, IV/13, 16, 27).

Second, we find concrete proposals for understanding the role that is expected from those who hold positions of power in a church or community
(IV/13). Insofar as Melbourne did speak of ways to use power in the Church,
there was general agreement. But when the issue was raised as to whether the
power structure itself should not be questioned, unanimity disappeared immediately. From the conference's missionary perspective, any power structure—even that within the Church—eventually appears as creating a "centre"
and a "periphery". The debate on the women's requests and the almost complete lack of reflection on the role and existence of children as signs of the
kingdom proved once more how much at the periphery of church life these
groups are, at least with regard to the decision-making processes. But here we
reached one of the crucial points of disagreement where this otherwise very
ecumenical conference had to step back: the problem of ministry.

Third, the search for a lifestyle adapted to actual situations, but clearly following Jesus' movement towards the periphery of society has implications for another classical mission theme, the integration of mission and church. Next year will be the twentieth anniversary of the integration of IMC into the WCC. The Melbourne Conference, through its participants, its discussions, its agenda, testified to the success of that integration. Some people even asked what distinguished Melbourne from an assembly of the WCC and whether there was still a need for specialized mission conferences.

I believe that the Melbourne Conference reached the maximum point of integration which can be responsibly accepted from a missionary point of view. Indirectly, it pleads for the maintenance—or creation—of a relatively independent sector *within* the life of the established and institutional church. Surely, nobody can seriously object today to the idea/fact that the whole church is sent into mission and that all it does and lives has to be seen as part of its calling—worship, parish life, diaconia, development work, pastoral work, catechetical instruction, intervention in political life, etc. I read in the Melbourne documents, however, a renewed call for a personal and communal lifestyle appropriate to that specific part of the churches' mission which is to overcome limits, to break walls and boundaries, to go out to the "periphery" and live with people there, which is more than to declare oneself in solidarity with them. The repeated reference to the *communidades de base*, to monastic life, to missionary orders, the presence of Urban Rural Mission groups and their active plea for a life at the periphery, show how strongly the kingdom message pushes us towards new experiments and discoveries of exposed pilgrim ways of being in mission. And while in certain places, the whole church is placed, or places itself, in such a peripheral situation (in time of persecution for example), it does not seem realistic to imagine that the whole church as institution with all its parishes, councils and bureaucracies, will live such a life. Even in the New Testament churches, that was not so. By definition, an institution develops ways to protect itself and its own continuity. The churches, incarnated in this world's history, cannot easily escape that fact, however faithful they are. Most church leaders and members of the hierarchy understand their responsibility as holding together, protecting the church from disruptive forces, from too risky experiments that might destroy it as an institution. And this is not to be seen in negative terms only. If it had not been so, no Christian tradition would have survived—humanly speaking. Many churches have, through the simple fact of their existence, carried the testimony to God's kingdom.

But this is not the only way for churches to live their missionary responsibility. And that is why we need to keep *within* the institutional church an institutional place carrying the inheritance of the IMC and its members bodies—in a new way. It may be the task of the mission agencies, where they exist, to function as a kind of communication channel between frontier communities and individuals and the central church authorities, a window through which new individual or communitarian missionary experiments of crossing established limits can enter and fructify the whole life of the church without being immediately cut off by cautious authorities. This would mean that mission agencies and departments—as well as CWME—would turn away as much as possible from inter-church aid and development programmes—others do that well enough—from money-sending activities, and become places for information and exchange, centres of network. Their specificity would be, in cases where financial or other co-operation with other churches is requested, to help experiments to live their life, even if they are of very short term. Where mission agencies or departments do not exist, there may be need for the churches to reflect on ways in which to allow those "crazy" enough to cross frontiers to have sufficient independence from the central decision-making organization of the churches. This is a plea for the continuation of "specialized" mission bodies *inside* the church structure—with clear delegation of competence.

The presence at Melbourne of Urban Rural Mission groups was a vital element in the conference. One could have hoped to have had more and other "crazy" people—more monks, more young people who had participated in the Taizé youth council, more charismatic groups, more Pentecostals, more people engaged in cross-cultural mission (yes!)—and fewer people representing the central structure of their churches. This is not of course in any way a moral judgement; it rather points to the problem of finding the right place for a missionary conference within the whole spectrum of churches' life. For the next missionary conference, CWME should have more freedom to invite frontier people to come and should depend less on consultation with central church authorities for determining the participants in the conference. Twenty years after integration, we need to watch that missionary freedom is granted and accepted *within* church institutions. Otherwise mission experiments will happen more and more outside, as is already the case.

The last point I want to raise will clearly show why such freedom is essential. One question has already appeared in the first post-Melbourne discussions though it had already been touched upon during the preparatory process. It is the significance of Christ's *kenosis* as the necessary way of accomplishing his mission. Christ refused to impose God's kingdom by taking power and ruling humankind and all creation as the just ruler (cf. temptation story). He manifested God's way of reigning by giving up his being equal to God, becoming a Jew, a Galilean, living among the poor and disenfranchised, dying on the cross in our place. The symbols of God's kingdom are not the sword and crown, but bread and wine—the broken body of our Lord. The call to the disciple is nothing less than to follow that way—in absolute opposition to any reasonable search for accomplishment and success. It is not a call to powerlessness, but to a life that has its source in the power of the Holy Spirit—the life-giving, forgiving, healing and community-building power, a non-coercive power, a non-violent power. Possible implications for personal lifestyle could easily be drawn from a study of the lifestyle of Jesus and his disciples—if transposed into specific cultural contexts of today. The matthean version of the beatitudes give the picture of such a missionary—and the whole Sermon on the Mount develops what it means. We will have more difficulty in discovering the institutional consequences which communities and churches must draw from a recognition of the necessary kenotic way of being in mission that Jesus is calling us to follow. Some paragraphs of the Melbourne report try to formulate the question (IV/8, 11 on non-violence, I/7c and 20a, last lines), and it was raised in the plenary debate by Bishop John V. Taylor. But Melbourne did not touch the question; it probably has too many challenging institutional consequences to be dealt with by such an official meeting.

But one can easily discern that real crossing of the limits put by humankind to God's saving and healing activity—today's version of what Paul calls the Law—is only possible through the abandoning of security, wealth, power, through a kenotic approach. Whenever this is forgotten, the crossing of barriers becomes a crusade of conquest, which bears counter testimony to the way God himself crossed the barrier between himself and humankind. That is what Melbourne's final message tries to communicate when it says: "The Triune God, revealed in the person and work of Jesus Christ, is the centre of all peoples and all things. Our Saviour Jesus Christ was laid in a manger 'because there was no place for him in the inn' (Luke 2:7). He is central to life, yet moves toward those on the edge of life. He affirms his lordship by giving it up. He was crucified 'outside the gate' (Heb. 13:12). In his surrender of power he establishes his power to heal."

The missionary consequences of this are developed in section IV's paragraphs 20 to 25 which may be seen as a summary of Melbourne's vision of world mission.

Jacques Matthey
Conference Secretary

PLENARY PRESENTATIONS
Your Kingdom Come
SORITUA NABABAN*

Praise be to the Lord, our God and Father, who in his mercy has safely gathered us here together. We have come from all parts of the world, from our various and different situations, bringing along the experiences of our churches, our groups and of ourselves—all these in the different "earthen vessels" of our cultures and nations. At the same time we have come to this place with expectations and hopes shaped by our respective spiritual and religious heritages. And this is rightly so.

For since 1978 we all have been invited "to join in a period of prayer, reflection, search and obedience" under the conference theme "Your Kingdom Come". We have been invited as a generation to "seek first the kingdom and its righteousness, believing that all else that is necessary for human existence will be added". We have been invited to "affirm our trust in, and dependence upon, the God who is Creator, Redeemer and Saviour, Lord of Lords and King of Kings". We have also been invited to "pray confidently, for the kingdom is already in our midst", and yet to "pray expectantly, for the kingdom in all its fullness is still to come".

Because our situations and experiences are so various, so different, we know that in our understanding of the theme there will be different emphases. But let us beware the danger of dramatizing these differences, of confronting them one with the other. Rather let us share in love and humility, in joy and hope, our experiences and concerns, our insights and visions, knowing that our Lord and our King wills that we should be one in order to carry out his will. We are here that we may share these experiences directly and personally, so that we may also fulfil the main task of this conference: "to provide opportunities for churches, mission agencies and communities to meet together for reflection and consultation leading to common witness".

And now I want to begin this process of direct and personal sharing with you—out of the background of the experiences and concerns, of the insights

---

*Dr Soritua A. E. Nababan, General Secretary of the Council of Churches, Indonesia, is Moderator of the Commission on World Mission and Evangelism of the WCC.

and vision of our churches and Christian groups in Indonesia—by inviting you to meditate with me on the theme itself. There are three things I would like to point out.

First: Our theme is a part of the Lord's Prayer, the only prayer taught by Jesus to his disciples and followers as recorded in the New Testament. Jesus teaches his disciples the right prayer and the right way to pray. The right prayer embraces the biggest things and the smallest daily affairs, but also the most momentous, including eternity itself. The right way to pray demands simplicity, concentration, discipline, patience and obedience. With the Lord's Prayer, Jesus teaches his Church—all his disciples through the ages—the right prayer and the right way to pray. As such it becomes the normative prayer, the prayer against which, in a sense, all our prayers are tested. For it is the right prayer of the new era, of the new relationships brought about by the arrival of the kingdom.

But Jesus not only teaches what and how to pray. He lives in prayer. It is urgent for us to recognize that all important decisions and events in the life of Jesus are taken and happen in prayer. The Gospel of St. Luke shows this clearly: from the baptism of Jesus to his crucifixion. The apostles and the early church, too, lived and acted in prayer. In all their important decisions they turned to God in prayer. Mission is born out of the obedience which follows Jesus Christ's word when he says: " pray therefore the Lord of the harvest to send out labourers" (Matt. 9:38).

As we confront these biblical insights, which are exposed by the prayer nature of this theme, with the realities found in the life of the churches and our congregations, a variety of questions come to the surface: could it be that the time and energy consumed in the polarizing debate on the understanding of mission in the last two decades, which weakened the church's witness in the midst of a hostile world, is caused by the fact that our supposedly important decisions are not taken in prayer, or that our prayers are not tested by the Lord's Prayer in their contents and attitudes—and that a possible way out of this polarization is to join in the right prayer, prayed in the right way? Could it be that the diminishing enthusiasm and zeal for mission in its comprehensive understanding—and not in a one-sided fanatic activism—in so many of our congregations and groups, in spite of the integration started in 1961 in New Delhi, is caused by the fact that mission is uprooted from its very root: prayer! And indeed, when congregations and Christian groups pray, rightly tested by the Lord's Prayer, mission happens on the way, and in a kind of headlong holy rush!

What we are reminded of by this theme is that whether our conference fails or succeeds in achieving its aim depends on how we live during these days in the right kind of prayer and praying in the right way. In all our studies, discussions and common search, in all our intellectual and spiritual pursuits, we must not forget the very nature of the theme—a call to prayer.

Secondly, to pray "Your Kingdom Come" is to pray for the impossible from a human point of view, both in our personal as well as in public life. *In the personal sphere,* to pray "Your Kingdom Come" means to ask and therefore to work out the end of the reign of one own's will, richness, power, welfare, honour—all these dreams of the highest values of life dictated by our inherited cultures. It is to give up inherited cultural identity for a totally new, transformed identity, which is neither western nor eastern, neither Asian nor African nor Latin American, which is in fact "Christian" in its very nature and expression—a Christ-like identity. To illustrate it more personally: I am a member of the Batak tribe, and it is our sacred doctrine to understand that each Batak is a king's son or daughter—prince and princess—and that every Batak basically is a king. To pray "Your Kingdom Come" in the midst of the reality of the Batak life, is to ask and therefore to work out the end of the kingly rule of every Batak. Therefore, it is to ask the impossible in human terms. *In public life,* to pray "Your Kingdom Come" is to ask the full revelation of what Christ did: "He disarmed the principalities and powers and made a public example of them, triumphing over them in him" (Col. 2:15). It is to ask and therefore to work for the end of the powers which are the ordered structures of society and the spiritual powers which lie behind them and undergird religious structures, intellectual structures, moral structures, political structures—the religious undergirdings of stable ancient and primitive saints, all the "ologies" and the "isms", all the codes and customs, all the tyranny of the market, the school, the courts, race, and nation. Or in the light of the Guatemalan experience, to pray "Your Kingdom Come" is to ask and therefore to work out the end:
— to all that destroys life in the world
— to all that forces human beings to live like animals
— to the interests of those who make the poor work like beasts
— to the violence of the political structure of the political system, the educational system, the economic system, all of them approved by people who call themselves Christians
— to what makes people turn themselves into machines and their lives into merchandise
— to all that makes people slaves to themselves and others.

It is apparent how impossible, how risky, how dangerous it is to pray "Your Kingdom Come".

And still Jesus teaches his Church—all Christians—even today, to pray this prayer. For he has won the victory over all those powers in the manifestation of his suffering power in transforming and changing, renewing and replacing. And we find ourselves between the "already" and the "will be", liberated to listen to his command, to follow him obediently, to pray and to work. And even if we have still to suffer now, we know that it is not the last word. The last word belongs to the King of kings. Therefore we are not to sit and watch the powers do what they want, but we are called to put ourselves at the disposal of the King to carry out his will. This theme is a call to *ora et labora*, to pray and to work, not that we force God to implement his plan according to our plans or the world's plans. We are invited to erect actively the signs of his kingdom: justice where injustice rules, peace where war and revenge prevail, joy and hope where tears and disappointments govern, and mercy where mercilessness and unimaginable torture is at work.

Thirdly, as we discern the signs of the times in our century we see that the whole world is full of dreams and struggles for freedom and liberation. We notice the growing yearning of humanity in general for a common life based on justice and well-being. We witness the birth of freedom movements from foreign oppression, liberation movements from poverty, from economic and political oppressions. Development too should be understood as a liberating process aimed at justice and well-being, particularly for the poor and the oppressed. We know that behind these movements at the deepest levels are dreams, yearnings for justice and well-being. Initiators and supporters of these movements come from various religious and ideological backgrounds. But we also know the millions who are not aware of these movements, who are losing even their right to their places in the world, who are dying, suffocated under the injustice and poverty of the world, those who live without human dignity, whose dreams are fading and disappearing. In the midst of the signs of the time, to pray "Your Kingdom Come" implies the urge for all Christians and for the whole Church to proclaim to all creation that the time is fulfilled and the kingdom of God is at hand; and that therefore there is a need to repent and to believe in the Gospel (cf. Mark 1:15). To all creation, to the whole creation, not just to those who have not yet religion, not also only to those who have nothing to lose—but to every creature. For it is in the kingdom that has come, is at work and is still to manifest fully its power, that the dream, the joy and the ideal for justice and welfare are justly assured and it is in the same kingdom that the dead are brought to life, the dry bones are brought to their feet (cf. Ez. 37:10).

To pray "Your Kingdom Come" is to discern the urgency of proclaiming the Gospel holistically by the whole Church to the whole world. Holistically, because the partial Gospel leads to new suffering; the whole Church, because conflicting proclamations betray the Gospel itself, and hinder people from seeking the kingdom and its righteousness; the whole world, because it is the world that God loves and which Jesus died to save.

Finally, as we enter this decade of the eighties with him who is the King of kings, let us strive to act obediently that we may be able to call the worldwide Church to join in the prayer that his kingdom might come, in all its implications willed by the Lord.

We pray confidently—for the kingdom is already in our midst.

We pray expectantly—for the kingdom in all its fullness is still to come. May all our work and decisions be taken in prayer, as we yearn to pray "Your Kingdom Come".

From Edinburgh to Melbourne

PHILIP POTTER *

It is a joy for me to associate myself with all those who have welcomed you to this World Missionary Conference. The World Council of Churches is proud to be the inheritor of the great missionary movement which launched the decisive stage of the ecumenical movement at Edinburgh 1910. It was, therefore, natural that when the World Council was formed in 1948, the International Missionary Council was declared to be "in association" with it. One of the functions of the World Council was, from the beginning, "to support the churches in their task of evangelism". Since the integration of the International Missionary Council with the World Council in 1961, this function has been expressed comprehensively as follows: "to facilitate the common witness of the churches in each place and in all places", and "to support the churches in their worldwide missionary and evangelistic task". The nearly 300 member churches in over 100 countries are committed to this task, and the purpose of this conference is to deepen and further that commitment.

We are also happy to meet in Australia, which has played such an active role in the missionary movement, especially in the Pacific, Asia and Africa. Australia was well represented in the Edinburgh Conference and in the Continuation Committee which followed. Certainly this is the largest ecumenical gathering ever to be held in Australia. Let us pray that it will be a blessing for us who have come and for our Australian hosts who have so generously received us.

I have been given the daunting task of introducing the work of this conference by indicating the significance of the missionary movement from the meeting of the Edinburgh Conference in June 14-23, 1910, to our meeting here in Melbourne. The 70 years, which we shall rapidly pass in review, have seen radical changes in the world and in the life and witness of the Church. These have been noted in the very helpful issue of the *International Review of Mission* on "Edinburgh to Melbourne" (Vol. LXVII, No. 267), and more briefly in the brochure introducing this conference. My only qualification for

---

* Dr Philip Potter, Dominica, is General Secretary of the World Council of Churches.

speaking tonight is that for nearly half of these 70 years I have been involved directly in the work of the International Missionary Council and the Commission on World Mission and Evangelism, first as Missionary Secretary of the British Student Christian Movement in the late 1940s; later as secretary of the WCC Youth Department with which the IMC was associated; as a secretary of the Methodist Missionary Society in London; and as Director of CWME. I have had the immense privilege of knowing personally and of having been inspired by several of the missionary leaders from Edinburgh onwards. Perhaps the most important influence on my life was my own local church on a small island, Dominica, in the Caribbean. The central event in our church year was the missionary meeting and from my earliest years I was taught to pray for the work of mission and collected money for the world mission of the Church. This sense of belonging to "the Holy Church throughout all the world" and of participating in a small way in the proclamation of the Gospel of the kingdom of God and his justice has been deeply engraved in me, long before I became acquainted with the vast literature of mission.

Our theme, "Your Kingdom Come", has been at the heart of the missionary movement throughout Christian history, and not least in this century. The Student Volunteer Missionary Movement of the late nineteenth century was born in what was called "The Morning Watch". Prayer and Bible study were the basis of facing the missionary challenge to proclaim the kingdom to those who had not heard it. It was in the context of responding to the demands of the kingdom that people like John R. Mott spoke of "the evangelization of the world in this generation". As early as 1901 Mott wrote:

If the Gospel is to be preached to all men it obviously must be done while they are living. The evangelization of the world in this generation, therefore, means the preaching of the Gospel to those who are now living. To us who are responsible for preaching the Gospel it means in our lifetime; to those to whom it is to be preached it means in their lifetime... The phrase "in this generation", therefore, strictly speaking, has a different meaning for each person.

Mott (the twenty-fifth anniversary of whose translation to "the land of larger dimensions", as he loved to say, we celebrate this year) declared in 1924: "I can truthfully answer that next to the decision to take Christ as the leader and Lord of my life, the watchword has had more influence than all other ideals and objectives combined to widen my horizon and enlarge my conception of the kingdom of God." The Edinburgh Conference did not speak of "the evangelization of the world in this generation", but it was under the deep constraint to get on with the job. At the opening of the conference, the Archbishop of Canterbury, Randall Davidson, ended his appeal to his "fellow-workers in the Church Militant, the Society of Christ on earth" with the words:

> The place of missions in the life of the Church must be the central place, and none other. That is what matters. Let people get hold of that, and it will tell—it is the merest commonplace to say it—it will tell for us at home as it will tell for those afield. Secure for that thought its true place, in our plans, our policy, our prayers, and then—why then, the issue is His, not ours. But it may well be that if that come true, "there be some standing here tonight who shall not taste of death till they see"—here on earth, in a way we know not now—"the Kingdom of God come with power".
>
> (*History and Records of the Edinburgh Conference*, p. 150)

The theme of the kingdom, affirmed in a context of prayer, has been dominant in all the world missionary conferences up to the last one in Bangkok 1972 on "Salvation Today". It is not surprising that the clearest expression of the kingdom was in the prayers that the participants at Bangkok composed as they wrestled with the salvation which Christ offered. Here are excerpts of two prayers:

> Father, so many of the forms of this world are passing away... Help us to see that your Son has come into this world to transform it as Lord... Let not this world be changed without me being also changed. Convert me and I shall be converted. Let your judgement come in the Christ who is to come. And let us hasten his coming in the community that seeks his justice. Maranatha. Amen.
>
> O God...
> You have sent your Son in one place and time, We praise You!
> Be present in every time and place, We pray You!
> Your kingdom has come in his salvation, We pray You!
> Let it come always among us, We pray You!
>
> (*Bangkok Assembly*, 1973, pp. 81, 83)

The first reflection I want to make is that the missionary movement and the world missionary conferences have always been based on worship, prayer and Bible study in the presence and hope of the kingdom. Commentators and critics of the ecumenical movement often forget this profound sense of always being in the presence of the King and Saviour of the world. At Edinburgh the central act every day was the period of intercession at midday, apart from other acts of worship. In the message addressed to the "members of the Christian churches in non-Christian lands", the last paragraph begins: "A strong co-operation in prayer binds together in one all the Empire of

Christ." Jerusalem 1928, Madras 1938, Whitby 1947, Willingen 1952, Ghana 1957, Mexico 1963 and Bangkok 1972 were all celebrations of God's kingly rule in prayer and meditation on his Word. This conference will be in the same living tradition.

What, then, do we learn from this living tradition of prayerful reflection and action on the missionary calling of the Church to proclaim in word and act the kingdom of God? I would like to concentrate on three issues which have impressed themselves on me in relation to the concerns which are before us in this conference.

The first is the relationship between the kingdom of God and the kingdoms of this world. The matter can be put in other ways, like the relationship between salvation history and world history, or between the text of the gospel of the kingdom and the context of the world in which the Gospel must be preached. (This issue was only articulated at the Willingen Conference in 1952.) What strikes one forcibly is how difficult our fathers and mothers in the faith found it, at Edinburgh and Jerusalem particularly, to relate what was happening in what they called Christian lands to what was going on in non-Christian lands, as they were fond of saying.

Let us take the year 1910. The dominant mood of the conference was one of "abounding optimism", as the missionary historian, Kenneth Latourette, put it. It was the age of western imperialism. It was the time of "the white man's burden". This phrase was the title of a poem by Rudyard Kipling addressed to the USA to take up their responsibilities as they joined the imperialist club at the end of the nineteenth century. The first verse of that poem says:

> Take up the White Man's burden—
> Send forth the best you breed—
> Go bind your sons to exile
> To serve your captives' need;
> To wait in heavy harness,
> On fluttered folk and wild.—
> Your new-caught sullen peoples
> Half-devil and half-child.

The tone of this verse was that of what was classified as "Social Darwinism". Darwin's books, *On the Origin of the Species* (1859) and *The Descent of Man* (1871) had analyzed the human situation as a perpetual struggle for survival with some races, regarded as superior to others in the evolutionary process, asserting themselves over the weaker races. The English sociologist, Herbert Spencer, coined the phrase, "the survival of the fittest", which he applied to the necessity of the stronger nations, through their industrial, financial and military power, imposing their will and way over other peoples. At best, these western empires felt they had a mission, as advanced peoples, to bring civilization to the backward peoples.

The churches and missionary agencies saw it as their duty to bring the best that they had, the Gospel, to these peoples as the most effective civilizing influence. The first speaker at the Edinburgh Conference, Lord Balfour of Burleigh, described the great opportunity before the Christian West in these noble terms:

> Nations in the East are awakening. They are looking for two things: they are looking for enlightenment and for liberty. Christianity alone of all religion meets these demands in the highest degree. There cannot be Christianity without liberty, and liberty without at least the restraint of Christian ideals is full of danger. There is a power unique in Christianity of all religions to uplift and to ennoble, and for this reason, that it has its roots and its foundations in self-sacrifice and in love.

Lord Balfour went on to hope that the mission to other countries could well affect relations of nations and churches in the West. He said:

> It is a thought not without its grandeur that a unity begun in the mission field may extend its influence and react upon us at home and throughout the older civilizations; that it may bring to us increased hope of international peace among the nations of the world, and of at least fraternal co-operation and perhaps a greater measure of unity in ecclesiastical matters at home.
>
> (*History and Records of Edinburgh Conference*, p. 145)

It is touching to read the record of that conference which gave such concentrated and dedicated attention to what was happening in Asia, Africa, the Middle East and the Pacific. But they did not apply their prophetic assessment and judgement to the situation of their own countries and churches, except to lament the lukewarmness of Christians as regards the world mission. And yet, the situation in Europe was at that time perilously moving into a cataclysmic conflict. The western powers were competing with each other for the division of the world for investment, raw materials, and export markets. The doctrine of free trade was described as "the free fox in the free chicken run". But this competition was also expressing itself in the arms race and growing conflict in the West itself. The French socialist Jean Jaurès wrote in 1905:

> From a European war a revolution may spring up and the ruling classes would do well to think of this. But it may also result, over a long period, in crises of counter-revolution, of furious reaction, of exasperated nationalism, of stifling dictatorships, of monstrous militarism, a long chain of retrograde violence.
>
> (*OEuvres*, ed. M. Bannafous, Pour la Paix II, 1931, p. 247)

This prophecy has been abundantly fulfilled in these past seventy-five years. It is our present condition in the 1980s—the context in which this conference is being held.

Of course, the participants at Edinburgh were not unaware of these dangers. W. H. T. Gairdner in his interpretation of *Edinburgh 1910* noted recent events which affected the world mission. There was the Boxer Uprising in China in 1900 against the carving up of their country by foreign powers, including Japan. Japan defeated Russia in 1904-5 and trees of victory were planted in several Asian countries. Britain and Russia tried to compose their rivalry by signing an agreement in 1907 in which Tibet was neutralized, Afghanistan was left in the British sphere, Persia was divided in zones of influence with a neutral zone in-between. Britain, France, Germany and Russia were moving inexorably into war.

Another participant in the Edinburgh Conference as a steward was William Temple. He and others had been to a student conference the previous year on "The Social Problem" in class-divided Britain. At the end of the conference, with deep Christian sensitivity, they declared: "We are the social problem." That "we" meant the privileged class to which they belonged. The Edinburgh Conference would have gained in depth and relevance if a similar stance could have been taken, because the issues at stake were moral and spiritual. John R. Mott was being perhaps too confident in saying in 1911 that the Edinburgh Conference "has familiarized the Christians of our day with this idea of looking steadily at the world as a whole, of confronting the world as a unit by the Christian Church as a unit". Perhaps this is far truer today than it was then. We can, therefore, be thankful that Mott and his colleagues at least made a beginning.

The point I want to make is that when we are motivated by God's kingly rule, then we are bound, like the Old Testament prophets, to see the world as a whole. The prophets' understanding of God's kingship over the world drove them to declare God's judgement not only on the nations which did not know or accept him, but particularly on Israel as the bearer of his covenant word. For example, Isaiah, who saw the King, the Lord of hosts, in the temple, was renewed to see the world and his own country in a new way—the way of judgement and of hope. That is why he could speak of "that day", the day of the final revelation of God's Kingdom, in these beautiful terms:

In that day there will be a highway from Egypt to Assyria, and the Assyrian will come into Egypt, and the Egyptian into Assyria, and the Egyptians will worship with the Assyrians.

In that day Israel will be the third with Egypt and Assyria, a blessing in the midst of the earth, whom the Lord of hosts has blessed, saying, Blessed be Egypt my people, and Assyria the work of my hands, and Israel my heritage.

(Isa. 19:23-25)

I have dwelt on Edinburgh 1910 in order to show the need for relating the text of God's kingdom to the total context of our world and not only as part of it. If time had permitted I could have indicated ways in which the other conferences, including Bangkok, failed to allow the full weight of the kingdom to open their eyes to the missionary task, in its integral relationship of home and abroad. We can be grateful that we, the inheritors of the increasing awareness of Christians over the years, will have an opportunity at this meeting to let the message of the kingdom be our guide for discovering God's mission for the coming years in all its starkness and wholeness.

The second issue I want to bring to your attention is the extraordinary similarity between the concerns debated at Edinburgh and since, up to this meeting. Naturally, these concerns are perceived with greater clarity today, thanks to the boldness and wisdom of our predecessors. I have had an opportunity of consulting not only the reports of the world missionary conferences, but also the minutes of the Continuation Committee after Edinburgh and of the IMC and CWME. It is a heartening and also humbling experience to realize how open these men and women were to what God was leading them to say and to do. I will attempt to refer briefly to several of these concerns.

The Missionary Message

The Edinburgh Conference did not find it necessary to struggle with the missionary message. Christ and their obedience to his call brought the participants together. Lord Balfour, in his opening address, appealed to the Trinitarian basis of the faith as Christians sought "to call the human race into one fellowship, to teach the way of eternal life". He said: "The fatherhood of God, the love of the Son, the power of the Holy Ghost, the purity of Christian life, and the splendour of the Christian hope are common ground." There were addresses on "Christianity, the final and universal religion" as redemption and as ethical ideal. Dr Henry Sloan Coffin, coming out of the social gospel tradition, was the one who spoke most fully about the kingdom of God. He said:

Christianity finds its ethic, as its religion, in Jesus Christ. Its God is the God revealed in Jesus' religious experience—His Father, the eternally Christlike God. Its ethical ideal is the kingdom of that God—the kingdom which Jesus proclaimed and for which He laid down His life. This kingdom is a redeemed social order under the reign of the Christlike God in which every relationship is Christlike, and each individual and social group—the family, the trade-organization, the State—comes not to be ministered unto, but to minister, is perfect as the Father in heaven is perfect, and the whole of human society incarnates the love of God once embodied in Jesus of Nazareth.

(*History and Records of the Edinburgh Conference*, p. 164)

The Edinburgh Conference was more concerned with what it described as "a close and continuous study of the position of Christianity in non-Christian lands" and addressed itself mainly to the approach to other faiths. The question could well be asked whether the conference would have been so sure of the message if it had more consciously come to terms with the situation of both church and society in the West. The great insights of the prophets on the character and purpose of the living God came out of the white heat of involvement and struggle with the storms of the world's history around them and beyond.

The Jerusalem Conference had no alternative but to face the challenge of expressing the message of the Church in its mission to the world. The carnage of World War I and the bitterness it evoked had destroyed "the abounding optimism" of eighteen years before.

The phrases "Christian lands" and "non-Christian lands" could no longer be used. Those who dared to proclaim the Gospel to people of other faiths would have to do so without reference to any shining examples of countries which nevertheless had had centuries of exposure to the Christian faith. Another factor exposed at Jerusalem was the different ways in which Christians in the West interpreted the Christian message. It was too early to point out that historical and cultural factors influenced this interpretation.

It was interesting that at the end of the long series of papers on Hinduism, Confucianism, Buddhism, Islam, there was one on "Secular Civilization and the Christian Task" by Professor Rufus Jones who began his paper by saying:

No student of the deeper problems of life can very well fail to see that the greatest rival of Christianity in the world today is not Mohammedanism, or Buddhism, or Hinduism, or Confucianism, but a worldwide secular way of life and interpretation of the nature of things.

He added a note: "I am using 'secular' here to mean a way of life and an interpretation of life that include only the natural order of things and that do not find God, or a realm of spiritual reality, essential for life or thought."

(*Jerusalem Report: The Christian Message*, p. 284)

Jones significantly ended his paper with the call for a fresh vision of the kingdom of God in terms of daring to live and act according to the prayer of our Lord that God's kingdom come and his will be done on earth as it is in heaven—a position which was hotly debated between Anglo-Saxons and Continentals. Jones appealed to his fellow westerners:

Go to Jerusalem, then, not as members of a Christian nation to convert other nations which are not Christian, but as Christians within a nation far too largely non-Christian, who face within their own borders the competition of a rival movement as powerful, as dangerous, as insidious as any of the great historic religions. We meet our fellow Christians in these other countries on terms of equality, as fellow workers engaged in a common task.

It was not surprising that it was the same William Temple, whom I mentioned earlier, who drafted the message which all accepted, though all interpreted it in their own way. In the midst of a world of insecurity and instability, of relativism in human thought, of suffering and pain, rising nationalism and the yearning for social justice, human brotherhood and international peace, the conference declared:

> Our message is Jesus Christ. He is the revelation of what God is and of what man through Him may become. In Him we come face to face with the ultimate reality of the universe; He makes known to us God as our Father, perfect and infinite in love and in righteousness; for in Him we find God incarnate, the final, yet ever unfolding, revelation of the God in whom we live and move and have our being...
>
> Christ is our motive and Christ is our end. We must give nothing less, and we can give nothing more.
> *(Christian Message*, pp. 480, 486)

The Minutes of the Committee of the IMC in the years which followed show that the message was a central concern of the churches and mission agencies, issuing in an intensive reflection on the task of evangelism. All this culminated in the great statement of the 1938 Madras Conference on "The Faith by which the Church Lives", based as it was on the churches all over the world grappling with the realities around them fearlessly and candidly. The Madras Conference asserted that "world peace will never be achieved without world evangelization" and summoned the churches "to unite in the supreme work of world evangelization until the kingdoms of this world become the Kingdom of our Lord".

There have been several expressions of the missionary message since, and we shall no doubt be adding our own at this conference. I only want to make a few comments on this effort at articulating together the message which we proclaim which might be of some relevance to us here. First, the biblical revelation has always been the rallying point of the missionary movement. It was Hendrik Kraemer who in his great, though controversial book on *The Christian Message in a Non-Christian World* (1938), spoke of biblical realism. For him the Bible and the Christian faith has an intense realism which proclaims and asserts realities. "It does not intend to present a 'world view', but it challenges man in his *total* being to confront himself with these realities and accordingly take decisions... The Bible in its direct intense realism presents no theology. It presents the witness of prophets and apostles... To take biblical realism as the fundamental starting point and criterion of all Christian and theological thinking exposes all problems to an unexpected and revealing light" (pp. 64-65).

It was in taking seriously the biblical revelation that our understanding of mission has been deepened. The revelation of God is one of the Father who created the world and humanity in his own image, who sent his Son to redeem the world and sent his Spirit to interpret and make real his creative and redemptive work. God is the true missionary. The mission is God's, not ours. Moreover, as we have learnt since the Willingen Conference of 1952, the basis of mission is the Trinitarian revelation of God in creation, redemption and fulfilment through Father, Son and Holy Spirit. Mission is cosmic in its scope, concerned with bringing the whole creation and the whole of humanity within the sphere of God's purpose of good. It is this Trinitarian understanding of mission which enables us to explore fully the meaning of the kingly rule of God and his justice.

Secondly, the message must be articulated and communicated in the context of the culture of people, their whole way of thinking, believing and acting. We owe a great debt to the men and women who clearly perceived from Edinburgh onwards the importance of taking culture and religion seriously. The minutes of the Continuation Committee and of the IMC show what a battle it was to get the Bible translated, education conducted, and literature produced in the languages of the people. The colonial governments in many countries were bent on imposing their own language and culture. The first meeting of the IMC in 1921 enunciated the principle that "Christianity can succeed only as an indigenous movement". Biblical realism demands the encounter with culture and other faiths in dialogue. Kraemer himself, in the years that followed the Madras Conference, found that he had to speak no longer of the communication of the faith *to* people of other faiths and cultures, but rather *with* them. It is in this spirit that we were able to say at Bangkok, "Culture shapes the human voice that answers the voice of Christ". It is also in this spirit that dialogue with people of other faiths and ideologies is conducted. Those who gathered at Edinburgh in 1910 would rejoice to see the day when there were such rich and varied expressions of the Christian faith around the world and where dialogue with people of living faiths has reached such integrity and depth. Our task is to bring all these experiences and expressions under the judging and renewing purview of the kingdom for the sake of God's mission today.

The Church, Mission and the Kingdom

At this conference we shall be discussing the Church as witnessing to the kingdom, and the kingdom as the *raison d'être* of the Church. At Edinburgh there was a deep consciousness of the need to renew the Church to take up its missionary task. The sense of urgency which was sounded there meant, however, mobilizing all the forces of mission in spite of the churches in the West. It was the era of foreign missionary societies and boards supported by a faithful minority in the churches. Exceptions like the Moravians were highly commended. But it was to the churches in the mission lands that the conference issued the most direct appeal: "It is you alone who can ultimately finish this work: the word that under God convinces your own people must be your word; and the life which will win them for Christ must be the life of holiness and moral power, as set forth by you who are men of their race." This was a clear acknowledgement that the Church exists for mission and that the base of mission is the local church. It is interesting to observe that it was through the missionary movement that this essential missionary character of the Church has become accepted during these years. The World Studies on Churches in Mission and the study on the Missionary Structure of the Congregation in the 1950s and 1960s conducted by CWME have been extremely fruitful for promoting this process.

The debate about the Church and the kingdom has in many ways been exaggerated. It is true that there was a tendency in the Byzantine and Roman churches to equate the Church with the kingdom, especially as the kingdom was almost equated with the holy empire both East and West. Happily this is no longer a matter of controversy. The missionary movement was reproached for making the Church rather than the kingdom the centre of mission. A closer study of the documents reveals that what motivated the accent on the Church, especially at the Madras Conference in 1938, was not the concern to make the Church central, but to call the Church to its central evangelistic task through its total life at a time of competing ideologies, nationalism and of totalitarian regimes claiming the absolute allegiance of peoples. It was rather a valiant attempt at asserting the crown rights of the Redeemer and that the Church which is his Body must transcend all loyalties which may take precedence over the sovereignty of God. This is a challenge which is very much with us in the 1980s and I hope we will not shirk it in this conference.

What is certainly true is that the eschatological understanding of the kingdom as not only present but to come is a constant call to the Church in each place and in all places to renewal and unity. This was clearly stated in the paper prepared for the Second Assembly of the World Council of Churches in 1954 on "Christ—the Hope of the World". It declared:

> Our unity in Christ belongs to the ultimate structure of reality. This is the goal to which all history and all creation move. In pressing forward towards this goal we are one. Let us not forget that when we stand before our Lord at the end we shall stand before our Judge—the Judge of His Church as well as of the world. His judgement will bring about a separation that goes much deeper than all our present divisions and cuts across them all...

The Church's visible structure passes away with the age, but as the chosen people of God it will enter into the glory of the Kingdom of God that is to come... Here at last the Church will know fully what it is to be one in Christ.

(Report of Advisory Group, pp. 20, 24)

This vital aspect of the relation of the Church and the kingdom certainly needs to be carried further in this conference.

Evangelism and Social Concern

At this conference we shall be discussing the plight of the poor, human struggles and power. It has become fashionable in some quarters to be violently critical of CWME and especially of the World Council of Churches for being too concerned with social justice rather than with justification by faith. This kind of criticism has been made since Edinburgh 1910. I am sure, however, that the participants at Edinburgh and at subsequent meetings would endorse the statement in Bangkok:

The salvation which Christ brought, and in which we participate, offers a comprehensive wholeness in this divided life. We understand salvation as newness of life—the unfolding of true humanity in the fulness of God (Col. 2:9). It is salvation of the soul and the body, of the individual and society, mankind and "the groaning creation" (Rom. 8:19). As evil works both in personal life and in exploitative social structures which humiliate humankind, so God's justice manifests itself both in the justification of the sinner and in social and political justice. As guilt is both individual and corporate so God's liberating power changes both persons and structures. We have to overcome the dichotomies in our thinking between soul and body, person and society, humankind and creation. Therefore we see the struggles for economic justice, political freedom and cultural renewal as elements in the total liberation of the world through the mission of God. This liberation is finally fulfilled when "death is swallowed up in victory" (I Cor. 15:55).

(Bangkok Assembly, 1973, pp. 88-89)

The Edinburgh Conference was confronted with many major social evils that it could not ignore. The opium trade was a matter of deep concern. Bishop Charles Brent, then a missionary in the Philippines, would be chairing an international conference on it at The Hague the following year. He was also the founder of the Faith and Order movement for the unity of the Church. At Edinburgh he spoke on the sufficiency of God which gives courage to dare and courage to bear. Strong reference was made at the meeting to the oppression and wanton destruction to human life being perpetrated in the Congo by the Belgians and their associates. There was a strong discussion on this in the Continuation Committee when apologists for Belgian brutalities tried to say this was beyond the competence of the Committee.

At Edinburgh, too, V. S. Azariah of India had raised a very delicate issue which hurt and angered many. He started his address on the problem of co-operation between foreign and native workers as follows: "The problem of race relationships is one of the most serious problems confronting the Church today. The bridging of the gulf between the East and West, and the attainment of a greater unity and common ground in Christ as the great Unifier of mankind, is one of the deepest needs of our time." The Continuation Committee took up the challenge, as it did on such matters as labour relations in new industries in Asia and Africa. J. H. Oldham, that guiding genius of the missionary movement at and after Edinburgh, undertook studies on "Christianity and the Race Problem" (published in 1924), on education, land rights, and industrial labour in Africa. In fact, Oldham was not present at the Jerusalem Conference in 1928 because he considered it top priority for the sake of the Gospel and missionary witness that he take part in a commission of enquiry on these matters in East Africa. In the 1920s Oldham, Paton and noted economists like R. H. Tawney were drawing attention to the economic and political power structures which maintained racial and social injustices, especially in the poorer nations.

The IMC took a bold step in 1930 by setting up a Department of Social and Industrial Research and Counsel in Geneva. This was strongly contested by some European countries, and Mott and William Paton had to find the funds privately to maintain this department under the leadership of the far-seeing, competent and devoted J. Merle Davis. A monumental volume on the economic basis of the church was prepared for the Madras Conference in 1938.

It is out of the work of this department that such matters as Urban and Rural Mission in CWME and the practical work of organs of the World Council's Unit on Justice and Service sprang.

Moreover, after World War I, when German missions were orphaned, new concerns arose about the relation of missions and governments. Efforts were made to get a clause on religious and missionary freedom in the Covenant of the League of Nations. It was in this context that the missionary leaders in the neutral countries during World War I drew up a statement on the supranationality of missions which they submitted to diplomatic representatives of the warring powers in 1917. It is interesting to note here that even the most conservative and hostile mission groups appealed to the IMC to help them in matters of religious liberty, and that meant precisely very difficult and protracted political negotiations.

Co-operation and Unity

Perhaps the most difficult issue on the agenda of the missionary movement has been the relations of missions and churches in the evangelistic task. There were two major tasks—to persuade the missionary agencies to work together and to develop relations of partnership with the indigenous churches. At Edinburgh, among the very small band of participants from Asia, two of them challenged the conference in ways that caused deep consternation. Cheng Ching-Yi said: "Speaking plainly, we hope to see in the near future a united Christian Church without any denominational distinctions... The future China will largely depend on what is done at the present time... The Church of Christ is universal, not only irrespective of denominations, but also irrespective of nationalities." V. S. Azariah raised his voice against the racist and paternalistic attitudes of missionaries towards nationals in India and elsewhere. He said to a stunned audience: "You have given your goods to feed the poor. You have given your bodies to be burned. We also ask for love. Give us FRIENDS!"

The Continuation Committee took up the challenge and John R. Mott did much to develop National Christian Councils, particularly in Asia, and to promote better relations between missionaries and nationals. The Jerusalem Conference was the first of its kind in human history when representatives from all over the world could sit together on equal terms. Moreover, one year after the Edinburgh Conference, Mott visited Orthodox Patriarchates and pioneered the participation of the Orthodox in the ecumenical movement. At its meeting in 1912 the Continuation Committee received a report giving statistics on "Missions of the Greek Orthodox Church". A prominent American layman, Silas McBee, had persuaded Monsignor Bonomelli, the Roman Catholic Bishop of Cremona, and reputedly a close friend of the Pope, to send a message to the conference. This message is a remarkable document, antedating the spirit of Vatican II by over 50 years. He wrote:

The most desirable and precious of human liberties, religious liberty, may now be said to be a grand conquest of contemporary humanity, and it enables men of various faiths to meet together, not for the purpose of hating and combating each other, for the supposed greater glory of God, but in order to consecrate themselves in Christian love to the pursuit of that religious truth which unites all believers in Christ. United in one faith, the various spiritual forces combine in the adoration of the one true God in spirit and in truth.

(Gairdner: *Edinburgh 1910*, p. 210)

We have made valiant efforts over the years to develop relationships in mission which are consonant with our calling as sharing a common life in the Body of Christ. At all the world missionary conferences up to Bangkok these issues have been hotly discussed. But we have not got very far in the ecumenical sharing of resources and in our partnership in the Gospel. The power of money and of other resources has prevailed. It is our earnest hope that this conference will carry us further along in our quest for true co-operation and unity.

The third major issue I wanted to bring to your attention as we survey these 70 years is the inter-related character of the various parts of the ecumenical movement on mission. The YMCA and YWCA and later the World Student Christian Federation prepared the way for Edinburgh by creating relationships of friendship and co-operation across the barriers of nations, cultures, races and sexes. Edinburgh 1910 inspired the establishment of the Life and Work movement (1925) and the Faith and Order movement (1928). The work of these movements in turn played a big role in determining the content of the Jerusalem Conference in 1928. Indeed, the 1927 Faith and Order conference statement on the Christian message was incorporated in the Jerusalem statement. J. H. Oldham became the organizer of the World Conference on Church, Community and State in 1938, which was followed by the Faith and Order Conference. These had a profound influence on the Madras Conference, which itself prepared the way for the active participation of Third World churches and Christians in the formation of the World Council of Churches in 1948 following the Whitby Conference in 1947. The Willingen Conference of 1952 had some effect on the Lund Faith and Order meeting when the principle was enunciated that the churches should act together in all matters except those in which deep differences of conviction compelled them to act separately. And so it has continued until now. The basic conviction behind this was expressed at Amsterdam in 1948 when the World Council of Churches came into being: "The whole Church with the whole Gospel to the whole person in the whole world." One of the purposes of this gathering here in Melbourne is to demonstrate this inter-related character of our calling to mission and to further the cause of mutuality and justice in partnership.

This has been a long pilgrimage, from Edinburgh to Melbourne—and well should it be, because momentous events have taken place both in the world of peoples and nations and in the churches through the missionary movement. What is remarkable about this period is the extraordinary boldness, courage, courtesy, faith, hope and love displayed by all those who were involved in this great movement. It was William Carey who had said: "Expect great things from God. Attempt great things for God." He was planning a world gathering on mission for 1810 but his dream was not fulfilled until 1910. It was J. H. Oldham who used to say: "We must dare in order to know." In these 70 years many things have been dared in obedience to the Gospel of the kingdom of God. We can do no less today.

The times in which we live call for, what Bishop Charles Brent said at Edinburgh, "the courage to dare and the courage to bear"—to dare to speak and act for the sake of the kingdom and to bear one another's burdens as those who seek to proclaim and live the way of the kingdom. This is my hope for this conference and for the decisions and actions which will follow. For all this we must begin, continue and end with the prayer: "Your Kingdom Come". Over 50 years ago, William Paton, that intrepid missionary apostle, ended a book, *The Faith for the World*, with the story of a Telugu girl in India who was learning to pray and who folded her hands and said: "Our Father, our Father, Thy Kingdom, Amen." May this be our prayer throughout this conference.

The Role of Students in the Missionary Movement
Emidio Campi*

It is a joy and a privilege to take part in this opening ceremony. I extend to you very warm greetings and wishes from the World Student Christian Federation (WSCF).

During this conference we shall be remembering that seventy years ago a momentous event took place in the life of the ecumenical movement—the opening of the World Missionary Conference at Edinburgh. It so happens that this year we shall also recall another ecumenical anniversary: the founding of the World Student Christian Federation eighty-five years ago at Valdstena, Sweden. I do not mention this fact in order to suggest some kind of ecumenical "right of seniority". My point is slightly different. There is a unifying factor, a spiritual logic in these two anniversaries. Edinburgh 1910 expresses the commitment to the integration of the missionary dimension in the total calling of the Church. Valdstena 1895 expresses the dynamism of the greatest surge of student commitment to mission in the history of the Church. Together, these two anniversaries sum up and epitomize the enthusiasm, the hopes and the limitations of the nineteenth century missionary movement.

It is, therefore, not surprising that the planning and preparation of the 1910 conference was largely the work of the Student Christian Movement (SCM) and the WSCF. This can best be seen in the life and work of the two men to whom the Federation and the ecumenical movement in general are deeply indebted: John R. Mott and J. H. Oldham. At the time of the Edinburgh Conference, which they organized, they were respectively General Secretary of the WSCF and Study Secretary of the British SCM. And when the World Missionary Conference resulted in the Continuation Committee, later to become the International Missionary Council, it was not surprising that J. R. Mott became its first chairman (holding that office until 1941) and J. H. Oldham its first secretary.

Other examples could easily be given to show the strategic role that the student movement has played in the emergence and development of the modern

---

*The Rev. Dr Emidio Campi, Italy, is General Secretary of the World Student Christian Federation.

missionary movement both in nurturing its leadership and in providing the initial testing ground for new visions. Three call for explicit mention.

The Orthodox churches were not represented at Edinburgh in 1910. But the very next year the WSCF organized a World Conference at Constantinople with the specific aim of breaking through the barriers of ignorance and misunderstanding which had kept East and West separated for many centuries and entering into fellowship with Orthodox Christians. Surveying the delegates and observers who attended that conference, John R. Mott asked: "When, since the early Councils, has there come together a gathering representing so nearly the entire Christian Church?" This student meeting provided the inspiration for new contacts between eastern and western churches. Historians of the ecumenical movement record the fact that at this meeting at Constantinople, people like Nathan Söderblom, Bishop Germanos of Thyatira, Nicolai Velimirovic came to understand that it was part of their vocation to prepare the way for an ecumenical movement in which the Orthodox churches would participate fully.

In the exploration of new ways to be relevantly engaged in the world, the WSCF has served as an experimental laboratory in the re-thinking of the relationship between Christian faith and political involvement. The possibility of Christian witness in the struggles for liberation has been widely debated in the Federation during the last two decades or so. In this debate, traditional sources of conflict have simply vanished into the air. We have learned that it is not incompatible to be believers who live our vocations within the context of the struggles for human liberation. It is possible to prefigure a new type of Christian community that participates in the difficult but not utopian task of building a new society and, at the same time, confesses Jesus Christ as the Lord of history. Even more momentous has been the growing realization of the need for "doing theology", taking into account political, economic and social factors. The risk of calling things by their right names was fully accepted. Political theology, liberation theology, materalist reading of the Bible, approaches by social psychology and other social sciences to the analysis of various manifestations of Christian faith have been, along with other traditional theological methods, courageously experimented within the Federation and in the related programme, "Frontier Internship in Mission".

As we have expanded the membership to more than ninety countries, mostly from Africa, Asia, Latin America, the WSCF, as the first world ecumenical organization, took the bold step in 1968 of regionalizing its work. This was not only a practical programmatic measure, but also a way of looking seriously into the question of how an international Christian movement may be more authentically rooted in the life of different areas of the world, and how the emphasis on local involvement alters the self-understanding of the Christian community as an international body.

Obviously, students today look with some amusement at the pictures of gentlemen in cutaways who convened at Edinburgh in 1910. The solemn and sonorous phrases of the addresses and reports of 1910 belong to a style very different from the direct expression of youth today. Students today see that the 1910 Conference was a world conference only in name. Most of the churches in what is now called the Third World were still under the tutelage of the western churches. The philosophy of history which stated that "the best years are ahead" (J. R. Mott's famous dictum!) does not carry conviction with the present student generation facing the problem of survival of human life on this planet. Particularly, the watchword of "evangelization of the world in this generation", which permeated the thinking and the deliberations at Edinburgh, would be classified today as an example of triumphalism that is quite out of fashion.

Is the Edinburgh Conference representative of an era irrevocably gone, the missionary equivalent of Thomas Mann's prophesy for western civilization? I do not think so. The Edinburgh Conference was not the "Magic Mountain" from which one descends only to die. It was rather a sentinel, alerting people to the coming of new things. It was an appeal from students to students and to the churches for the realization of a vision that transformed and will continue to transform the life of the churches. Young men and women who later became leaders of the ecumenical movement were brought into the ecumenical fellowship through that appeal. However differently interpreted, there can be no doubt that, since Edinburgh 1910, very close personal, theological and ministerial links have existed between the student and missionary movement in our common search for finding ways of being relevantly obedient to the challenge and call of God in historical situations.

I have mentioned these well-known facts in order to point out the unique relationship between the student and missionary movements, and now I would like to make a suggestion regarding the future work that we may undertake. Its simplicity, perhaps its seemingly commonplace character, would be easily dismissed unless it is seen in this context.

The suggestion is this: because the university/student world has been and will remain for the immediate future one of the primary places where education is consciously undertaken, and because it attracts people from all walks of life, from varied social, political and economic origins, who hope to gain not only the qualities but also the benefits that education brings, it is imperative that in conceptualizing and articulating the missionary task of the future, this conference gives critical consideration to the needs of students, faculty and other members of this world, integrating questions related specifically to university life into its planning. I am suggesting that this conference recognize the strategic place that this university/student world occupies in contemporary life.

Such a suggestion, of course, is nothing new. It is in fact embedded in the very founding of the missionary movement. John R. Mott used to repeat that the "student world is a strategic point in the world's life". This world which is the training ground of future leaders, breeding place of new ideas and transmitter of old ones, the working place of some very common, some very odd, some very pedantic and some exceptionally bright and alert people, this world, with its peculiar ethos, its special needs and challenges, according to our common founding fathers, constitutes a very strategic point in the evangelization of the world. The church must therefore penetrate it, must learn its language and partake of its life, and must recruit its members for the church's task.

Of course, more recent experience has taught us that the romanticism of the earlier evangelical zeal towards the university and students was not viable. The university, we have learned, is as much a defender of the status quo as the critical trail-blazer of a new society. But, if more recent experience precludes any romanticism, this does *not* mean that the student/university world has become less important and crucial in our societies. On the contrary, as we face the last two decades of this amazing twentieth century, its importance looms as clearly as ever. It calls us more than ever to give attention to it, and to seek within this milieu a more vigorous expression of Christian witness than was expressed in the past. Of the many factors that may be mentioned to support this concern, two, I think, are important to bear in mind: a) the extraordinary growth of student population; b) the incredible control and manipulation of science and education towards ends that are antithetical to human liberation and total development. Can we, in this context, ignore such a crucial and important arena for Christian witness to the kingdom of God? Can we neglect the obvious strategic importance this arena holds in the economy of human liberation in our time?

To some extent the Student Christian Movements can provide some initial responses to this challenge, but more *visions, farsightedness* and *involvement are required from the entire Christian community* if this arduous task is to be accomplished. As we look back at the road travelled during the past seventy years and the challenges lying ahead, this should not be an impossible request. Indeed, in renewing tradition we best show our respect for it.

Your Kingdom Come: A Missionary Perspective
EMILIO CASTRO*

Seven years ago, in Bangkok, the findings of the World Mission Conference on "Salvation Today" were summed up in the phrase: "We are entering into the era of world mission." This simple affirmation referred to several facts: the churches were present everywhere; there was no longer a central place from which mission was initiated; every church in every place was called to be a committed missionary community; the local churches were not required to be repetitions of a model developed somewhere in some central place, but should illustrate the manifold answers that the human soul is capable of giving to the call of God in Jesus Christ. Because missionary responsibility belonged to every church in the world, Bangkok did not shy away from raising the issue of *moratorium*, a halting of relationships of financial support among churches, because this, too, could enhance the obedience of the churches.

"World mission" also therefore implies an attitude of dialogue in relation to other religions and ideologies. Dialogue is a way to describe God's attitude towards humankind: serving, suffering, calling, hoping. This dimension of the Gospel is rediscovered today as churches increasingly find themselves side by side with people of other convictions and discover the importance of joining forces with them in facing common problems. They are learning that the testimony to Jesus Christ can only be rendered in normal daily life, in the midst of relationships of friendship, respect and collaboration.

The biblical concept of salvation was related in Bangkok to all aspects of life, showing how the search for justice and peace, reconciliation among people, belongs to the very heart of God's saving will for humankind. Consequently, churches were called to assume their missionary vocation responding in different contexts, committing themselves to the proclamation of salvation *in relation* to the present needs of their respective societies.

The findings of Bangkok met, in the churches, both receptivity and opposition. Looking back, however, it is clear that the conference's agenda,

---

*The Rev. Emilio Castro, Uruguay, is Director of the Commission on World Mission and Evangelism of the World Council of Churches.

and its main affirmations, were soon taken up in all currents of Christian thought. I make no claim that the Lausanne Congress on Evangelism or the Synod of Bishops of the Roman Catholic Church were taking up the agenda of Bangkok! What I am saying is that because we worship the same God and read the same Bible, and live in the same world, it is impossible to avoid the same topics and, in large degree, similar conclusions! We have today, after Bangkok, a body of common convictions set forth in documents, but even more clearly, a growing experience of common witness.

We have come together in Melbourne under the topic "Your Kingdom Come". You are involved in that "world mission" that Bangkok sought to describe. You come from all confessional backgrounds. In the preparation of this conference, Roman Catholics, Orthodox and Protestants have worked together side by side. You represent churches from the most diverse cultural settings in the world and you belong to diverse frontiers or areas of responsibility. Some of you have policy-making roles in the direction of missionary societies and agencies. Others are fully involved in grass-roots communities fighting in the name of Jesus Christ for the creation of more human conditions for life. Some of you come from local parishes; others are members of the churches' hierarchies. Because we are in this period of "world mission", it is fitting that representatives of *all* aspects of the churches' life should come together to face their common missionary and evangelistic vocation.

It will be essential to the success of our conference that we allow concrete local experiences to illustrate and question our theoretical discussions. An international meeting provides occasion for reciprocal questioning, for the sometimes polemic and often passionate mutual correction. We hope, especially, that we will learn from the experience of those who are working with the poor of the earth. Generally speaking, history has been written by the winners. The history of Christian thought has not escaped this rule; it has been written by those who have been winners of wars and are winners in the economic structures of the world. We hope that new aspects of the Gospel of Jesus Christ will appear as we read his Word and meditate on the kingdom from the experience and perspective of the poor of the earth.

We gather here around a prayer of Jesus, "Your Kingdom Come", and so we pray together. We gather around a Bible text, so we shall study the Word of God. We have come to find inspiration and help in the fulfilment of our missionary task, as we discover new callings, new challenges.

Let me now make my personal contribution to the debate, remembering some of the dimensions of the theme "Your Kingdom Come" that have emerged in the process of preparation, which we hope may be relevant for each of the four sections and the conference as a whole.

First, Bangkok emphasized cultural identity. It said "culture shapes the human voice that answers the voice of Christ... The Christian faith must be at home in every context and yet it can never be completely identical with it. Therefore there will be a rich diversity."

These affirmations are now recognized everywhere. But Bangkok paved the way for stating this old missiological problem in new terms: what is the theological value of our traditional cultures? It is not only my right or my duty to respond from within my culture to the calling of Christ, but I must consider the history of my people, the stories of my parents, in the perspective of the kingdom of God. To see their relation to God's providence, to redemption in Jesus Christ. Am I to believe that God's concern for the people of Taiwan or Korea began only 60, 80 or 90 years ago when western missionaries arrived with the Gospel of Jesus Christ?

In Latin America, we celebrate, on the 12th of October, "Discovery Day". That has traditionally been considered the beginning of our history. We are learning now to look at history from other perspectives, to see it through the eyes of those who in the European view were being discovered, but who, from their own perspective, were being invaded, massacred, subjected. Traditional Indian cultures are still there, present among the Indians of the high mountains, real in the collective unconscious of our people. Very often, our preaching and teaching as Christian churches has made people ashamed of their own ancestors, and they have hidden the practise of their cultural and religious traditions out of fear of being, if not persecuted, at least ostracized. We have even denounced as syncretism all manifestations of Christian faith where elements of traditional cultures or religions were present. This is an old problem in theological debates. I hope that we will have a word of encouragement to say to those who are trying to recover their traditions in the perspective of the Christian faith.

As Christians who have received the revelation of God in Jesus Christ, we should be able to see signs of the kingdom in every culture, in every nation. The Old Testament recognizes the action of God in other nations. As the people of Israel were the chosen vessels for his revelation, so Cyrus was chosen to be the historical liberator from the Babylonian captivity. Jesus said: "There are many other sheep of mine, not belonging to this fold, whom I must bring in and they, too, will listen to my voice" (John 10:16). In the struggle for his kingdom, God has used, and uses, various cultural and historical means, and the Church of Jesus Christ has the particular task of disclosing the final revelation of God in Jesus Christ. But this revelation entitles us, not to despise, but to cherish all achievements in the history of peoples that correspond to kingdom values. As the wise men came from the Orient, bringing their offerings to the child in Bethlehem, so will the cultural richness of humankind also be brought to the throne of the Lamb who reigns.

We must not, of course, idealize our cultural past. Sin was also a reality then; sin is still a reality today. But Jesus' attitude of sympathy and compassion for the multitudes was the source of his judgements and his calls to repentance. The invitation to repentance comes with the Good News of the kingdom. To link our history and culture with the story of Jesus Christ surely will produce both judgement and change. We are not proclaiming an easy continuity between history and the kingdom. But, just as we ourselves, as servants of Christ, pass through death and resurrection with the earthly body while preserving continuity with our personal identity, so we also hope that through death and resurrection, by going through the fire, those manifestations of the kingdom which have permeated our history and are present today in our human cultures, will also be accepted as our offering on God's altar. This hopeful approach to cultures will bring with it new possibilities for evangelism: we come from Jesus to see our cultures. We look from our cultures to Jesus. We try to link our history to his story. Evangelization happens in this way, planting the seeds of the Gospel of the kingdom in the soul of our culture, where we already discern manifestations of the presence of that kingdom. There, the Gospel will fulfil its role as salt, leaven, light, by transforming, enriching, evangelizing the very frame and structure of the life of our nations.

A non-imperialistic evangelism, a faithful evangelism that aims at the transformation and permeation of societies from within, looks to the kingdom that is coming as the recapitulation of all things in Jesus Christ. That recapitulation will include our lives and also our cultures. I am sure that all four sections will need to deal with this issue, but particularly sections I and II which should look to the culture of the poor, finding there hidden treasures of the Spirit among them and, without romanticizing, seeing what it means to announce the Good News of the kingdom that is promised to them and to whose service they are called in faith and repentance.

Secondly, after Bangkok, the Russian Orthodox Church sent to the World Council of Churches a letter commenting on the conference. In it, they mentioned one particular concern: salvation has meant traditionally, and in the daily life of the Orthodox Church, entrance into eternal life. And while they recognized the importance and the duty of Christian participation in social issues, they wanted to highlight the reality of salvation as hope beyond death, as life in God. A critical remark of this kind might need to be addressed to us here, because we are looking at the kingdom in close relation to the historical events of the world. Bangkok, of course, did not deny eternal life. It perhaps took it for granted as the fundamental conviction of the Church, and concentrated instead on calling our attention to immediate priorities and responsibilities.

Perhaps today, with the prayer "Your Kingdom Come", we can and should be more explicit. We do not, of course, want to escape our historical responsibilities. We want to encourage people to participate fully in the shaping of their respective societies. But precisely because we believe in the historical responsibility of Christians and of all human beings, and in order to find inspiration, courage and vision for the historical task, we confess our faith in a kingdom that is not limited to the horizon of our historical death. The missionary movement was committed to overcome all distances, to cross all borders, to open all frontiers with the message of the kingdom. Today we want to recover the biblical meaning of time, and to reaffirm that our past, and our future, the future of our nations, our societies, but also our personal future, beyond death, belong to the economy of the kingdom. To die is not to be lost to the kingdom, because God in Christ has overcome even the last enemy, death itself. Those who die in the kingdom's struggle are also participants in the hope of the kingdom that is coming. We make passionate speeches in remembrance of those who have been the victims of repression and those who have paid the price for victory. But these words of remembrance, can only promise a historical memory. And, without being cynical, we know that this can only be true for the few. The many are forgotten. But we want to remember today those who die in their carpentry shops, in schoolrooms, in planting seeds that produce food for the people, in taking care of children, in creating loving relations in their neighbourhoods, who organize themselves in the struggle for justice, those who are not able even to name their real enemies. We are thinking of the peasants in El Salvador who are being killed every day in the mountains of that small country, without any mention in the press apart from their number. We are remembering with gratitude the ministry and death of Archbishop Romero of El Salvador. His sacrifice and the sacrifice of the many other Salvadorians is fruitful not only for the historical destiny of the Salvadorian people, but also, in the total economy of the kingdom, for the working out of God's eternal plans to bring all things to newness in Jesus Christ.

Our vision of the kingdom overcomes time and death, and invites us to believe that those who have surrendered their lives belong to that "cloud of witnesses" who follow the historical struggle, and through God's love we are in relation with them. How then can we make a contradiction between our entering into historical struggles and our belief in eternal life with God? It is precisely because we discern the ultimate within the struggles for the penultimate that we engage seriously in those struggles, surrendering even our lives because we know that our failures, too, can be used by God as he used the Cross of his only begotten son Jesus Christ to advance the redemption of humankind, to bring the kingdom.

When the sacred words of our Christian faith recover their biblical dimension, they will also recover their historical dimensions; the Good News of the kingdom will then be recognized as such, will become polemic, will invite us to enter into an historical struggle that culminates in the total transformation of creation.

Thirdly, we have encountered a difficulty in our biblical preparation for this conference: the relation of the message of the Apostle Paul to the teachings of the Gospel and to the Old Testament. While in the Old Testament and in the Gospel we have a clear historical line, a calling to manifest faith in historical action, the impression has been given that in the Apostle Paul we have a more individualistic message, a message of a more spiritual kind. We seem to move from the realm of collective history to the realm of existential personal decisions. While the kingdom is the main theme of the Gospel, it seems that the personal relation to Jesus, conversion, faith, grace are the new reality that the Apostle Paul describes.

I hope that our discussion of the prayer of Jesus, "Your Kingdom Come", will help us to understand the fallacy of this division. While various theological interpretations are evident in the pages of the Bible, its overwhelming theme is that God takes seriously the totality of human life and human history, so seriously that he sent his only begotten Son to live in the midst of that history, to suffer from it, to die for it, to bring redemption to it. If we look more closely at the Old Testament references, in Jesus' teaching about the kingdom—and in particular at his manifesto in Luke 4: "He comes to announce the acceptable year of the Lord"—we will discern a direct reference to the teaching of the Old Testament on the Jubilee Year, that moment once every fifty years when the land was redistributed and when every family, every tribe had the chance of a new beginning. It was not justice based on merit, but pure grace, a redistribution of land to create a new beginning in history. The kingdom that Jesus announced is not based on retribution but on the offering of grace by a God who provides for every one of his children an opportunity for a new beginning in life.

Is that not precisely the message of the Apostle Paul when he speaks of salvation through grace and justification by faith? These old themes of our Christian traditions, salvation by grace, justification by faith, co-operation with God, find in a theology of the kingdom their just and fair place. We are incorporated into that liberating movement of the Divine Spirit which in Jesus Christ breaks all the chains of yesterday, freeing history to attain its full potential. Our missionary obligation is to announce the kingdom of freedom, and to invite all to participation in the transformation of all things in the perspective of the kingdom.

I quote here our Vice-Moderator Jacques Maury when he says: "I can accept the forgiveness of my sins without great difficulty. That belongs to the traditional teachings of my Church. That has been incorporated in our liturgical life. I accept it as an affirmation of my faith in the sacrifice of Jesus Christ. But it is very difficult for me to accept the collective forgiveness of the white race. My share in the guilt of a situation of oppression and colonization has a long history, and consequences even longer. How can I accept the forgiveness of the white race when the consequences of our sin are still evident?"

There are situations, historically speaking and from our human point of view, that cannot be fully corrected. How shall we escape from paying the bills of yesterday? How can we be open to a new beginning?

When the people of Latin America look towards the future and consider it closed because of a situation of oppression that seems hopeless, they exclaim—like the disciples in their last interview with the risen Christ: "Oh Lord, how long? When will you bring back the Kingdom to Israel?" But they also hear the promise of the Lord: "Times and seasons are in God's hand, and you will receive the power of the Holy Spirit, and you will be my witness." You will receive the possibility of a new beginning, struggling for the transformation of all reality. Perhaps the old law of jubilee was never applied historically in Israel. We cannot and we should not make a direct transplant from the Bible into our historical situation. But the utopia promise of the jubilee is taken up by Jesus and converted into an historical dynamic, in a beginning of new life, in a living principle for our human struggles.

To pray today "Your Kingdom Come" is to raise the banner of concrete hopes; it is to announce freedom to the captives.

Fourthly, Jesus came *proclaiming* the Gospel of the kingdom of God, Good News to the people. The Kingdom is to be announced. That was central in Jesus; that should be central to us. "As the Father sent me, so I send you." We are here in a conference on evangelism. This kingdom of God for which we pray must be announced and announced as Good News. John R. Mott, urging the "evangelization of the world in this generation", perhaps succumbed too easily to the optimism of the Victorian era. But his watchword pointed to the fundamental Christian vocation: we are called to announce to every creature the Good News of a new day in Jesus Christ, the Good News of new possibilities for human life, the Good News of the promise of God's Kingdom coming to us. We know the difficulties. How can the Church announce the Good News if the very same Church appears historically to have been an ally of the bearer of bad news? How can we come with the proclamation of the message of redemption and freedom in God's kingdom, when so many people have seen slavery coming to them through colonialism, even in the name of the Christian faith?

We should remember the statement made by a Hindu observer in the Assembly of the World Council of Churches in Nairobi in 1975: "I think that I understand what this is all about. You would like all of us to come to be like you are, Christians. Thank you, I am not interested. Because, from you people, from the West, has come colonization, imperialism, pollution, the atomic war, etc." For him and for many, the close union over the centuries between Western expansion and the Christian community makes it almost impossible to distinguish between the guilt of Christianity and the guilt of the West. No doubt there are churches with different histories, less associated with these sins of Christianity; and perhaps other observers will not pronounce such categorical judgements. We all recognize, however, the ambiguity of our situation, especially when we measure our Christian life against the excellence of our Christian declarations. But surely the centuries of Christian presence in the world have added another dimension of difficulty to the proclamation of the Gospel. The Church is taken for granted. There is a certain familiarity with the words of the faith. Those words have been tamed. They appear to refer to some kind of religious experience which can be compared with the experience produced in other ways and in other religious traditions. The sceptical phrase that was mentioned in relation to Jesus, "Can anything good come from Nazareth?", can now be applied to the Church. Today perhaps we could even say: "It is from Nazareth, from the Church that something new may come!" Christian language is so tame that it no longer brings with it revolutionary power. It provokes neither fear nor turmoil. Yes, we recognize all these difficulties, and could add others. And our temptation may be to keep silent. Bishop Wickham of Sheffield once called the Church to silence for a couple of generations, in order to recover the right to speak to the working class in England! It may be possible to keep silent for the sake of better communication, but we cannot keep silent because of our failures. For, finally, we do not preach ourselves, but call people to look *beyond* us to the reality of the kingdom.

We are under the command that "this Gospel of the kingdom should be proclaimed to the ends of the earth". We also believe that the promise of the kingdom belongs to the poor of the earth. Who are we to deprive the masses of people of the world of the knowledge of the preference which God has for them? The Gospel of the kingdom is not our private property to be disposed of as we wish. It belongs to those to whom it is addressed. It belongs to those who are outside the Church. I do not have the right to keep silent forever. On the contrary, I must constantly look for better ways to proclaim rightly, to announce the Gospel of Jesus Christ. Even more. If out of our Christian missionary vocation we do fully participate in the struggles of the world, in solidarity with the poor, unavoidably questions of motivation and meaning will need to be faced.

I Peter 3:11 says: "Be always ready with your defence whenever you are called to account for the hope that is within you..." Just as we cannot preach the Gospel of the kingdom without facing the questions of grace and judgement, life and death, justice and peace, so we cannot enter in the historical struggles of the kingdom without being challenged to name the Lord Jesus and to give witness to him.

The proclamation of the Gospel of the kingdom includes an invitation to join the kingdom, to participate in its struggles. Evangelism, then, becomes revolutionary engagement: repentance becomes a transformation of our practice, our faith, a commitment to the King. Surely critical questions must be faced about our being Christians and about our being Christian churches. Is that repentance which is called for by the proclamation of the Gospel expressed first of all in us who call ourselves Christians?

Are the methodologies of proclamation we use coherent with the content of the Gospel? Section I will be especially concerned with the Church as witness to the kingdom. Their fundamental question will be: "What fruit of Church life, what Christian style will make us proclaimers of the kingdom?" But of course the conviction that the Gospel of the kingdom is entrusted to the Church to be proclaimed will oblige all sections to do some serious thinking.

Fifth, we proclaim that the kingdom has come in the King, Jesus of Nazareth. Leslie Newbegin has reminded us that it is easier to say "Your Kingdom Come" than to pray "*Maranatha*, Come Lord Jesus". With the expression "kingdom", we are related to all the dreams of humankind: it would be difficult to find a people whose religion, or ideology, does not expect a new day in the future. But when we confess our faith in Jesus Christ as Lord, we make a particular affirmation: we are calling people to recognize in the events of Golgotha and of the garden tomb, the redeeming and saving power of God with consequences for all humankind. To add a new God to the Pantheon of gods in the Roman Empire was not difficult. Romans had learned to live with their kind of religious tolerance. We live in a pluralistic world, where in the name of tolerance we try to avoid all absolute pretensions, although the religious and ideological map of the world indicates the tragic result of those pretensions! As Christians, we recognize values in all the peoples of the earth and in all religious movements. We also confess our own Christian limitations. We do, however, render testimony to Jesus of Nazareth, in whose death we have found sacrificial love, in whose resurrection we have the assurance that even our worst enemy, death itself, has been defeated.

How do we proclaim Jesus as Lord, Jesus as the King in this pluralistic world with any credibility? The affirmation of the Kingship of Jesus sounds imperialistic today, although in the time of Herod and Pilate, it sounded simply like a ridiculous pretension.

How can we express today loyalty to a King who was born in a manger and died on a Cross, who tried to transform all human realities, not through the "fiat" of his will, but through participation in the struggles of humankind, becoming one among us, sharing our sufferings and hopes? The announcement of the King Jesus Christ sounds today like a manifestation of intolerance and pride. The Apostle Paul, claiming Jesus as Lord, was able to speak of himself and of the Christians in very humble terms: "My brothers, think what sort of people you are whom God has called. Few of you are men of wisdom by any human standard. Few are powerful or highly born. Yet to shame the wise, God has chosen what the world calls folly and to shame what is strong, God has chosen what the world calls weakness. He has chosen things low and contemptible, mere nothings to overthrow the existing order" (I Cor. 1:26-28). The exclusivism of our proclamation disappears when we announce Him who gave his life for all. The pride and sense of possession of the Christian community disappears when we confess *our* sins, the special sins of Christians. The pride disappears with the knowledge that the King, Jesus Christ, is not a possession to cherish but a cross to take up, a mission to participate in, a love to show.

The difficulty of recognizing Jesus was already evident in the Gospel, most markedly when the disciples of John the Baptist came to see Jesus and asked: "Are you the one who is to come or are we to expect some other?" Jesus answered: "Go and tell John what you see and hear. The blind recover their sight. The lame walk. The lepers are made clean. The deaf healed. The dead are raised to life. The poor are hearing the good news. And happy is the man who does not find me a stumbling block" (Matt. 11:2-6). The question remains: Is Jesus the One who was supposed to come? Is He the One who is sent by God to respond to the needs and expectations of all people? Which are the signs by which He is recognized? They are always the same: the poor, the marginalized, those without power, are blessed. We can only offer one possible proof: self-surrendering love. How far from this are our beautiful apologetic systems!

We who would also give witness to the King, who manifested his kingship by taking the towel and basin to wash the feet of his disciples, give evidence of that self-surrendering love whenever the cross is the inspiring centre of our lifestyle and a servant solidarity with the poor is shown. Then our proclamation of Jesus as Lord can be made in the hope that the miracle of faith, conversion, will become a reality.

The question then becomes very personal: whom do I serve? The honesty of our proclamation is proved as all our old loyalties are shaken. While we respect and rejoice in the values of other religions and other *weltanschauung*, we witness to Him in whom we find the first fruits of the kingdom, and we invite everybody to look towards Him.

Let us finish this introduction by noting three fundamental things: First, our central theme is a prayer, "Your Kingdom Come". We are in a spiritual struggle and we are searching here for spiritual resources. The struggles to overcome oppressions have economic, social and political manifestations that should be considered on their own merits. But at the root there is a spiritual reality: principalities, powers of evil that need to be combated with spiritual powers and spiritual realities: the power of love, the power of hope, the power of the Gospel. To pray, to worship, is essential for our Conference.

Second, the purpose of our Conference is to help each other in our missionary vocation and especially in its evangelistic dimension. How can the churches be better servants of the kingdom today? How can they announce the coming of that kingdom? Can they help all human beings to discern beyond ourselves the full manifestation of the love of God in Jesus Christ? We shall need to discuss social, ethical issues, and ecclesiological issues. But our task will not be completed if we do not challenge with clarity our missionary vocation, our evangelistic responsibility, our discipleship.

Third, in our search and in the answers that we hope to find, we commit ourselves as persons and as communities. We are not specialists who provide recipes for others! We are Christians who share our attempts to be faithful in our different circumstances, bringing here the anguish and the glories of our respective crosses, expressing our convictions with passion, and the discussion will always be heavily emotional. So that the expression of our findings in documents should not necessarily be limited to conceptual or academic styles. The cry, the poem, the prayer, the story, even silence may be used in order to transmit the reality of our search and the agony of our agreements. May God bless us, as we attempt the impossible.

The Gospel of the Kingdom and the Crucified and Risen Lord
METROPOLITAN GEEVARGHESE MAR OSTHATHIOS*

Where are we now?

We pray, "Your Kingdom come, Your will be done on earth as it is in heaven" and live with the motto, "My kingdom come, my will be done in my place as it is in West Germany or USA or China or Soviet Union". We say we have a Gospel of the kingdom to preach, and preach everything under the sky except "Jesus Christ crucified" (I Cor. 1:23). If at all we preach a crucified Christ, he is a domesticated Christ who puts no stumbling block before our luxurious lifestyle, callous provincialism, and selfish denominationalism. We are deeply convinced that the kingdom of God is abundant life on earth and our risen Christ has no nail marks on him. Even if he has nail marks on his palms and feet, we can afford to be his followers as he has paid the ransom on our behalf. The various theories of atonement we have created are mostly substitutionary and so there is no need of bleeding Christians or cross-bearing missionaries due to the finished work of Christ. We need not repeat St. Paul's experience, "Now I rejoice in my sufferings for your sake, and in my flesh complete what is lacking in Christ's afflictions for the sake of his body, that is the Church" (Col. 1:14). Dietrich Bonhoeffer's eloquence against cheap grace and the plea for costly grace is enjoyed and quoted by all of us with no change in our *praxis* of enjoying freely and cheaply the costly grace earned for us by the One who cried on the first Good Friday, *"Eli, Eli, Lama Sabachthani"* (Mark 15:34). We believe that salvation wrought by the crucified and risen Christ is free and unmerited as a reaction to the wrong Roman Catholic teaching on the Treasury of Merits and conveniently forget the injunction of St. Paul: "Work out your salvation with fear and trembling; for God is at work in you, both to will and to work for his good pleasure" (Phil. 2:12).

Is God really at work in us or we ourselves at work in us? We have separated the last commission from the double commandment to love God absolutely and the neighbour as we love ourselves, because the former is easy

---

*His Eminence Metropolitan Geevarghese Mar Osthathios is Principal of the Orthodox Theological Seminary, Kottayam, Kerala, India.

and the latter very hard and utopian. We do conveniently forget that the sin of the rich man was nothing other than allowing his neighbour Lazarus to remain poor while he was himself rich. The gospel of the kingdom committed to us seems to be either Liberation theology with no stress on the eschatological dimension or Black theology which puts all the Blacks who are oppressed on the side of God and all the whites as oppressors against God, knowing in our heart of hearts that there are oppressors among the Blacks also just as there are oppressed among the whites. We all have our partial gospels, either in the form of a Christ-Monism, with no role for the Holy Spirit or the charismatic gospel with no social concerns, or the Unitarian gospel with hardly anything more than what our Jewish and Islamic friends preach. The Roman Catholic Church has its infallible Pope, the Protestant brethren the infallible Bible, the Orthodox the infallible Tradition with a capital 'T' and hardly anybody has the full implication of the Trinitarian faith with the equality that it demands.

Some of us present the Good News of the kingdom as bad news of eternal hell to all the non-Christians who do not accept Christ as their personal Saviour and get baptized to their own brand of Christianity. Certainly that was not the approach of our Saviour to the Samaritan woman. As pointed out by Karl Barth and others, those who preach eternal hell preach it for others and not for themselves. Our lingering fear of syncretism is due to the lack of faith in the transforming Christ, the Logos at work in all religions and ideologies, and the "far-off Event to which the whole creation is moving; the Alpha and the Omega"[1]. If the writer of the fourth Gospel was afraid of syncretism, he would not have borrowed the Hellenistic Logos concept and made it richer. The Cappadocian Fathers were not afraid of syncretism when they used words like *phusis*, *hypostasis*, *ousia*, etc.

The greatest tragedy of our existence is the inner contradiction between our sacramental theology and practical life. To quote a passage from my book, *Theology of a Classless Society*:

> According to St. Paul, if there are divisions among us, it is not the Lord's supper that we eat. Unity in faith alone would not make us one. How can one organ of the body be lean and another fat and then call itself the body of Christ? "When you meet together it is not the Lord's supper that you eat. For in eating, each one goes ahead with his own meal, and one is hungry and another is drunk. What! Do you not have

---

[1] Rev. 1:8; 21:6; 22:13. Is it accidental that Christ is Alpha and Omega in the first, ultimate and penultimate chapters? No, he is the End in the Beginning, Beginning in the End and First and Last all through. Read the writings of Teilhard de Chardin, esp. *The Phenomenon of Man*, *The Divine Milieu*, and *Letters from a Traveller* (Collins, London).

houses to eat and drink in? Or do you despise the Church of God and humiliate those who have nothing?" (I Cor. 11:20-22). The Holy Eucharist is for those who have an intimate sharing fellowship which prompts them to share the material wealth also with those with whom they communicate.

An African friend at the Nairobi Assembly shouted: "In our culture, the brothers eat together; and if we do not eat together, we are not brothers." He is perfectly right. Brothers share the father's property alike and the members of the church must share the Father's property alike before they share in the body and blood of Christ. There is no depth in the inter-communion practised today. Communion is a *koinonia* and must be so practised and the class-structured church has no right to communicate together.[2]

Where are we now in our missionary achievements, then? The following caricature of *Matthew* 25:42f is partly from some unknown person in Latin America and I have only enlarged it:

I was hungry and you said, "Population explosion";
I was sick and you built mission hospitals into
    which I cannot afford to enter;
I was naked and you made costly clothes I cannot
    afford to buy;
I was homeless and you built palatial houses for
    yourself and dehumanizing huts for me;
I was in prison unjustly and you fought for human
    rights for yourselves;
I was thirsty and you made Coca-Cola to exploit
    my thirst;
I was a stranger and you practised apartheid and
    caste-ism against me;
O Lord, I am tired; I cannot endure it any more;
O Lord, give me strength to change the world.

How did we arrive here?

May I pinpoint five of the rules which brought us here.

We have drifted away from the joyful burden of the wooden cross to the proud glory of the golden cross. This happened decisively with the Edict of Milan in 313 A.D. and the gradual change of the suffering church to the rul-

---

[2] Osthathios, Geevarghese Mar: *Theology of a Classless Society* (Lutterworth, Guildford and London, 1979). (Forthcoming editions include an American edition by Orbis, an Asian edition by C.L.S., Madras, and a German edition by Lutherisches Verlagshaus, Hamburg.)

ing church. The true essence of Christianity had then to be maintained through the monastic movements, which also slowly became worldly to a great extent. The model of the Master is still there for us to follow: "Perceiving then that they were about to come and take him by force to make him king, Jesus withdrew again to the hills by himself" (John 6:15). But, will we dare to do so and return to the centre, namely the way of the cross?

A similar drift has taken place from the model of Joseph Barnabas who submitted his whole wealth for the sharing community to the model of Ananias and Saphira who were not ready to take the whole risk, but wanted some material security for themselves (Acts 4:34-5:11). If this was due to the waning of the eschatological hope, the church must regain that hope and share all its resources for the needy world till it can be said, "there was not a needy person among them".

This can also be called a drift away from the cross. *Kenosis* is to be seen as a joyful aspect of Christianity and not a higher and higher standard of life.

We have arrived here by the divisions of the church started with the Corinthian church. The three questions St. Paul asks them are as relevant today as they were in the first century: "Is Christ divided? Was Paul crucified for you? Or were you baptized in the name of Paul?" (I Cor. 1:13). With the dangers involved in all generalizations and sweeping statements, may I be permitted to say that we are far away from the Church of Jesus Christ and belong either to the Petrine Roman Catholicism or the Pauline Protestantism or the Johannine Orthodoxy today. With due apology, may I ask the various churches to examine their own canons within the one Canon of the Bible whether it is Petrine supremacy or justification by faith alone or speaking in tongues or adult baptism of the Parousia or something else? Is it truly necessary to exalt Peter from the college of apostles, as St. Peter called himself a "fellow elder"? Was Luther right in calling the epistle of James "the epistle of straws"? Is there no possibility of surrendering our particular faiths to what St. Paul called "one body, one spirit, one hope, one Lord, one faith, one baptism, one God and Father of all" (Eph. 4:4f)? The gospel of the kingdom of the Triune God committed to us to preach is not watered down to the gospels of Augustine, Aquinas, Luther, Calvin, Zwingli, Anabaptists, John Wesley and hundreds of others. Like St. Paul each of them is now asking us, "Was I crucified for you? Were you baptized in my name?" What we need to regain is the lost kenotic and cosmic dimensions of the Christian church. From the need-based society of the early church we have drifted away to the greed-based society of the modern world.

— On the theological front there was a drift away from the *Nicene-Constantinopolitan* Creed to a number of denominational confessions such as the Augsburg Confession of 1530, the 450th anniversary of which is being celebrated this year with the initiative of the Lutheran churches, Thirty-Nine Articles of Faith (1563), the Westminster Confession of the Presbyterian faith (1643), the Heidelberg Cathechism of the Calvinists (1562). All these had a corrective role to play and so were of real value, but the ecumenical theology cannot dilute the faith of the fathers of the undivided church as enunciated in the Nicene Creed accepted by all the churches. "So then brethren, stand firm and hold to the traditions which were taught by us, either by word or by letter" (II Thess. 2:15).

— The nineteenth century drift to Modernism or Liberalism was also a passing phase with a corrective role, but Jesus of Nazareth, crucified and risen, is more than they understood him to be: He is the Second Person of the Blessed Trinity. Johannes Weiss' essay on "Jesus' Proclamation of the Kingdom of God", first published in Gottingen in 1892 and later published by the SCM Press in 1971 with a Foreword by Rudolf Bultmann, shows the "eschatological character of the person and proclamation of Jesus" but almost totally ignores the passion of the Saviour. Albert Schweitzer's *The Mystery of the Kingdom of God* connects the secret of Jesus' messiahship with the passion. As he points out, "We must go back to the point where we feel again the heroic in Jesus. Before that mysterious Person, who, in the form of his time, knew that he was creating upon the foundation of his life and death a moral world *which bears his name*, we must be forced to lay our faces in the dust, without daring even to wish to understand his nature. Only then can the heroic in our Christianity and in our *Weltanschauung* be again revived."[3]

What then is the whole Gospel of the kingdom?

May I be permitted to mention seven aspects of the Gospel of the kingdom, granting that you can add to them.

— Christ is not for a part of humanity, but for the whole of humanity. "For I am not ashamed of the Gospel; it is the power of God for salvation to everyone who has faith, to the Jew first and also to the Greek" (Rom. 1:16). This includes the illiterate and sophisticated Indians, Chinese and Africans, as well as the people of the West. The Gospel of the kingdom is not the part-truth of the part-church, but the whole truth of the whole of humanity, because Christ the Logos is at work everywhere to bring all to the Incarnate Logos.

— The present is the opportune moment to believe and be saved, but Christ descended into Hades to show that even the disobedient departed ones

---

[3] Albert Schweitzer: *The Mystery of the Kingdom of God* (Adam and Charles Black, London, 1956), 274f.

must be given a chance to accept the Good News (I Peter 3:19; 4:6). "At the name of Jesus every knee should bow, in heaven, on earth *and under the earth* and every tongue confess Jesus Christ as Lord to the glory of God" (Phil. 2:10f). Though reward is in accordance with one's service in the world, salvation is free for all those who believe in Christ in history or beyond history.

— "The fullness of the blessing of the Gospel of Christ" includes the body, mind and soul and hence the Last Commission was to heal, exorcise and preach and thus uplift the total person. This personal dimension is only a part of the total mission of "making disciples of all nations" (Matt. 28:19). The personal and the social are included perfectly in the Blessed Trinity and that is the ultimate ideal to which Christian mission is to be directed.

— The eternally active mission of love in the Holy Trinity, which overflowed in creation of one family, "God has made of one blood all nations of men to dwell on all the face of the earth" (Acts 17:26), could not remain in Heaven leaving fallen humanity to its destiny, but descended again to the world to redeem them through his passion, death, resurrection, and he again descended into the Church at Pentecost to create an egalitarian sharing humanity of the redeemed children of God. The same agape that empties itself on the cross to create one family in the model of the triune Godhead is the distinguishing mark of Christian mission at all times.

— The pentecostal sharing was not forced on them by outward pressure, but by the "expulsive power of a new affection" combining in it the privilege of freedom and the responsibility of justice. The model communities that are thus created will not have a needy person among them because they enjoy sharing the spiritual and material wealth of the Heavenly Father among all his children.

— It is impossible to have a Gospel without the hope of Easter, as Jürgen Moltmann has ably explained in his famous *Theology of Hope*.[4] The delayed second coming of Christ is not cancelled and so we can always live in hope and preach the Gospel of resurrection. "For this slight momentary affliction is preparing for us an eternal weight of glory, beyond all comparison, because we look, not to the things that are seen, for the things that are seen are transient, but the things that are unseen are eternal" (II Cor. 4:17f).

— The full Gospel is that of the Father, the Son and the Holy Spirit, one God, world without end. Though the Holy Trinity is to be adored and not to be scrutinized, it is impossible not to explain it. The Fathers of the undivided Church have written volumes on this topic, though they knew they were not exhausting its essential mystery. I beg to submit that the all-inclusive

---

[4] Jürgen Moltmann: *The Crucified God* (SCM Press, London, 1974).

Godhead is an eternal Nuclear Family with unity and distinction within Himself. If the term Father can be used for God without sexism, the Holy Spirit can be called Mother without sexual connotation. If the Son is not eternal, the Father and Mother cannot be eternal. In the unity of the Godhead there is co-equality, co-eternity and co-essentiality. The theological foundation of a classless society is the classless Godhead Himself as a classless Nuclear Family. We are being adopted to the divine Family through the Son to share his riches equally.

The Compassionate God and not Nirguna Brahma (Attributeless Absolute)

The God of Aristotle and the Brahmen of Sankara are not compassionate. *Apatheia* is the mark of the God of the philosopher. I am glad Jürgen Moltmann was not afraid of being called guilty of the heresy of Patripassianism when he called his excellent treatise of the suffering and death of Christ *The Crucified God.*[5] To quote from it, "As Abraham Heschel shows in a comparison with Greek philosophy, with Confucianism, Buddhism and Islam, the Israelite understanding of the *pathos* of God is unique... What the Old Testament terms *the wrath of God* does not belong in the category of the anthropomorphic transference of the lower human emotions to God, but in the category of the divine pathos." Agape of God is not a lower or negative emotion, but the positive, infinite, eternal, absolute, ontological nature of God. It is not necessary to interpret *'Neti, Neti'* (not this, not that) of Brahman as *Nirguna,* but only as the absence of negative attributes in God, as Ramanja criticized Sankara's Nirguna Brahma concept.

The God revealed in Jesus Christ, however, is beyond evil, but not beyond good. We are not limiting God when we say that God is love. "The apathetic theology of antiquity was accepted as a preparation for the trinitarian theology of the love of God and of men."[6] Goodness is positive and evil is negative. Love of God is positive, though *eros* is negative. "God is light and in Him there is no darkness at all." The rays of the sun harden the clay and melt the butter. God is love and his love can be wrath on the wicked to purify him. Even the punishment of God is saving punishment.

Not only India, but the whole world is waiting for the Good News of the saving love of the Triune God. Emil Brunner should not have said that the Trinity is not to be preached. If we have to baptize in the name of the Trinity, we have to tell the catechumen why we do so. As Moltmann said in another book, "The material principle of the doctrine of Trinity is the Cross. The formal principle of the theology of the cross is the doctrine of the Trinity. The

---

[5] Ibid., 171f.
[6] Ibid., 170.

person who wants to say who God is must therefore tell the passion story of Christ as the story of God."[7]

This Gospel of the kingdom of the compassionate God who died on a cross is not only to be preached through radio and television, but also to be manifested in the life of the preacher and the community to which he belongs. St. Paul said, "Rejoice with those who rejoice, weep with those who weep" (Rom. 12:15), but we rejoice while others weep and weep while others rejoice because we have lost the Christian virtue of compassion somewhere on the way. Is it possible for a Christian with the mind of Christ to eat a square meal while others are hungry, put on costly clothes while others are naked and live in luxurious houses and hotels while their fellowmen are dwelling in the slums like animals? Do we at least have a guilty conscience when we do so and are we praying for a compassionate classless society full of the love of Christ and His concern for the hungry, the sick and the marginals? The parable of the householder who hired labourers for his vineyard (Matt. 20) manifests not only his concern for the unemployed, but also his readiness to pay extra to those who could not work full-time, taking into consideration their need, and not only their work. The parable of talents in *Matthew* 25 and *Luke* 19, is to reward people for their extra work and to punish the idle ones. In none of the parables is there any dole to the unemployed, because that would make them parasites and destroy their talents.

The compassionate services of the Mother Theresas of the Christian church around the world show the beauty of the face of Christ brighter than many sermons preached. But our deeds of charity are not to pacify our conscience and justify the class-structured church and society we have today.

The Lamb Slain from the Foundation of the World (Rev. 13:8)

Jesus Christ had a cross not only from Bethlehem to Golgotha, which had its climax when he "died for sins, once for all" (I Pet. 3:18), but also in his compassionate heart ever since the fall of the angels and the fall of Adam. William Barclay, writing about the death and sacrifice of the king, points out five things, viz., Jesus expected to die, he chose to die, his death shows the length to which loyalty must go, and the length to which God's love will go and finally the death of Jesus was for us.[8] This precious death of Christ is the driving force that sets the missionary-wheel rolling. To quote Albert Schweitzer, who went to Equatorial Africa with the saving mission, "As

---

[7] Jürgen Moltmann: *The Experiment of Hope* (SCM Press, London, 1975), 81.
[8] William Barclay: *The King and the Kingdom* (St. Andrews Press, Edinburgh, 1969), 183-7.

Jesus gave up the ghost, the Roman Centurion said, 'Truly this man was the Son of God'" (Mark 15:39). Thus at the moment of his death the lofty dignity of Jesus was set free for expression in all tongues, among all nations and for all philosophies.[9]

The following touching quotation is from an unknown source and I am quoting it from memory:

"Whenever I am fast asleep, I am startled by a cry;
The first time I heard it, I went out and saw a
  man in the throes of crucifixion;
I said to him, I cannot endure your cry; shall I
  remove the nails from your hands and feet
  and take you down from the Cross?
He said, 'No, let them be. Go and tell every man,
  every woman, every child you meet;
There is a man on the Cross, waiting for them to
  ʈʌʞɛ hɪm down."

The crucified and risen Lord has the nail marks on his hands and feet and daggermark on his chest, as noted by St. Thomas the Apostle. The Death-of-God theologians, though wrong on a number of points, were right in insisting that the Descent into Hades is not yet over and will continue till the last person is won back to Himself. How can a compassionate father be satisfied even if only one of his sons remains a prodigal? "If you then, who are evil, know how to give good gifts to your children, how much more will your heavenly Father who is in heaven give good things to those who ask him?" (Matt. 7:11).

The pre-incarnate Logos "was in the world and the world was made through him, yet the world knew him not" (John 1:10). The Incarnate Logos "came to his own home, and his own people received him not" (1:11). Zachariah the prophet had already answered the question of those who mocked Christ and asked him, "Prophecy to us, you Christ! Who is it that struck you?" (Matt. 26:67), by saying, "What are the wounds on your back? He will say, the wound I received in the house of my friends" (Zech. 13:6). Also see the suffering servant passage in *Isaiah* 53.

The question that must again be asked is whether we can afford to live without the cross, trusting in the ransom or satisfaction or penal theory of atonement or whether we have to give greater stress to the innumerable passages in the Gospels which say that cross-bearing and following the Master is expected of us also (Matt. 16:24; Mark 8:34; 10:21; Luke 9:23).

---

[9] A. Schweitzer: *op cit.*, 252.

The Joy and Triumph of the Mission Under the Cross

The major cosmic christology passage of *Colossians* 1:15-20 ends with the phrase, "Making peace with the blood of the cross". Every Christian is called upon to run the race, "looking to Jesus, the pioneer and perfecter of our faith, who for the joy that was set before him endured the cross, despising the shame, and is seated at the right hand of the throne of God" (Heb. 12:2). The life of Christian martyrs from St. Stephen to Father Mathew Mannaparampil who was recently killed by the robbers at Sasram Bihar in India shows the joy and triumph of mission under the cross. We have come to an age when hardly anybody sheds a drop of tear at the death of a millionnaire while thousands weep at the martyrdom of even a humble missionary who dies saying, "please kill me, but not my poor colleagues".

To quote Moltmann again, "There are many kinds of bread, according to the persecuted South Korean Cardinal Kim. There is the good white bread of friendship, but there is also the black bread of suffering, of loneliness, and of poverty. This is the bread in which splinters of wood have been mixed. This black bread of suffering should be fraternally divided. This must come first... The hunger of India is our hunger. The despair in Chile is our despair. The prayers in Korea are our prayers. Ecumenism always begins with a fraternal sharing of suffering under the cross. [10] The joy of a mother who shares the sufferings of a hungry sick child and slowly brings it to health is something she alone can experience. There is a joy and triumph in her redeeming suffering. She enjoys the sufferings because of her deep love towards the child. "God so loved the world that he gave..." If we love the people of God created in the image of God like ourselves, we will also give whatever we have to their well-being and enjoy the same. "It is more blessed to give than to receive" (Acts 20:35), said our Lord.

The mission under the cross is the glory of the feet-washing of the disciples. Our Lord must have enjoyed the laying aside of his garments and girding himself with the towel and washing the feet of even Judas Iscariot (John 13:1-11). The command, "You also ought to wash one another's feet" is not a ritual to be performed on every Maundy Thursday, but the continuing mission of service in which the Master acts like a slave and all behave like a brotherhood, a sharing fraternity, a classless society.

"Unless a grain of wheat falls into the earth and dies, it remains alone" (John 12:24). The church is not a privileged class, but a brotherhood of servants, eager to serve all in need. The missionary's style of life is ever to be modelled in the pattern of that of the Master. "Let the manner of your life be worthy of the Gospel of Christ" (Phil. 1:27). "Let this mind be in you which

---

[10] J. Moltmann: *The Open Church* (SCM Press, London, 1978), 90.

was also in Christ Jesus." (2:5). "As the Father has sent me, even so I send you" (John 20:21) shows that the mission is ever the continuation of the Incarnation and the extension of the Cross of Christ to the ends of the earth. The apostles were not to perpetuate any priesthood or prophecy or kingship, except that of the crucified and risen Christ. "We are treated as imposters, and yet are true, as unknown, and yet are well known; as dying and behold we live; as punished and yet not killed..." (II Cor. 6:8f). This is the triumph of the Cross.

The Gospel of the Kingdom is the Doing of the Will of God

What is the will of God for each of us and CWME in the problematic world in which we live? If we pray "Your Kingdom Come" we have to surrender our particular wills to the one will of God. Those who have the missionary vocation should call themselves apostles according to the will of Jesus Christ (I Cor. 1:1). The will of God is our purification and the surrender of all our abilities and resources for the solution of the multifarious problems of our churches and the world. We will have to pray the same prayer of our Saviour, when we are sweating blood in our Gethsemanes, "My Father, if it be possible, let this cup pass from me; nevertheless, not as I will, but as thou wilt" (Matt. 26:39). The will of God is abundant life for all, and not plenty for a few and penury for the majority. "Your abundance at the present time should supply their want, so that their abundance may supply your want, that there may be equality" (II Cor. 8:14). Furthermore, as disunity is a real obstacle for mission, the ecumenical movement must enlarge its horizon with Catholic substance, Protestant principle and Orthodox ethos.[11] The pyramidical hierarchy must pave the way for collegial hierarchy as the Holy Trinity is the model for union. Still another area in which the whole of Christendom must exert its influence on the governments is about the immediate need of disarmament and "beating of their swords to plowshares" (Isa. 2:4). The expense of one costly bomb of today is said to be sufficient to erect apartments for the two million slum-dwellers of Calcutta. Thinkers like Arnold J. Toynbee are showing the need of a world government, but the rich nations are diametrically opposed to it, for they are more concerned about maintaining their own living standard than the coming of the kingdom of God in the whole world.

The citizens of the kingdom of God are to be freed from selfishness, ultra-nationalism and personal ambitions.

"None of us lives to himself, and none of us dies to himself. If we live, we

---

[11] I am indebted to my teacher Paul Tillich for the first two phrases and the third is the title of a book on Orthodoxy.

live to the Lord, if we die, we die to the Lord; so then, whether we live or whether we die, we are the Lord's" (Rom. 14:7f). As the whole world and the fullness thereof belongs to the Lord, we are only stewards and should not claim anything as our own. "As each has received a gift, employ it for one another, as good stewards of God's varied grace" (I Pet. 4:10). The developed nations must be satisfied with zero-point development till the developing nations catch up with them. Multinational corporations must stop the exploitation of the poor countries and try to help them with their scientific know-how. International trade regulations and tariff rates must be remodelled for the development of the developing nations. "The rich must live simply that the poor may simply live." Conscientization that is being advocated by Paulo Freire's *Pedagogy of the Oppressed*[12] has to be implemented in every country. "Render unto Caesar the things that are Caesar's and to God the things that are God's" (Matt. 22:21) is not an unconditional permission to pay taxes, but a conditional one as the image and inscription of human person is that of God and so he does not have to act against his conscience. Our ultimate loyalty is to God and not to the government. "Our citizenship is in heaven" (Phil. 3:20) and everything else is subject to that. "We must obey God, rather than men" (Acts 5:29). We must, of course, check with the Word of God and the teachings of the Church to see whether our understanding of the will of God is authentic and genuine, or fanaticism.

Mission to the Right and to the Left

The promise and command in Deutero-Isaiah "You will spread abroad to the right and to the left" (Isa. 54:3) has to be interpreted with more than a geographical connotation. The Christian mission is also to be extended to the conservative rightists and to the radical leftists without being afraid of either. It is even possible that the immediate response will be from the thief on the left and not from the thief on the right. The atheism of communism cannot last too long and the materialism of capitalism is also likely to shift if the Gospel of the kingdom is presented to both with the practice of a theology of classless society. It is the Holy Spirit that creates repentance (metanoia) both to the conservative and to the liberal and we must challenge them with the scandal and the power of the Gospel, with the power of the Holy Spirit. When the atheist says, there is no God, he who sits in heaven laughs. A sincere atheist is preferable to an insincere atheist, because the former is likely to find God sooner than the latter.

---

12 Paulo Freire: *The Pedagogy of the Oppressed* (Sheed and Ward and Seabury Press, 1973).

If the horizontal cross-bar of the cross is beckoning those on the right and the left, the vertical bar is beckoning the rich and the poor, the high and the low, the ruler and the ruled, the employer and the employee, the living and the departed, to the salvation wrought by the cross of Christ for the whole of human race since Adam to the end of history.

The only way to do away with the various divisions between man and his fellowman without destroying the freedom of man is the voluntary acceptance of the way of the cross by all of humanity, with its profound and world-shattering implications. " 'When the cross has been raised to a banner and to a banner whose positive tenor is the kingdom of God', then there is inherent in it a 'revaluation of all public values', as Nietzsche acutely reproached Christianity—a revaluation which is as dangerous as it is liberating, and a revolutionary tendency." [13] Mission with the cross can stop the war with the bomb between the right and the left or between the rich and the poor, for the cross reconciles all to a sharing family of profound solidarity.

We have to christianize politics also because politics is the art of the possible. I am glad that many of my evangelical friends like Ronald J. Sider [14] have begun to express a social concern, which was previously absent in that tradition. The Church is the mission and the Church has a mission in every realm of life. A holistic view of mission cannot be satisfied with the old "pie in the sky, when you die, bye and bye", nor with the historical here-and-now without the Easter hope. Christian men of incorruptible character must enter politics and try with the help of God not to be corrupted by the corrupt politics in which they are placed. They must be like the Lord, who did not become unclean by touching the leper, and the leper became whole. Let us remember that political and ecclesiastical leaders could find political reasons to crucify the Lord of glory, and not just the breaking of the Sabbath. The politicians would like to keep the church out of politics except when it is to their advantage. During the recent Parliamentary and Assembly elections in Kerala, 15 Roman Catholic bishops issued a statement calling upon the faithful not to vote for atheists. Four non-Roman Catholic bishops including myself, with some other clergy and laymen asked the faithful not to vote for "ahumanists" saying that the devil is not an atheist (James 2:19) but an "ahumanist" and a wicked person. In both the elections the Leftists won. I believe that Jesus Christ is the Lord of Principalities, Powers, Marxism, Capitalism, Maoism and all the evil forces of the world and they will

---

[13] J. Moltmann: *The Church in the Power of the Spirit* (SCM Press, London, 1977).
[14] Ronald J. Sider: *Christ and Violence* (Herald Press, Scottdale, Pa. 1979).
(See the Chapter "Cross and Violence", reprinted in the Preparatory CWME document No. 3.)

ultimately be defeated by him. Let us conquer the lion in his den, for Christ is the Lord of lords and King of kings.

Let Us be Crucified to be Raised to Glory

Koyama wrote, "Either the Church preaches the Crucified Christ, or else it crucifies Christ as it preaches." [15] I must go further and say that we must be crucified like the Master if we are to be raised to glory. St. Paul's command, "Be imitators of me, as I am of Christ" (I Cor. 11:1) must be ours also, having suffered as he suffered (II Cor. 11:21-33).

Christianity without the cross is Christianity without a crown. The tragedy of the churches today is their unwillingness to be humiliated for the sake of others and their desire for exaltation for themselves. The Faith and Order document of Bangalore on hope said that hope is to take risk, but we are not ready to put it into practise. Is this CWME Conference ready to announce that if any of the governments launches a third world war, we are ready to go and die with the people who are bombed and actually do so, saying that our loyalty to Christ and the suffering world is greater than our loyalty to our particular country? If the rich nations are not heeding the call of UNCTAD to share 1% of their income for the poor nations, are the rich churches in every country ready to do at least that much to share the poverty of the poor while sharing our riches with them? If Bangkok called for a moratorium on mission, shall we call a moratorium on our luxuries? Bangkok announced, "Mission in six continents has ended, mission in one world has started." Shall we add to it, "Self-denying (kenotic) and cosmic mission has started." Christ Our Lord identified himself with the poor, but we do not and so our mission is not succeeding. The contradiction between what we preach and practise is the greatest stumbling block, at least among the youth of today. CWME can decide to have no more "five-star hotel" conferences and stick to it and ask the delegates to live a simpler lifestyle voluntarily and share the savings for lifting the standard of at least a few of our brethren.

We, in India, have some of the rich, Christians and non-Christians, who are seeing to it that the poor will ever remain poor and illiterate and not conscientized or educated lest they loose their cheap labour that can be exploited for their own benefit. Much of the help of the government to the Harijans is going to the middle-man or the caste-Hindus. There are a few Christian missionaries who raise the standard of such Harijans and it was for that crime that Fr. Mathew Mannaparampil had to become a martyr. But India needs more Father Mathews to bear the cross that the Harijans may wear the

---

[15] Quoted from Koyama in the Preparatory Document of CWME on "Your Kingdom Come", No. 4, sent from Geneva, 21 August 1978.

crown. The poor can never become richer unless the rich become poorer, either voluntarily or by the force of a totalitarian government. The way for the first alternative is the cross and the way for the second the sickle and hammer. If the cross-bearing of the Christians will not bring about a just classless society by the force of Christian love, God may permit the sickle and the hammer to do so as he chose Cyrus the heathen to fulfil his purpose once. In any case the Nazarene is bound to win ultimately.

Then the seventh angel blew his trumpet, and there were loud voices in heaven, saying, "The kingdom of the world has become the kingdom of our Lord and of his Christ and he shall reign for ever and ever." And the twenty-four elders who sit on their thrones before God fell on their faces and worshipped God, saying,
"We give thanks to thee, Lord God almighty,
who art and who wast, that thou hast taken
thy great power and begun to reign,
The nations raged, but thy wrath came, and
the time for the dead to be judged, for
rewarding thy servants, the prophets and
saints, and those who fear thy name, both
small and great, and for destroying the
destroyers of the earth..." (Rev. 11:15-18).

The Crucified Lord:
A Latin American Perspective
JULIA ESQUIVEL*

We have been asked to speak from our own Christian experience in Central America. We shall try to share with you the reason for our hope in the Lord of history, of how a people in bondage builds with unbreakable faith its own resurrection through the power of the true and only God in it.

It is only from this real, concrete, difficult, incredibly painful perspective that what we are about to say has evangelistic worth. For this reason, before we begin this reflection it is necessary for you to become acquainted with a little bit of our concrete reality.

Central America is a small isthmus that unites North and South America. The six republics comprising Central America total only 25 million people. This belt of America, however, in spite of its smallness, has already begun to savour the marvelous experience of the resurrection with the victory of the people of Nicaragua.

The assassination of Monsignor Romero of El Salvador is only one proof before the entire world of the spread of one pharaonic project of death. Those who dare to raise their voices asking for justice—demanding that repression cease, denouncing the fact that jets made in the United States fly over the indigenous communities of Guatemala carrying bombs destined to exterminate the Indian nations, denouncing the spraying of napalm over the agricultural lands of the Ixiles, and the killing of the Quichés Indians by machine gun—are silenced in the same manner that the voice of the prophet Oscar Arnulfo Romero was silenced while he was raising the bread and wine asking for the Lord's blessing.

What we are going to say is therefore the word of God, to the extent that our people read the history of salvation illumined by the reading of the Bible and by events, with a faith that is generated by the Spirit of God. It is the denunciation by the people which, enabled by the Spirit, breaks the structures of sin and injustice which attempt to change the glory of the Immortal God for deified systems.

---

*Ms Julia Esquivel is lay leader, Bible study organizer, Guatemala.

In my country an average of seventeen political assassinations, committed by the government and the army, occur daily. Last year there was a total of 3,252 assassinations according to the records of the police themselves. Most of those assassinated were poor people, workers, those who had no possibility of purchasing food from one day to another because they depended on their daily work for each day's sustenance. Whenever they miss a day of work, that is a day without food, and yet they share their bread with their brothers and receive it like manna from heaven. It is necessary for us to remember that Guatemala is a country occupied by 12,000 soldiers, by twelve different types of police. Military recruitment in Guatemala is brutal and the training itself produces inhuman and savage degeneration, converting those who undergo it into beasts at the service of a regime of injustice.

In order to be faithful to the truth we must say all this and say also that we are alive only by the grace of God and the love of our brothers and sisters.

The Institutionalized Image of God

We learned in Sunday School and at the seminary that God is omnipotent, just, and that he punishes sin and protects the just. We also learned that we the "evangelicals" were the chosen people and that our God, the God of the Reformation, sustained order in this world in spite of the power of evil.

We learned to choose from the Bible those passages which gave us personal security, which guaranteed us well-being and tranquillity here on earth. We were almost convinced that social and economic well-being were signs of our friendship with God and, as if this were not enough, we had a heaven prepared and assured for eternity. Jesus, the Son of God, was presented and offered to us as "my personal Saviour". We needed to guard, take care of and enrich that holiness and purity while we walked as pilgrims in this world. We sang hymns with North American folk music in which we repeated: "The world is not my home...", "beyond the sun I have a home, home sweet home, beyond the sun...". In this manner we lived and constructed a false reality, detached from the people from whom we were separated by this type of evangelization. We thus converted the call and blessing given to Abraham for all the people of the earth into a contract of individual security for a small, isolated and protected elite, which now calls itself the evangelical or Christian Church. This description encompasses an important portion of the institutional Catholic Church which has been allied with the governmental power in order to assure its own existence, at the expense of the life of the people.

In spite of this kind of spirituality in which many of our friends live in Central America, Jesus is born, lives and suffers on the cross and experiences his Easter. Increasingly, each day, the nostalgia for the kingdom that is to come is felt and foreshadowed in concrete accomplishments, although not yet fully completed. Easter, especially in Nicaragua, is grasped as an anticipation of that kingdom, in a community of believers which is participatory, organized and joyful and which discovers every day, in its struggle against the old oppressive ideology and in the fraternity and vigour, the faith of Abraham as it offers at the altar of an efficacious love its best sons. Such an offering in the case of our martyrs is total and unconditional for the life of the people. It is the faith confessed by our brother Romero when he said, "If I am killed, I shall rise up again in the Salvadorean people."

In the midst of repression and death, the resurrected community is being lived already because the news of liberation and hope is clearly revealed to the poor. The captives break their chains of fear and individualism; the blind begin to have a vision of a New World, and the approximation of the realization of a new man is perceived and proclaimed along with the coming of a new earth and a new society. A God unknown until recent years is proclaimed—a God who was weak within an unorganized people, a people who had vacillated like sheep without a shepherd, and who today become strong: that people has organized itself and marches towards an earth of peace. This unknown God begins to appear. We have seen that his shoulders which were bent under a heavy weight have begun to straighten. This God has unveiled for us the disfigured image of the idol of development, consumerism and the great Mammon.

We had learned that God is a pure spirit; this affirmation in practice came to mean pure air, that is, empty words, empty of their basic meaning. We have been discovering that in practice we have invented a god that sanctifies the system, the same god that blesses consumerism and converts it into a collective obsession. It is the god that decides the price of oil or coffee or sugar; the same god that creates apartheid in South Africa and in other places. It is the same god that created and maintained that monster called the Shah of Iran and that created and maintained a similar monster called Somoza in Nicaragua. It is the same capricious, blind and mute idol that produces the scandalous wealth of a fat developed world at the expense of the exploitation, robbery and death of people in Chile, Haiti, Paraguay, Argentina, El Salvador and Guatemala. That god wraps himself with any flag, even anticommunism, or disguises himself with religious piety in order to defend us from atheism, or takes on the new attire of human rights...

The God of Jesus, forger of our history

To the extent that the people of faith in Central America have unmasked the god of death, the real God, the God of Jesus, the God of Abraham, Isaac and Jacob, has begun to be accessible to the poorest. He has revealed himself in events and in the communal reading of the Bible. That God has been described in the People's Mass of the Nicaraguans:

> You are the God of the poor,
> The human and humble God,
> The God that sweats in the street
> The God of the worn and leathery face.
> That is why I speak to you,
> In the way my people speak,
> Because you are God the worker,
> Christ the labourer.

Brothers, sisters, that God who perspires in the streets, who shouts through the people asking for freedom, that God who suffers with the people (the suffering servant of today—Isa. 53), that God whom we find in sumptuous and cold temples is the God of the sweaty and pallid face of the tortured peasant of Latin America. He can only reign through a people, in a people that transforms itself, its paths, its life, its history and its future. That is the Justice-God, the Fraternal-God, the Liberation-God who appears also to us in the Exodus of the people of Israel and in each exodus of the people of the earth that march full of faith towards the kingdom of Life.

This God unknown in the temples of development, consumerism and capital, whose glory has been usurped by the economic powers, substituted for by technology at the service of wealth, is the God who changes the laws of the transnational free enterprise (the creation of abundance for some and death for many) for laws that safeguard and defend life. It is the God who shall inexorably change the laws of the mighty in order to plant in the hearts of the people the law of love, the law of life (Ezek. 37:24; Isa. 33:22). It is the God who changes hearts of stone into hearts of flesh. It is the God who changes individualism for fraternal communion. Such communion emerges from suffering, from the struggle, and can be seen in the organization of the people who collectively and in solidarity are breaking through the frontiers of geography, sex, race and classes in Central America. It is the God who creates a human family in all the countries of the earth. It is the God who reminds us since the time of his friend Abraham that each nation is a chosen one, that each one has its Easter in Jesus (Eph. 2) and that Easter is the starting point so that bread, that is, all the resources of the earth, may be shared and distributed for the benefit of all mankind. That God, our Father, offers to us a fatherhood which of necessity manifests itself in society as a real fraternity which means co-participation in work and in production for the subsistence and maintenance of the life of the people.

The history of salvation shows us the God who reveals himself in the events of the daily lives of human beings, fishermen like James, searchers for a different future like Abraham, leaders of the masses like Moses, ordinary women like Mary, carpenters with faith like Jesus; but *all of them* discontent with the models of society in an unjust world that subverts the will of God (Rom. 12:2). All these people dream of a different world and a different earth, of a world of peace and brotherhood.

In this manner God links his action and his name to women and men who dare to exchange their own personal history for a communal project; they are connected to the God of Life. Thus, through concrete actions (defending a mistreated Hebrew in the case of Moses, or daring to have a fatherless child in the case of Mary) by daring to move without knowing where they were going (Heb. 11) they became friends with that God, they became the Word of God, the action of God among his people. Abram becomes Abraham when he makes an alliance with God that will benefit all the people of the inhabited earth and agrees to be a co-participant in an ecumenical project. In the same way, Jacob becomes Israel, Saul of Tarsus becomes Paul and Jesus of Nazareth, the Christ. And this Christ, fullness of God, in whom God reveals to us as Life, the Word, the Mediator, is the God of the people of Nicaragua, of the peoples of El Salvador and Guatemala, the God of the poor, the human and humble God, the worker God, he who raises our hope beyond any death, he who shall not be mocked by any idol no matter how powerful it may be because he has conquered death.

This God, who on many occasions in the past and in many ways spoke to us through the prophets, has spoken to us in a definite way through Jesus of Nazareth. This Jesus also promised us that through his Spirit we would accomplish even greater things than he. He assured us that he had many other things to teach us, that in his time we could not understand. That is why he promised us the Spirit of Truth which would lead us to all truth (John 16:12-15), and would reveal to us things to come (John 16:13).

Therefore, although Jesus did not leave us in writing a finished plan completed down to the last details, he planted in us instead the seed of truth and life. In this way he opened the way that leads to the kingdom that he announced, and announces today, amidst the people who struggle for liberation.

This experience appears clearly in Jesus. He himself at the beginning of his public life performed many miracles: he calmed the tempest, cured the sick, healed the blind and made the crippled walk. He had power over sickness, physical pain and death. In addition he multiplied the bread for his followers until there was bread left over.

As a result of this he was seen by the masses that followed him and did not have yet a common project, as insurance for a peaceful life, safeguard against risks, work and danger. He was seen as a leader who could make them forget and even accept their slavery under the power of the Roman Empire. Up until the multiplying of the bread in which he used his power to alleviate the pain of his people, who followed him as a pleasant leader, the peoples were tempted by a false image of the Son of God and they wanted to turn him into a king, a rival of Herod, into the king of easy bread, king of the bread without commitment. These people were still a mass brought together by individual interests, and wished to put upon him only the responsibility for their future. He escaped to the mountain to talk about this with his father (John 6:15).

In the same chapter, after he removed himself from the temptation of his disciples, when the people found him they asked for more signs, and he confronted them harshly by making them see that they were not interested in signs, that they only wanted to fill their bellies easily. Although they followed him, they continued being enemies of his cause, his cross, his project (Phil. 3:17-19). He asked them to believe in him: "This is the work of God that you believe in him whom he has sent" (John 6:29).

Further on, in a difficult dialogue which is like a sword that cuts deep into the soul and the spirit down to the very marrow, he spoke to them about his project, his father's project, of a plan that had to do with his physical body and blood, a plan that is beyond the power of Herod or Caesar but that calls in question the way in which they exercise power. That is to say his imprisonment, his tortures, his beatings, his pain, his crucifixion; he who defends life and is life and proclaims the kingdom of love encounters death due to the hate of his enemies. The disciples themselves could not understand this scandalous end resulting from his vocation (John 6:60). Others say: This language is very hard! It is heresy, who can stand up to it? (verses 60-71). Knowing what they are thinking, he asks them: Is this a scandal to you? What about when you see the Son of Man rise to the place where he used to be? It is the Spirit who gives Life!

So the king of easy and over-abundant bread, the king who gives things but not freedom disappears from the scene. Jesus refuses to utilize his power to satisfy an unconscious and dispersed crowd; he refuses to serve a multitude of isolated individuals. When he speaks about accepting the way of suffering and death, when he invites us to drink from his cup... when it had to do with following him to the cross, many left him (John 6:66).

Since then, in accordance with their personal projects and their economic and political interests, men have fabricated a god of their size, according to their image and likeness; a mutilated God, deaf and dumb, a dehumanized Jesus, a guardian of security, personal salvation and private property, a removed servant distant from the good and evil of their neighbours, from the oppressed majorities nearby and in the world at large. He is a national God with geographic and religious frontiers.

At the moment when Jesus spoke of his death, the disciples themselves who, before the masses, enjoyed power and prestige, began to be afraid and tried to persuade him away from the cross. But Herod, the princely priests of institutional religion, and the powerful plan his death because they see in him the incarnation of the ancient prophets (John 12:47-57). We know the reasons well, so well that they almost do not make sense to us anymore.

1. He has clearly demonstrated the emptiness of their religion and that they followed idols and not the God of Israel (John 8:44).
2. They do not want their religious institutions to disappear; therefore, although they know that he speaks the truth, they prefer to eliminate his forces instead of eliminating their own lies.
3. The high priest believed that it was necessary for one man to die for the people rather than for all to perish. (His word had to be sealed with his death and his resurrection.)
4. We know that he died for the people in order to achieve the unity of the dispersed children of God (John 12:52).

The subversive word and action of Jesus carried him to his death. The crowd that applauded him, motivated by individual interests, was easily manipulated by the powerful. This crowd, which awaited immediate miracles to satisfy their personal interests, had a distorted image of the kingdom, a kingdom that could be bought with praises and blackmail. They also had an image of a King and God that could be manipulated. But Jesus did not allow himself to be manipulated or used.

Jesus showed us through this that God could be found through him who is the *Way*, in the *Way of the Cross*, which is in living and dying for and with the *people united in a common project*, a marvellous and difficult dream that only the fearless can realize: the kingdom of God.

Salvation and the Kingdom

Jesus, the Christ, preached and announced the kingdom. He showed us that the history of salvation is one with the history of the world of men. Israel is only one example. For us today Israel could be Zimbabwe, El Salvador, Nicaragua or Guatemala. God has no religious frontiers.

Through his cross he broke down all frontiers and each country has its own history of salvation and, in building it, encounters or loses the God of Jesus who acts among men planting justice, the roots of the kingdom, which is the source of authentic peace. He is present and acts among the people as the Suffering Servant or as the Crucified King, but he can only truly reign when a family of human beings is created.

Jesus appears to us in the people, in their struggles, in their deaths, in their unity, in their hopes, and in their struggle for freedom. That is why we are able to understand the *Revelation of St. John* when it speaks of the triumph of the Word of God:

> Then I saw heaven opened, and behold, a white horse! He who sat upon it is called Faithful and True, it is he who judges in righteousness and makes just wars. His eyes are like a flame of fire, and on his head are many crowns; and he has a name inscribed which no one but himself understands. He is wrapped in a blood-stained robe. His name is The Word of God (Rev. 19:11-13; also Rev. 21:6-8).

Thus, the Reign of God is the ability to believe until death, and even beyond death, that God is our father and that we are brothers and sisters. It means living so as to break down all divisions, all injustices, to dry every tear, to love in such a way that we may share our lives, our work, our struggle and our dreams with all mankind. It means revealing that God to all, even though sharing that testimony may cost us our lives, because we believe that death no longer has any power over us.

He who believes that on the throne of God the lamb reigns who was slain for love does not dare kneel down before any god made of gold or stone. He dares to oppose any political project that produces injustice or death for the majorities. Although he may die, he has already been resurrected. The kingdom cannot be taken away from him because he carries it within himself with the violence and strength of God in the people, and he shall never die. That is the light of the everlasting fire.

For that kingdom Moses renounced the throne of Egypt and preferred to share the ills of the people of God. Others died after being beaten without accepting the transactions that would have rescued them, because they preferred resurrection. Others suffered the trials of mockery, beatings, and even the chains of prisons. They were stoned; others were tortured, burned, persecuted and discredited. Others are marked so that their movement can be controlled. Others are left without food and land. Others are shot while they bury their martyrs. Others flee to the mountains and find refuge in caves. But all of them, even though they continue to be oppressed and mistreated in the factories, the fields and the cities, march onward, lifting their eyes to the future towards Jesus from whom they derive their faith and who shall give them their prize. For his sake and for their sake we must resist until death, knowing that he has conquered the world.

"Therefore, be careful not to refuse God when he speaks to us. When God spoke to us in those days, the earth shook; this time I shall make not only the earth to tremble, but also the heavens..." says the Lord.

The kingdom we receive cannot be moved; let us guard carefully the grace given to us to celebrate a worship that is pleasing to God with love and respect. Our God is a fire that destroys! (Heb. 11).

In conclusion

— The cry "Your Kingdom Come" can only come from the perspective of the poor who have this hope as a community.

— Whoever takes up the way of solidarity and commitment with the poor can pray "Your Kingdom Come".

— The kingdom of God suffers violence and only those who dare to live daily this conflict, who nail their own interests to the cross, will attain it.

— In Latin America it is Christ who is being crucified and only this experience of death can generate hope among the people who moan under the cross and cry out, "Come, Lord, we are desperate!".

The Eschatological Royal Reign of God

ERNST KÄSEMANN*

According to the New Testament, both John the Baptist and Jesus began their ministry with the proclamation: "Repent! for the kingdom of God is at hand." The fundamental theme of their work is to announce that final era in which God steps forth from his hiddenness and here on earth announces his kingdom to all. The authenticity of the Gospel is to be measured by this message. Christians and church communities are credible only as long as people hear issuing from them the passionate cry: "Your Kingdom Come!". This means, however, that we also have to include within this theme the whole Bible, all our traditions and hopes, and even world history.

What is meant by the eschatological royal reign of God?

People have often longed for or feared the end of the world. The New Testament proclamation of the nearness of the divine kingdom is inconceivable without Judaism, whose fathers confessed in *Exodus* 15:18: "The Lord shall reign for ever and ever" but who in *Isaiah* 26:13 see earthly realities threatening the deepest conviction of their faith: "O Lord our God, other lords than thou have been our masters, but thee alone do we invoke by name." They find themselves caught up in the conflict between the one true God and the ruling powers which compete with him in this world and even appear to triumph over him. So the question arises: to whom does the earth and its creatures really belong? In this situation both the Baptist and Jesus reply: "Repent! For the kingdom of God has drawn near." In the New Testament the term "repentance" always carries the Hebrew meaning and not the Greek. It signifies not a change of mind but a turning back, a return. What appears to be a condition is really a consequence of the promise of the kingdom which has drawn near, an invitation rather than a command. We are permitted to return to and to renew a hope that was in danger of being lost, to back God's future and so to line up with the company of the hopers instead of succumbing to despair. God comes to his earth and to his human

---

* Professor D. Ernst Käsemann is Professor Emeritus of New Testament at Tübingen, Federal Republic of Germany.

creatures. He has not written them off as his creation. He will establish his sovereignty among his enemies, unmask the idols, humble the proud in the dust, create justice for the oppressed. When the Jews spoke of God's kingdom, they meant in the first place the revelation of him who does not abdicate his sovereignty and who exercises his rule perceptibly everywhere. This is not without its echoes on earth, of course, as is illustrated by the angels, shepherds and wise men of the Christmas story. As at Easter and Pentecost, there is tumult and conflict throughout the world. In the midst of the rebels who refuse obedience to their Creator, a community of believers is formed. This is a feature of the last days: when God draws near and breaks into the realm of the powers and authorities of this present age, the earth becomes the battlefield and we are all drawn into the conflict over the one true sovereign of our life and of the life of all others. God and the idols now constitute the main theme of world history, and no one can remain neutral here.

In saying this we certainly go beyond the message of John the Baptist. John spoke of the coming judge of Israel. His baptism was meant as a sign of protection for those who renewed the covenant with God at the very last moment. But, for Jesus, the inauguration of the royal reign of God is essentially a saving event, commencing with the Beatitudes, an event which brings the forgiveness of sins, relief for the tormented, freedom for the captive, and by mighty deeds destroys the works of the devil. For Jesus, the judgement is only the obverse of the grace which the self-righteous despise and reject, the end of the violation of the creation by the devil and his demons. So we find in *Luke* 10:18: "I watched how Satan fell, like lightning, out of the sky" and in *Luke* 11:20 the explanation given for proclaiming the nearness of the kingdom is that "by the finger of God" Jesus drives out the demons. The preaching of the Baptist is turned inside out, therefore, without our being able to explain how this has happened. The very appearance of the Nazarene on the scene is already instinct with this mystery of his mission. Between the Baptist and the one who brings the eschatological kingdom there are two key differences. Firstly, God's royal reign is not merely imminent but has already begun in Jesus' message and ministry. And secondly, when the power of the devil has been shattered, salvation is no longer limited in principle to the frontiers of Israel. A new world begins. Pentecost hoves in sight; when the heavens open, the Holy Spirit acquires ecumenical elbow room, and the Pantocrator is glorified even by the Gentiles.

The kingdom of Christ

In a famous dictum, Origen called Jesus the *autobasileia*, the royal reign of God in person. Whatever objections there may be to this dictum, it is just this that marks the distinction between the Christian view of the kingdom of God and the Jewish view. Judaism had already stressed that the coming of the king is determinative for the message of the kingdom, so that the latter is not simply a new structure. Judaism had also connected the eschatological kingdom with the appearance of a messiah on the scene, even if this view was not universal. This messiah was generally thought of, of course, only as a forerunner, i.e. as one who brought political liberation to Israel. But in the Christian message, the Saviour had become not just the flesh of Israel or exclusively that of its pious members, but the flesh of all humanity, and is now and to all eternity the mediator and revealer, the face of God, so to speak, turned towards the earth and its creatures. The Fourth Evangelist calls him the way and the door, the shepherd, the bread and the water of life, the unique word of the Father and sole interpreter of the Father. In Peter's Pentecostal confession in *Acts* 2:36 we read that God has made this Jesus the one Lord and Messiah. In *Corinthians* 15:24 Paul speaks of him who will abolish "every kind of domination, authority and power" and who then gives world history its meaning: "he is destined to reign until God has put all enemies under his feet". The impressive hymn of praise in *Ephesians* 1:20f celebrates the Risen One who has been enthroned at God's right hand in the heavenly realms, "far above all government and authority, all power and domination, and any title of sovereignty that can be named, not only in this age but in the age to come". The *Revelation to John* sums it up in 11:15: "The sovereignty of this world has passed to our Lord and his Christ, and he shall reign for ever and ever." As far as Christianity is concerned, there is no eschatological divine reign of which Jesus of Nazareth is not the centre. According to *Luke* 4:43, it was his earthly task to proclaim the Good News of the kingdom; for his disciples he became the presence of this kingdom with all its wealth of gifts and powers. This is what they meant when they said: "We saw his glory." We must now see the consequences which this entails for us.

I have already pointed out that Christianity and Judaism separate here, as do also Gospel and world view or religious utopia. For us the kingdom of God is not primarily theory but praxis. Nor is it a praxis concerned mainly with changed conditions, new possibilities and goals. From the New Testament, the Christian, standpoint, the kingdom of God denotes that praxis in which Jesus of Nazareth is our Lord and the Saviour of the world. For us, the First Commandment, "I am the Lord your God... You shall have no other gods before me", assumes concrete form. This command no longer sounds forth from the clouds, as it did at Sinai. It has become a human being, crucified, risen, Son of the heavenly Father and at the same time the new Adam. Others may turn him into a stereotype hero and pattern of their own desires, into the pioneer of human, social and political ideas. We are not to despise that but neither can it suffice us. For he and he alone is our Lord and, as *Acts* 4:12 says succinctly, there is salvation in no one else. He and he alone wrests us from the power of all the idols to whose mercy we are otherwise abandoned. What sounds like a command is actually a promise. You no longer need to have any other gods before me, no longer need take these gods seriously, fear them, pay them tribute. He makes us free, just as happened to Israel in Egypt. His sovereignty creates free human beings and a fellowship of free human beings.

As Christ's kingdom, the royal reign of God begins on earth as the kingdom of the crucified, which places his disciples with him under the cross. Only those who, unlike the fanatics and ideologues, refuse to bypass Golgotha are ever really liberated by him and received into his fellowship. My own generation in Germany has learned at first hand that it is possible, like Israel, to be delivered from Egypt and led through the wilderness, only in the end, even as a Church, to dance around the golden calf. Even before Jesus had set out on his way, the tempter offered him all the kingdoms of this world and their glory. And even the man from Nazareth, he too had to reach out for the protection of the First Commandment: "You shall do homage to the Lord your God and worship him alone." This "alone" led to the cross and this "alone" remains the test for us all, including us Christians. Unmistakably resisting all ideological temptation, Jesus describes himself in *John* 18:36f as a king whose kingdom, while not of this world, nevertheless spreads out into this world as a realm of truth, i.e. of the sole sovereignty of God. God's truth is hostile to everything which comes on the scene in its own name, for its own glory, by its own power and intellect, i.e. trusting in itself and seeking to impose its own will. The limits of conceivable paradox are transcended when the return of the Son of Man is described in *Luke* 12:37 as analogous to the feet-washing in *John* 13. He who appears in the heavenly glory will once again gird himself like a slave in order to serve his own, in the way he had once done on earth. For this is his law and his badge, since, according to *Matthew* 20:28, "he did not come to be served, but to serve, and to give up his life as a ransom for many". But the disciples are not above their master who, according to the hymn in *Philippians* 2:6ff abandoned his equality with God and took the form of a slave, as foreshadowed in the prophecy of the despised and suffering servant of God of *Isaiah* 53. According to *Philippians* 3:10, the power of his resurrection is experienced in the fellowship of his sufferings, which brings us into conformity with his death. Again, according to *John* 12:24, the grain of wheat must die in order to bear much fruit. Grace does not reduce the price. "The man who loves himself is lost, but he who hates himself in this world will be kept safe for eternal life." The king of the heavenly kingdom is still travelling the roads of this world. When he is sought in the wrong places and proclaimed under false colours, he has been completely misunderstood. Only where deliverance is needed is he to be found, i.e. according to *Psalm* 107:10, only among those who sit "in darkness, dark as death, prisoners bound fast in iron". It is here that the Christian process of teaching and learning must begin, and be continued afresh each day, just as the same *Psalm* says at the close: "Let the wise man lay these things to heart, and ponder the record of the Lord's enduring love." The servant came among the earthly rulers and he also summons his servants into the world of the tyrants and idols which destroy the creation. He does so in order that his blessings may there establish, according to *Romans* 14:17, the kingdom of justice, peace and joy, inspired by the Holy Spirit.

The work of the royal reign of Christ

Jesus gives a very striking answer to the people who warn him of Herod's plan to murder him: "Listen: today and tomorrow I shall be casting out devils and working cures; on the third day I shall reach my goal." Yet no one can fail to notice that time and again our gospels narrate the healing of possessed persons, that this continues in the *Acts* of the Apostles, and that the New Testament letters, especially the *Revelation to John*, celebrate the triumph of the Risen Christ as redemption from captivity to the powers and authorities, meaning by this, all who torment and seduce the world and individual human beings, alienate them from their humanity and hurl the proud and the despairing into hell. The recurring confession found in such baptismal hymns as *Colossians* 1:13 is no accident: "He rescued us from darkness and brought us away into the kingdom of his dear Son." We may criticize and demythologize the language and ideas of an antique worldview as out of date. We must indeed do so, since only in this way can we have a true perception of the reality of our contemporary life and present world. But this reality does not abrogate the experiences of the first Christians; it heightens them rather. The white man's affluent society may find demons amusing but this is only because, in its blindness, deafness, insensitivity and stupidity, it looks no further than the shadows cast by its own technological achievements, its brutally defended privileges and traditional prejudices. The mountains of unacknowledged and unexpiated sin in its own domain as well as in the world beyond it pile up higher and higher. Inured to conformity, our churches support with pious words the optimistic prognosis of politicians and economists. Unwelcome critics, not to mention rebels, are blasphemously urged to display more confidence, more hope, more courage and, of course, more discipline, so as not to endanger the existing balance of power. People refuse to see or to be told that our hour has long since struck, and that when it says in *I Corinthians* 7:31, that "the whole frame of this world is passing away", this means us! In the opinion of most people, the sovereignty of God and the kingdom of Christ are metaphysical constructions floating above the clouds like islands of the blest, or, at best, only make sense in churches and in private edification. To most church members it seems heresy to assert that the sovereignty of God and the kingdom of Christ are not intended merely to keep citizens obedient to traditional laws and systems, submissive to the authorities, and that Christianity wherever it is found must be an active leaven and the voice of the oppressed, an alert and critical conscience against avarice, against the pillage of the earth, the violation of its creatures, the underwriting of the present state of things. Certainly we read in *I John* 5:19 the words "we know... the whole godless world lies in the power of the evil one", but we leave it to the "good Lord" to put this right, especially since in the white man's world the prospects do not appear all that grim, prosperity and enjoyment are perceptibly increasing and the sense of reality, except in the case of money and success, is diminishing to an appalling degree, suffocated perhaps also by propaganda and demagogy. We daily repress the knowledge that our earth is a kind of hell for the majority of its inhabitants and relegate the statement in *John* 1:5 that the light shines in the darkness, that Jesus died in "no man's land", to our bulging file of pious phrases.

All this has to be challenged, if one is to be in a position to deny the worldwide political dimension of the Gospel. Of course, Jesus was not a revolutionary. Nevertheless his appearance on the scene has revolutionary consequences which were inescapable. For when someone is called King of kings and Lord of lords (as Jesus is in *I Timothy* 6:15), and announces his claim to his creation, when truth and falsehood contend together for every individual human being, when the crucified snatches his kingdom out of the hands of tyrants and usurpers and destroys the works of the devil on earth, a universal conflict breaks out. When, therefore, the demons appear in the New Testament as the real enemies of Christ and every Christian service in its deepest sense must consequently be regarded as a kind of exorcism, as the expulsion of evil spirits, it is this universal conflict which is being described. The rule of the Spirit of God on earth in the realm of the demons always takes the form of the exorcism of these demons and victory over them.

Any version of Christianity is incredible which, while professing belief in the Holy Spirit, fails to carry his power and victory into every deepest hole and corner. What our world needs everywhere today is this exorcism of its demons. For it is only when the heavens open and the Spirit descends that God's good creation comes into being and continues in being.

For far too long we have made Christianity into an inward and private affair, the Holy Spirit into merely the power of sanctification in the Church, comforting ourselves and others with the prospect of eternal life beyond our temporal afflictions, at best doing no more than whispering the passionate cry of hope and protest against all that exists, which we find in *II Peter* 3:13: "We have his promise and look forward to new heavens and a new earth, the home of justice." Mission has meant for the most part the salvation of souls. Diaconia has been the demonstration of love for the weak and the suffering. Our charity has been the price we have paid for being better off than so many others near and far. All this was an embodiment of *caritas* and provisions for the journey. The new earth remained a dream; co-operation in changing the structures was left to outsiders and mostly fanatics. The proclamation of the resurrection of the dead was normally, therefore, only a message of personal survival after death, for which tombstones were in order but none of the victory signs that represent a threat to civil order. Like the triumph over fallen Babylon in *Revelation* 14:8 and 18:2, the Spirit who brings the dead bones to life (*Ezek.* 37) and the beatitude in *Matthew* 5:6 declaring that those who hunger and thirst for justice are to be satisfied already here on earth, were revolutionary dreams. We prayed the Magnificat from *Luke* 1:51ff without taking its words seriously: "The deeds his own right arm has done disclose his might; the arrogant of heart and mind he has put to rout, he has brought down monarchs from their thrones, but the humble have been lifted high. The hungry he has satisfied with good things, the rich sent empty away."

If Jesus' conviction (Matt. 12:28) that he cast out demons by the Spirit of God was true, then all this must be radically changed. In *Matthew* 10:8, appealing expressly to the kingdom which has drawn near, he charges his disciples: "Heal the sick, raise the dead, cleanse lepers, cast out devils!" His work is to be continued through us. Our time is to continue to be messianic time. We are not forgetting that he himself did not heal and liberate everyone who came to him. The earthly paradise in no way began with him, and what he actually did brought him in the end to the cross. Through him, the reign of God was carried into the demonic kingdom but not finally and universally completed there. He established signs showing that this kingdom had drawn near and that the struggle with the powers and authorities of this age had begun. We are not called to do more, but neither are we called to do less. But this means that instead of leaving the demonic kingdom in peace we attack it here, there and everywhere, as witnesses of the resurrection from the dead, as instruments of the Spirit of God who does not share his sovereignty with idols but fetches his originally good creation back to himself in order that a new heaven may appear upon a new earth.

Kingdom and Church

It cannot be seriously doubted that Jesus saw in his own words and deeds the arrival on earth of the eschatological kingdom of God, and that his disciples after Easter were counting with each successive day on the end of the world. While at first it was the restoration of the ancient people of God alone which filled the horizon of their commission, already the group around Stephen were aware of being sent on a worldwide mission. The church became the community of disciples made up of Jews and Gentiles alike. We, however, seldom realize—and perhaps do not wish to—just how complicated a process this was, and how many of the problems that still bother us today find their origins in it. Outside Palestine the early churches had for the most part no defined, still less any comprehensive relationships with each other. For their teachings, their ethics and their forms of organization they depended on the whole on their founders, and then later on travelling prophets and their own leaders, so that inevitably differences and indeed contradictions crept in.

Only the second and third generations knew any Holy Scriptures, and it is questionable whether all could afford to buy an Old Testament or even a few books from it. Confessions and catechetical teachings were handed down orally. This is why there is variety in the texts of the eucharist or of the Lord's Prayer, why the Easter stories and the traditions of the four Gospels are so different. It led to conflicts in which the community of the early Christians threatened to break up. On at least two fronts it was not at that time possible to reach any permanent theological understanding. Those Christians who held to the Torah and those who felt themselves free from the laws of Moses, since the quarrel in Antioch and in spite of the apostolic Council, never in fact overcame their controversy but only made it more acute. The intense expectation of the early disciples that the world would soon come to an end was never completely abandoned, and led to divisions inside the church: *II Peter* suggests that whole congregations are going wrong in their faith because of the delay in the expected return of Jesus; *I Thessalonians* 4:13ff shows Christians concerned about the fate of those of their number who have died; the *Letter to the Hebrews* shows how hope that has grown tired leads to paralysis in discipleship of Jesus. Yet there are also two other tendencies to be seen. There is the enthusiasm mentioned in *II Timothy* 2:18 and presumably presupposed in *I Corinthians* 15 which sees baptism as the anticipation of the resurrection, and therefore sees death as no more than the lifting of the earthly garment from off the heavenly being. Yet the majority of the churches are beginning to settle down within earthly horizons as a new religion with a specific morality and under the leadership of authoritative officers, until the time that God shall choose to reveal his heavenly kingdom. The plurality of theological systems in the early church, reflected in the New Testament, is undeniable. There is a corresponding pluriformity in the Christian community, already in the first century, which occasionally prevented dialogue, and which must not be idealistically softened under the heading of "conciliarity".

These facts still have precise implications for us today. Understood rightly, they permit, indeed demand theological insights for the contemporary situation of Christianity. Our confession of the *Una Sancta* can only be grounded in that Lord who died for all, calls all into his forgiveness, uses the sick and the dying in his service, unites by his Spirit those who are very different, judges those who even in their prayers conspire against one another and brings them under the command to repent. There has never been in the church any empirically provable unity in theology or in organization. Yet at all times repentance has been inescapably demanded, not only from believing individuals, but no less also from all Christian groups and denominations. Churches that do not repent deny their reality and reject the Lord who also had to die for them. They fail to stand under the cross where all our sins come to light and where we in our humanity are crucified with him. The Christian Church, which has only ever existed on earth in the form of theologically and organizationally various—at times conflicting—single churches, must therefore never simply be identified with the kingdom of God. Wherever there is expectancy of a new heaven and a new earth there will also be a passionate yearning for a deep renewal of the church. Each person and each church will do this yearning in her own way, but always rejecting any pious self-glorification or any idolatry of one's own community. The God who is to come is never replaced by existing institutions, his Holy Spirit never made redundant by human religious traditions.

Our place on earth is to stand under the cross. God's rule in this our time cannot be separated from the crucified Christ. All believers and churches are at best signs and instruments for the dawning of the end and for that fulfilment in which God alone will rule over the world and will destroy all enemies and rivals. Yet we are indeed to be signs and instruments of that end, if God is not to be blasphemed as untrustworthy. Seen in the light of this commission the pluriformity, without which there has never been any Christian oikoumene, takes on a positive character: when God comes to us no one goes away empty, no one is released from his service.

Each of us owes the common Lord a characteristically personal witness, in our own situation, in our own language and out of our own insight and tradition. Our witness is never worthy or capable of earning our own salvation, yet it is always in position as a fragile tool to pass on God's salvation in its own way to others and from the power of that salvation to stand up to the powers of evil. There is not yet found in the New Testament what we call "lay people" but only priestly members of the people of God. The Spirit of the Christ who is among us needs endlessly many and various functions in his earthly body in order to reach every place in our world and there to create ecumenical solidarity. God does not make people uniform. His kingdom creates solidarity among the unlike, since Christ died for all and can use each one of us in his service.

The kingdom of God today

Christianity does not live off preserves which our fathers laid down in earlier generations. Nor do we live in the perfection of the saints. We are thrust into the reality of today, whose worldwide dimensions must not be narrowed down by us into our own provincial, national, cultural or racial terms. For all the abundance of needs and possibilities, of gifts and services of which we are aware, we must ask, in conclusion: what is it that is ecumenically necessary today?

Three things are commended to us in the New Testament as necessary. "Preach the Gospel to every creature", we are told in *Mark* 16:15. There is no kingdom of God simply as a theory or as the fellow-feeling of pious souls. The kingdom is given only in the confrontation of the whole world with the Gospel, to the favour of every single creature. Love must be promised, guilt explicitly forgiven, blessing implored and shared, liberation proclaimed. I must experience that it is I who am truly addressed, that God speaks to me and wants to act through me. The earth must hear the voice of its true Lord as promise, claim and judgement. The miracles of grace can only be seen and believed by those who hear the word. One must be called by his name in order to become anything to the praise of his glory. The Gospel today defines Christianity as the resistance movement on earth of Jesus Christ over against the power of the idols and the despoilers of the creation.

God's royal reign is visibly represented when we are invited to the banqueting table of Jesus. Yet of course this can only come about when there is place there for all whom the Gospel calls to their Lord. The crucified master put himself in the hands of the godless, accepted even Judas as one of his guests, promised in *Matthew* 8:11 that many would come from East and West to sit with the patriarchs at the table of the perfected, assured all the needy of his brotherhood and promised the freedom of the reconciled in the midst of his enemies. According to *I Corinthians* 11:27ff, it is only the limitation or refusal of community in the body of Christ that makes us unworthy of sharing in his meal. To raise separating barriers at that precise point implies that heaven is not to be left open for all sinners and for all the disciples of Jesus; it is to retreat into the ghetto of a community closed to all but the pious, the ghetto of religious institutions. It is on the cross that the salvation of the entire world and with it the proper ecumenical openness is grounded. Is Jesus still the Lord of his table?

Ecumenical openness recognizes in the neighbour a brother of Jesus, and is therefore openness to all fellow-human beings. Christians cannot look in neutrality or silence at the appalling inhumanity which is turning the earth into an inferno. The gospel is watered down wherever body and soul are parted, salvation distinguished from earthly help for the suffering, where freedom is reserved for heaven hereafter, and so the Good News of Jesus falsified into an opium for the exploited, the tortured and the oppressed. The ideology of non-violence is hypocritical if it is directed not against the tyrants but against their victims. Moreover it becomes a superstition if it demands more than the possible renunciation of violence by individuals or groups.

For there have never been spaces on this our earth free from all violence, and today we are the witnesses of a worldwide class struggle in which rich societies, in an unstoppable lust of possession and with all their scientific and technological capacities, are defending their privileges and making whole continents pay for that with their blood. For too long the old churches have been in league with the powerful, and have supported themselves on a bourgeois middle class, while yet neglecting or even despising the cries of the damned in our world. God's royal rule today proclaims in the words of *Psalm* 12:6: "Because the needy are destroyed and the poor cry out I will arise, says the Lord. I will bring help to him who yearns thereafter." Will we too arise and set out with this Lord?

BIBLE STUDY

Your Kingdom Come: Notes for Bible Study
KRISTER STENDAHL *

The purpose of these notes is to assist in the Bible Study on the theme "Your Kingdom Come". The Lord's Prayer gives a most appropriate and challenging structure—since that prayer is a sustained cry for the coming of the kingdom. The various petitions will be enforced, deepened, and illuminated by passages from the *Gospel according to St. Matthew*. A significant result of the Bible Study would be this: As we leave the Melbourne Conference, we shall pray the Lord's Prayer with renewed sense, zeal, and purpose. By the grace of God in Jesus Christ, we shall be lifted into God's agenda by the very Spirit in which Jesus taught us so to pray. Or, to speak in the language of John's Gospel: "No longer do I call you slaves, for the slave does not know what his master is doing; but I have called you friends, for all that I have heard from my Father I have made known to you..." (15:15).

The Gospel according to St. Matthew is the first Gospel of the Church. Not only in the sense that it comes first in our Bibles, but also since it came to serve as the basic pattern for the Church's image and understanding of Jesus' life and work. In a sense, the other Gospels came to supplement in their distinct ways the basic record of Matthew. Matthew became in a special way the Gospel of the Church. That is not surprising. He is the born teacher, a wise "scribe who has been trained for the kingdom of heaven, like a householder who brings out of his treasure what is new and what is old"—a verse that is often seen as a self-portrait of the Evangelist (13:52). And Matthew has assembled and reflected on the words and deeds of Jesus Christ from the perspective and the experiences, the needs and the hopes of his community, of the church (he is the only evangelist to use that word; 16:18, 18:17).

He is in touch with "what is old", the promises and the insights of the Old Testament which he quotes more than the others. He is aware of "what is new", not only in Jesus Christ, but in the fact that the Gospel is now gathering the gentiles—"all nations"—or we should perhaps translate: "all gentiles" (28:19).

---

*The Rev. Krister Stendahl, Sweden, is Professor of Divinity at Harvard University Divinity School, Cambridge, Massachusetts, USA.

He is the evangelist who is most fond of words about the kingdom. He calls it the kingdom of heaven; retaining that sound awe for the word "God" is part of Jewish wisdom. Again, Matthew holds together "the old and the new".

The Lord's Prayer in *Matthew* is part of the Sermon on the Mount (Matt. 5-7). The teacher Matthew has structured his Gospel around five "sermons". Although we are accustomed to speaking about "The Sermon on the Mount", it is helpful to remember it as only the first of five "sermons". It is followed by the sermon on the apostolic mission (ch. 10), the sermon on how the kingdom comes (the parables in ch. 13), the sermon on church discipline (ch. 18), and the sermon against religious professionals (ch. 23), followed by Jesus' teaching about the end (ch. 24-25).

This structure of the body of the Gospel, prior to the passion and resurrection narratives, has its parallels in Jewish and Christian "handbooks" or manuals (e.g., the Manual of Discipline from Qumran, and the "Didache", the Teaching of the Twelve Apostles). Matthew's Gospel thus gives the Church a manual for discipleship. And the Church responded in gratitude by making Matthew's the first Gospel.

The Sermon on the Mount

The first sermon in Matthew deals with the glories and the demands of discipleship. The blessedness of discipleship is that we are liberated from all restraints of custom and compromise, worldly worries and calculations. The time is nigh when God mends his creation, when those who hunger and thirst for peace and justice will be satisfied and vindicated. I.e., the disciples are given the messianic licence to live the life of the kingdom here and now: Seek first the kingdom of God's justice—and the rest will somehow fall into place (6:33). The disciples are called to be sort of "guinea pigs" for the kingdom.

That is the more intensive righteousness (5:20), e.g., the high ideal of marriage without divorce (at which the disciples balked, 19:10); and the divine perfection of non-retaliation (5:39, 43-38). It is a posture made possible by the closeness of the kingdom.

When Matthew then comes to the three traditional religious duties (alms-prayer-fasting) he warns against concern for what people might think, but his main emphasis falls upon the prayer for the kingdom (6:9-13), *and* he underscores (vv. 14-15) how that prayer goes with, and presupposes a spirit of forgiveness, the very spirit which was one of the striking features in chapter 5.

As the sermon continues, it teaches in various ways the glories and the risks of discipleship. It includes the golden rule, coined by Hillel a generation earlier (again Matthew brings the old with the new). The sermon ends on the note of warning against false prophets and mere lipservice (7:15-23), and the solidity of Jesus' words as a foundation for our lives (vv. 24-27).

The Lord's Prayer

It is reasonable to consider the Matthean form of the Lord's Prayer (found also in Didache 8) as the form in which the Prayer was used in the life of the churches. The Lukan form (Luke 11:1-4) is shorter, and may well be a rendering closer to the style of Jesus' own life of prayer, especially the simple "Father". Matthew has "my Father" in the actual prayer of Jesus in Gethsemane (26:39, 42; see below). This preference of Luke's fits well with Luke's constant attention to, and interest in Jesus' life of prayer. For Matthew, the evangelist of the Church, the prayer is rather in the form in which the community had made it its own: Our Father who is in Heaven.

One more observation about the Lukan setting of the Lord's Prayer may be helpful—not least for our Bible Studies in Melbourne. Luke tells us that the prayer was given to the disciples in response to their request (11:1). John the Baptist had given his disciples a special prayer. Now Jesus' disciples wanted one also; a prayer that would be their "badge", their distinctive symbol. Jesus answers by giving a prayer which grows out of the themes familiar from Jewish prayers. Actually, there is nothing in the Lord's Prayer that could not be prayed whole-heartedly by a faithful Jew—then or now. (That does not mean that we should urge the Jews: "Let us say the Lord's Prayer together." Prayers gather unto themselves symbolic meanings, beyond the meaning of the words, and this is *the* prayer of the Christian Church.) The point is this: When the disciples desired a prayer to set them apart, Jesus gave them a prayer that constitutes our bond with Israel, as she prays for forgiveness from "our Father... who art gracious and dost abundantly forgive" (from the *Amidah*); who prays "Sanctified be his great Name in the world which he has created. May he establish his Kingdom... even speedily and at a near time" (from the *Kaddish*).

Our Father who is in Heaven

The western churches came to introduce the Lord's Prayer with the word(s) *"audemus* we make bold" to say: Our Father... Thereby they expressed the awe, the gratitude we feel for calling God our Father (cf. I John 3:1). While this address to God was not unknown to Jesus from his Jewish milieu, he lifted it up to a gracious prominence that has marked Christian spirituality ever since. Jesus' own relation to God as the only begotten, beloved Son intensifies the meaning of the word, and Paul reflects on the implications. He sees the perhaps ecstatic cry Abba-Father as a sign by which the

Spirit assures us that we are "children and heirs of God and co-heirs with Christ" (Rom. 8:17).

The church even retained the original Aramaic word Abba. It is sometimes argued that Abba would express a special tone of informality (like "dad"), but such speculation is unwarranted, since Abba is the standard Aramaic word for "father".

The Father-language is the glory of our Christian faith. But it seems that we have sometimes used it in ways which hurt our sisters. We have let it suggest that somehow God is "male", and somehow more in the image of males than females. In subtle ways the Father-language has reinforced male domination in church and society. We all know that such was not the intention—"male and female created God them". Such is the "image of God". We need to remind ourselves that when we say "Our Father...", we express a relationship of parent to child and not an idea of God as father over against mother. The opposite to father is rather unrelated coldness without involvement.

Hallowed be your Name

The meaning is not that we are urged to hallow or sanctify God's Name. A prayer is a prayer to God, not a veiled form of moral instruction. We pray to God for the time when the whole creation will recognize God for what he is in his holiness, and in his mighty acts.

The story about Jesus' entry into Jerusalem (Matt. 21:1-17) is one such act of recognition. Matthew—who knows the Scriptures so well—sees and hears many images from the prophets come together (Isa. 62:11, Zech. 9:9, Hos. 9:10) when the people greet Jesus in the words of the Temple Psalm that now took on a new and fuller meaning (Ps. 118): The one who comes in the Name of the Lord, the blessed one, is the Messiah, the Son of David. And the Hosannah (which in Ps. 118 means: "Save us, we beseech you") has become a shout of praise. It is as if salvation was now there—not a thing to ask for, but a thing to rejoice in.

As the acts of God are recognized and thus his name hallowed, so now the Holy Temple is cleansed from commercial profanation. The Holy Place is liberated for holiness, it is hallowed.

Matthew brings another facet to this moment of new holiness. The children keep chanting the Hosannah song—as children like to do. The serious religious folk take offense. Such behaviour is not in keeping with their understanding of holiness. But for Jesus this is in keeping with his sense of how in the affairs of the kingdom serious adults should emulate the openness of children, rather than the other way around (Hos. 9:10, cf. Matt. 18:3).

The hallowing of the Name, exemplified in this wonderful story about Jesus' triumphal entry, is pictured in many ways in the New Testament. Striking and important are *Philippians* 2:9-11, *I Corinthians* 15:28 (when God is "all in all"), and in *Revelation* 21:1-4.

Your Kingdom come

The three first prayers (Your Name—Your Kingdom—Your Will) are actually three ways of expressing the same urgent petition: the redemption of God's fallen and rebellious creation. Mark, Matthew and Luke are equally clear about the fact that Jesus used the term "kingdom" as his chief term for expressing what it was all about: The kingdom of God, of Heaven, is at hand—Repent.

It is important to take hold of this kingdom-language. It constitutes the essence of Jesus' message and mission. It stands out the more since it does not dominate the language of any of the other New Testament writings. Thus it is the more striking a feature in the teaching of Jesus.

Its relative absence in the other New Testament writings is not difficult to explain. For them the important and the tangible thing was Jesus Christ the Saviour. They knew him as their Lord and Saviour, as the first-born from the dead, as the one to come in glory. The Church witnessed to Jesus—but the Church also remembered that Jesus had not spoken so much about himself as he had spoken about the kingdom. We may ask humbly and eagerly: Why did Jesus choose—out of all the possible terms available—to center on the kingdom?

The simplest answer is this: it was a good term for expressing the full range of God's redemption. Contrary to the views of many modern exegetes, it does not point only to a "relationship" between the believer and God, but also to the whole of creation. Thus the Gospels see the miracles of Jesus as means of redeeming the creation from the destructive forces of illness, demonic possession, and even death. The miracles are not just illustration-stories about faith, they are acts of redeeming the creation, pushing back the frontiers of Satan. And the distinctive mark of the kingdom is justice (a word that should not easily be replaced by the more spiritual-sounding word "righteousness").

In praying for the coming of that kingdom we pray for a redeemed, a healed, a mended creation. Much theological and exegetical attention has been devoted to the question whether Jesus thought and taught about the kingdom as present or future or in the process of coming. And equal attention has been given to whether he thought and taught about the kingdom to be established and manifested within "time and space" or as a cataclysmic reality beyond the confines of history and the world. The very fact that the evidence for a clear answer to such questions is ambiguous and varied should perhaps teach us that the important point is not these—our clever analytical, speculations—but rather our undivided seeking of and prayer for the kingdom.

Wherever, whenever, however the kingdom manifests itself it is welcome: in a healed body, in a restored mind, in a juster society, in a human heart that finds the power to forgive, in the faith and trust of a Canaanite mother, in the death and resurrection of the Messiah, in a new heaven and a new earth where justice dwells... We have too long discussed and disagreed about the modes of the kingdom instead of being lifted into God's agenda by saying: Your kingdom come.

Your will be done

Again, we must remember that this is a prayer to God—not a disguised moral injunction or admonition. We are praying that God's will for the redemption, the salvation of the creation be done. In this prayer we have on earth pray that God lift us and all into his gracious and heavenly will and plan and overcome our resistance, our fears, our selfishness: Be it on earth as in heaven.

When Jesus prays on the threshold of his martyrdom—in the garden of Gethsemane (Matt. 26:36-46 par.)—his words are three times the very words he gave to us as our prayer of prayers: My Father (vv. 42 and 39)—Your will be done (v. 42)—that you may not enter into temptation (v. 41). Thus the Lord's Prayer is not only the prayer that Christ gave to us. It is hallowed, filled with meaning from his own prayer. We pray with him and he with us.

And here—in Gethsemane—God's will toward salvation is that of utter and incomprehensible sacrifice. Like—and unlike—the sacrifice demanded by Abraham, on Golgotha, "on the mount of the Lord, it shall be provided" (Gen. 22:14).

Thus the will of God is full of mystery. It is perhaps significant that the disciples sleep through this momentous struggle of Jesus Christ. It is as if Matthew wanted to say: When you pray "Your will be done" you should not think that God depends only on you, for you were asleep when the petition "Your will be done" was prayed in the most decisive manner. And yet we are invited to pray as he prayed...

Our daily bread give us today

The Greek word rendered "daily" *(epiousios)* has puzzled translators and interpreters ever since the early church fathers. For the word seems to refer rather to "the next day", to the future bread, even to the messianic banquet (Matt. 8:11, Luke 22:30). Yet it refers to bread that fills the stomachs of the hungry. For the kingdom-banquet was not just a symbol of spiritual bliss but also of the kingdom where there be no starvation. And in the meals of the early church the eucharist and the nutrition were held together as we can see from *I Corinthians* 11:17-33. The petition for the bread thus holds together material and spiritual needs without making one more important than the other. The daily bread was a token of the messianic banquet—and the messianic banquet a reminder of the sanctity of the daily bread. The eucharist and the grace at meals are distinct but also in continuity with each other.

This indispensable connection is central to the great farewell speech of Jesus, according to Matthew, the vision of the last judgement (25:31-46). The most holy act of all—to serve Jesus Christ—consists of feeding the hungry and caring for those who suffer and are persecuted. It does not even matter if one sees it as a service to Jesus Christ. What matters is acts of compassion for the least of his brothers and sisters in want, in pain, in prison.

Thus the point of this parable is not to satisfy our self-centred curiosity about the last judgement, and to figure out how we can beat the divine system so as to feel secure. Rather it is Jesus assuring the beleaguered and persecuted that they are so precious in his eyes that the whole world will be judged by how *they*, the oppressed, have been treated. So precious, so decisive, so "religious", so "theological" is the food for the hungry.

I believe that the spirit of Matthew 25 as a key to the prayer for bread is extremely well gathered up for many of us in the Latin American grace: O God, to those who have hunger give bread; and to us who have bread give the hunger for justice.

And forgive us our debts as we (have) forgive(n) our debtors

To this prayer Matthew's Gospel has supplied the perfect illustration, the story about the unforgiving servant (18:23-35), a story held together by the words "debt" and "debtors". (The traditional translation "trespasses" in the Lord's prayer is one of the beautiful but erroneous expressions in the King James Version. The Greek word is clearly "debts".)

The story about the unforgiving servant is the final section of Matthew's sermon on church discipline. The story speaks for itself and needs no comment. The magnitude of God's forgiveness makes it ridiculous for us not to forgive one another. If one asks whether Jesus intended to say that God is as touchy as the royal official in the story, then one forgets the joy in telling drastic stories which were part of the Jewish teaching tradition—just as in the case of the grumpy judge, who gives in to the pestering pleas of the widow (Luke 18:5).

For Matthew the mutual forgiveness of the Christians is important indeed. Thus he lifts up the principle of mutual forgiveness as *the* element in the prayer that needs special stress (6:14-15), and when Peter asks if seven times is enough (some rabbis had said that three times of serious backsliding was the limit, so Peter thought he was generous in a "Christian" spirit), Jesus says 490 (18:21-22). In the Sermon on the Mount the theme occurs once more in a striking manner, in connection with anger as akin to murder (5:21-26): if you come to the altar with a gift and remember that your brother or sister has something against you, lay down your gift and go and reconcile yourself with him or her.

Here the important point is that the text does *not* say: ... and you remember that you have something against them. What matters is that they have something against you. We all think that we are people of good will, but that is irrelevant... Decisive is whether the other is hurting...

The Lord's Prayer, as a prayer for the kingdom, requires a mutually forgiven community. Only such a community can pray the messianic prayer and share in the messianic meal. That may be the reason for this prayer being tied to the preceding one by an "and"—*und* forgive us... This point is even more clear if we read with the majority of the best manuscripts: "as we have forgiven...".

And lead us not into temptation, but deliver us from evil—or:
Let us not be tested beyond our strength, but deliver us from the Evil one

The word for temptation *(peirasmos)* has the whole range of meaning: temptation, test, trial. And so has the story of Jesus' temptation in *Matthew* 4:1-11, the testing of God's Son, by the temptations. Just as Satan of old in *Genesis* 3 argued from the gracious intentions of God (could it really be true that God has forbidden..., 3:1), so here Satan identifies with God's intention for Jesus to be the true Son of God. Satan proposes an effective missionary strategy with miracles and public relations that would prove the divine uniqueness without a place for doubt. And Jesus says no. In the *Gospel of Matthew* this encounter has a special dimension, for, in a way, all the things that Satan suggests and offers will be done—in due time, and for others.

Jesus answered, "Human beings do not live by bread alone" but he never said that to hungry people. Them he fed. He did throw himself into the abyss of death and was saved. He did receive "all authority in heaven and on earth" (Matt. 28:18)—all in God's good time. One comes to think of an old Christian hymn that Paul quotes: "He did not consider his being like God as something to use for his own advantage" (Phil. 2:7).

The testing of Jesus was by the temptation to abuse his strength, his gifts, his relation to the Father. It was the temptation of triumphalism, forgetting or bypassing the cross. One could perhaps speak about the temptation of secularization, of using worldly means and methods, Madison Avenue techniques for selling the Gospel. We all know that it works. But we should learn: one does not sell Jesus as one sells toothpaste. There is the cross, there is the mystery. And there is God's time, the right time.

But when the disciples prayed, do not test us beyond our strength, they did not pray from strength. Here is the non-heroic prayer. Not: when temptation comes, give me strength! Rather: we know that if Satan tightens the screws we have no chance. The spirit is willing, but the flesh is weak.

Thus, dear Lord, deliver us! "And if those days had not been shortened, no human being would be saved; but for the sake of the elect those days will be shortened" (Matt. 24:22). And Paul has the same non-heroic realism: If it gets too bad, God will supply an emergency exit (I Cor. 10:13), as he did for Paul in Damascus when King Aretas was guarding the city and Paul escaped "in a basket through a window in the wall" (II Cor. 11:33).

For yours is the kingdom and the power and the glory for ever. Amen.

Jewish prayers often concluded with a sentence of praise. Although the earliest manuscripts do not include such a sentence—hence the Roman Catholics usually end the Lord's Prayer with the words "but deliver us from evil", it stands to reason that the early Christians did use such formulas. The one that became standard in the later manuscripts comes from David's final prayer in *I Chronicles* 29:11. It is appropriate indeed as it again reminds us of the kingdom for which we pray, and of the power and glory which is so manifest in Jesus who gave us this prayer.

It also draws our thoughts to the way in which Matthew concludes his Gospel (28:16-20). Here is the great epiphany on a mountain—the traditional place of divine glory and revelation as it had been for Moses and Elijah, with whom Jesus is seen on the mountain of transfiguration (Matt. 17:1). Once more the vision is overwhelming. The words usually translated, "but some doubted", are perhaps better translated, "but they doubted", i.e., so great is the vision that "they could not quite believe it". Human difficulty to grasp underscores the heavenly intensity of the moment.

The "great commission" to the disciples is primarily a word of assurance. The mission of the church is now a global one in contrast to the limits set earlier (Matt. 10:5; 15:24). Thus it may be Matthew's understanding that now begins the great chapter of Gentile mission, for the Greek word *ethne* usually means "gentiles", not "nations". The Church is now the new witnessing community to be "a light to the gentiles, that my salvation may reach to the end of the earth" (Isa. 49:6). Thus the disciples had been told: "Let your light so shine before people that they see your good deeds and give glory to your Father who is in heaven" (Matt. 5:16). The fruit of the mission is that the world give glory to God, as the magi had done (2:10-12), and thus God's name is being hallowed.

The image of a Christian is and remains that of a disciple, like those who were taught by Jesus and learned from him. This is striking language since it is confined to the Gospels and Acts, while the other writings of the New Testament use other words like saints, believers, those in Christ, God's beloved, brothers and sisters, etc.

The act of initiation is baptism and that in the name of the Father and the Son and the Holy Spirit—the only distinct New Testament reference to what later became the structure of the trinitarian creed, a creed that is so overwhelmed by the abundance of God's grace that one dared to strain the precious language of monotheism.

And there is the teaching of all that Jesus had commanded—as Matthew, the teacher-evangelist, had so carefully gathered and structured those lessons.

As the Church faces her mission she is assured of two things: Her mission is rooted in and guaranteed by Jesus Christ as the glorified and exalted Lord of the universe. Through suffering and death God has now given him all power on heaven and of earth—not the secular power that Satan tempted him with—and tempts the church with.

Secondly, the Church is assured of Jesus' abiding assistance in her life, her mission, her suffering, her witness: "Lo, I am with you all the way until the end of time." That is the final word of assurance, and the "great commission" is first and last the "great assurance". It may even be that to Matthew this "I am with you" is an intensified echo of the other name given to Jesus: Immanuel—God With Us (Matt. 1:23). But all according to all that he commanded, according to the mysterious will of God, the agenda for the kingdom which includes both the resurrection and the cross of Christ—the whole Gospel.

A Paraphrase

Oh God far above and beyond our grasp, yet close to us like a parent:
Let the time come soon when you are recognized by all as God.

That is, when you establish your supreme and good and just rule over your whole creation.

Yes, let the time come soon when your gracious plan for salvation becomes a reality on earth, as it now is in heaven.

While we wait for that day, let us already now enjoy the foretaste of the messianic banquet as we share in the bread that sustains our bodies.

In order to make us worthy of that community, forgive us what we have done wrong to our brothers and sisters as we have already forgiven those who did wrong to us; for we know that we are and must be the mutually forgiven community, your community of these end times.

And see to it that we are not tested beyond our strength, for we know that Satan can destroy us—unless you rescue us out of his ferocious grip.

SECTION PLENARY PRESENTATIONS

Good News to the Poor—A Case for a Missionary Movement
RAYMOND FUNG *

On this occasion, I see myself as a reporter who has been sent to investigate a certain area and is now back to submit his findings. Or, if I may be slightly more presumptuous, a pioneer sent on an exploratory journey and now home to tell his story. Or, if you like, a missionary who has spent eleven years in urban industrial mission in Asia, among factory workers in Hong Kong and, from out of this particular involvement, is ready now to share his and his colleague's experience. I have gone, a first-generation Christian with a middle-class background, a personal knowledge of Jesus Christ, a desire to serve, but no serious experience of personal suffering and rejection—I have gone and have come back, and come back much changed. This is my report to the churches.

A Missionary Movement Among the Poor

I would like to report to you that a case can be made for a missionary movement among the world's poor, particularly the poor in the Third World. I would like to urge churches to help each other so that slum dwellers, factory workers, street labourers and farm hands and their families could be confronted with the claims of Jesus Christ. By missionary movement I do not mean that with which we associate imperialism and colonialism, that which results in Christian ghettos cut off from the larger community, and becoming strangers to the aspirations of their own people, or that which offers a gospel coated in opium, as in the not-so-recent past, or, more likely today, coated in the sweet sugary promise of success. I would like to make a case for a focusing of missionary attention on building evangelizing and witnessing communities of the poor which will discover and live their expressions of faith among the masses of the poor and the oppressed.

I think we in the ecumenical fellowship of the WCC have a specific responsibility in enabling the Good News to be preached among the poor. We claim our heritage from the first world missionary conference at Edinburgh seventy years ago. In the intervening years, we have chosen to interpret our task in

*Raymond Fung, formerly Director of the Hong Kong Christian Industrial Committee, is Secretary for Mission of the Hong Kong Christian Council.

the light of the poor and the oppressed to the extent of taking their side and participating in their struggles. This understanding and commitment is not a deviation from our original missionary calling, but a response to God's action in the twentieth century and beyond. And not just the twentieth century, but the first as well, for there can be no serious understanding of Jesus' mission without reference to his commitment to the poor and the rejected of society. The bias of the ecumenical fellowship towards the poor is no less a strategic step towards realization of the great commission of Jesus Christ. The reason, if anything, is a simple matter of numbers.

We cannot be serious, and do not deserve to be taken seriously, if we claim to be interested in global evangelization, of Asia, of Africa, of Latin America, and yet refuse to take as central to our evangelistic commitment the masses of the poor in the cities and villages all over the world. A middle-class church in a sea of peasants and industrial workers makes no sense, theologically and statistically.

On these bases, I would like to make the case for a missionary movement among the world's poor. Not in facile triumphalism, but in sombre recognition of an all-important job not yet done. This is a tremendous task. And we are all too aware of our shortcomings and the burden of history from which we cannot totally escape. But I believe that we Christians, together as a whole, have no choice. And after all, the ecumenical fellowship has chosen to be faithful to God specifically in terms of its commitment to the poor. We cannot go back. We have to press forward to bring to fuller fruition our heritage and God's calling. To go back is to betray both.

Let me further report that in trying to share the Gospel with the poor in the context of participating in their struggles for dignity and justice, we have made certain discoveries about the poor, about the Christian faith, and not least about ourselves. These discoveries have changed us profoundly. And so, I believe, will a missionary movement among the poor change the Church. Herewith some of our discoveries.

Human Sinned-Againstness

We wish to report to the churches that a person is not only a sinner, a person is also the sinned against. That men and women are not only wilful violators of God's laws, they are also the violated. This is not to be understood in a behaviouristic sense, but in a theological sense, in terms of sin, the domination of sin, and of our "struggle against sin... to the point of shedding our blood" (Heb. 12:4). We would like to report to the churches that man is lost, lost not only in the sins in his own heart but also in the sinning grasp of principalities and powers of the world, demonic forces which cast a bondage over human lives and human institutions and infiltrate their very textures.

Because of our involvement with the poor, we discover that a person persistently deprived of basic material needs and political rights is also a person deprived of much of his or her soul—self-respect, dignity and will. A fisherman deprived of his waters, a peasant of his land, becomes a person deprived physically and spiritually. Dangerous working conditions and lax safety and health protection systems resulting in death and injury not only take away the means of livelihood of thousands of working-class families, but forcibly reduce otherwise proud and independent persons into dependency and self-depreciation. I cannot forget the faces of the poor who sat on the ground helpless seeing their homes bulldozed away to make room for a summer resort. There was resentment and hatred on their faces, which turned inward and gnawed at their own soul. I wish to report that hatred is not found in the poor standing up to fight, it is found in the poor crawling into the corner of forced submission. I would like to report to the churches that the destroyer of the body may not be able to kill the soul, but it can, and too often does, rape and maim the soul.

Gospel to the Sinned-Against

As it is, I would urge that we do not lose sight of the sinned-againstness of persons in our theological understanding and evangelistic effort. We must rediscover the horror of sin on human lives. There has been too much shallowness in our understanding of sin in the churches' evangelistic enterprises. Could it be that many evangelists of our churches today have no notion of human sinned-againstness? Could it be that in our much-cushioned life we cannot dismiss it as alien or only secondary to theological and evangelistic consideration? Or could it be that having looked into our own Christian experiences and found that our faith has made us prosper, we honestly think we are not the sinned-against, and neither for that matter need anyone else be the sinned-against? If that is the case, then no wonder the poor who experience indignity and injustice every day don't give a hoot about our evangelism.

We would like to report that the Gospel should not only call on the people to repent of their sins, but also must call on them to resist the forces that sin against them. The Church must not only remind the people that God is separated from us on account of our sinfulness. The Church must also proclaim that God loves us and is with us even while we are yet sinners.

But how do we communicate this message? How do we make the Good News of Jesus Christ real and meaningful to the sinned-against?

Compassion

First, we wish to report that the Christian response to the sinned-against is compassion, not the popular unexamined notion of being sentimental and soft or pitiful, but in the proper sense—suffering with, fellow feeling, sympathy.

Matthew talks about Jesus "going ashore and saw a great throng; and he had compassion on them, and healed their sick". And Jesus told his disciples to feed the people: "I have compassion on the crowd, because they have been with me now three days, and have nothing to eat and I am unwilling to send them away hungry lest they faint on the way" (Matt. 14:14; 15:32). Luke paints a similar picture. When the Lord saw a woman whose son had just died, he had compassion on her and said to her, "Do not weep" (Luke 7:13). And when the Samaritan saw the man beaten and wounded by robbers, "he had compassion, and went to him and bound up his wounds..." (Luke 10:33). The parable of the prodigal son makes the direct connection between compassion and man as the sinned-against. Luke reports, "But while he (the son) was yet at a distance, his father saw him and had compassion, and ran and embraced him and kissed him" (Luke 15:20). And when Matthew summed up the work of Jesus in the first stage of his ministry in *Matthew* 9:36, he put it this way, "When Jesus saw the crowds, he had compassion for them, because they were harassed and helpless, like sheep without a shepherd." In short, Jesus had compassion on people because they were sinned against. And yet, even more significantly, immediately after this summary, Matthew recorded Jesus' appeal to his disciples for evangelism, "the harvest is plentiful, but the labourers are few; pray therefore the Lord of the harvest to send out labourers into the harvest". It is clear that the call to evangelism is a response to the call to have compassion on the sinned-against. Mark, in his corresponding passage in *Mark* 6:34, omitted the "harassed and helpless" reference but he made the necessity for compassion in evangelism even more clear. Mark reported, "Jesus saw a great throng, and he had compassion on them, because they were like sheep without a shepherd; and he began to teach them many things".

At this point, I think I am prepared to make a bold suggestion: that compassion for people is possible only when we perceive people as the sinned-against. If we look at people as sinners (as distinct from the sinned-against), we may have concern for them, affection or pity, but no compassion, i.e. suffering together with another, fellow-feeling, sympathy. Many of the evangelistic activities of today have little perception of people as the sinned-against. Many are thus devoid of compassion. We must recover compassion in our evangelism.

I would like to report that compassion requires the stance of personal involvement and of solidarity. It requires that we get close to the poor, so close that we can feel their pulse, and hear their sigh. That the poor become no longer "they", an object of our charity or service, but "you" with whom we share a common destiny and to whom we must account for ourselves. In short, compassion requires community with the poor. Sinned-againstness is a fundamental human condition shared by Christians and non-Christians alike. It provides a biblical, factual, deeply-felt basis for unity, whereas the corresponding understanding of people as sinners tends to separate. But the notion of the sinned-against enables the Christian to say to his or her neighbours, regardless of their attitude towards Jesus Christ, "You are my brother and my sister. We have a job to do."

Mission

That job is mission, the struggle of the Christian and his neighbours against the forces that sin against them. And it is this that makes the Good News of Jesus Christ real and meaningful to the poor, not only in terms of Christian presence, of sharing in their suffering, but also in terms of the Gospel empowering them to act. The landlord owns the village administration. The factory owner alone decides whom to hire and whom to dismiss. The tribal leaders are corrupt, for generations. The dictator has the banks, the police, the military and, yes, the media and the opinion polls in his pocket. It is hopeless to act. In exclusively economic and military terms, this may well be so. And it is foolish of anybody to underestimate the powers of the exploiter. But for those who understand these powers for what they really are, and call them by their real name: sin, or forces of sin, there is hope. Because we know that in Christian faith lies a resolution for sin, that sin is eventually self-destructive, and though sin's embodiment may look gigantically invincible it often has feet of clay. This understanding must be proclaimed.

In other cases, the poor do act, and sometimes do overturn forces of exploitation, and there are ideologies which motivate and unite. Here, the Christian understanding of human sinned-againstness is no less relevant, as it brings in realism, humaneness, and hope, should there be failure, and the will to continue, should betrayal occur. For the Christian who sees persons as the sinned-against, economic and political exploitation is spiritual exploitation, and so is the struggle, and so must be the solutions. The notion of the sinned-against enables us to see human exploitation at its most frightful fulness and depth, to the extent, paradoxically, that once it is seen that way, it becomes less frightening and less destructive.

Whatever the case, the Christian communication to the people takes place in the context of involvement and of solidarity, in compassion, in community. That is, the community of the sinned-against.

Evangelism

Secondly, I would like to report that in the community of the sinned-against something important very often happens; in the struggle against the forces of sin, the sinned-against soon comes to realize that he or she is also the sinner in such a way that he or she cannot respond with a "So what?". Together with the fact of being sinned against, soon comes the stark naked fact of his or her own personal sinfulness and the need for God. A struggle is no romantic place. It is an environment in which one comes to confront one's ugliness and emptiness, and is most open to God's forgiveness. To help a person become aware of his or her sinned-againstness does not absolve that person of personal responsibility. On the contrary, it makes that person see how he or she can and must be personally responsible, because the identity of the sinned-against is defined not only in terms of the exploiter, but also in terms of his or her fellow sinned-against, and in terms of God.

A factory worker found himself tempted to betray his fellowmen by not showing up at a picketline as had previously been agreed. A leader of 5,000 slumdwellers found herself trying to corner the best and the most timber for her own use from among the lot they managed to obtain from government to rebuild their burned-out squatters. The former challenged himself, experienced conversion and now claims the name of Christian. The latter was challenged and experienced conversion. I do not know if she is a Christian today. Or, take the case of a much-weathered village headman who has taken his people through thick and thin against the onslaughts of government and big business. After a series of lengthy and demanding negotiations in town, he was returning home with my counterpart keeping him company. As they waited for the once-a-day bus, the man said, "The crisis and the struggle is over for the time being. What do we do now?" My friend didn't answer him, knowing that he had not finished. "I want to pray to your God." They did, at that isolated bus stop on an unpaved road in rural Malaysia.

I would like to report to you that the context of a community of the sinned-against struggling against the forces of sin is an evangelizing context. It is in a community in struggle that evangelism takes place. It is impossible to overemphasize the importance of the community of the sinned-against in the evangelization of the poor. The most dwelt-upon methods of evangelism today—personal evangelism and mass evangelism—are futile among the poor because, among many other reasons, both presuppose a receiving community which is not available to the poor in most of our existing churches today. Of a definable 80 worker-Christians newly become members of local congregations in Hong Kong, only about one third remain in the churches after three months. The rest, still regarding themselves as Christians, have simply left. One made the painful decision when he was refused a place in the church's young adult Bible training programme. He is 28 but has only a primary education. He doesn't fit the church system of Christian education. To yet another, the final straw for her was the gossip in the congregation that she was a leftist on account of her active membership in a labour union, and talk of the likelihood of Communist infiltration circulated. At one point, I encouraged her to stay and fight it out. She looked me square in the eye, a few drops of tears glistening. "Is it worth it? One of your favourite pieces of advice is not to fight unnecessary battles." But most of those who have left the churches in which they received their baptism simply drifted away. They instinctively understand that the churches want them as spectators and even recipients of Christian services, but not as full members of a caring and sharing community. That is to highlight the fact that there are poor people in our churches. Their presence and their sinned-againstness by economic and political forces make it impossible for the pastoral ministry to be devoid of political dimensions. When the poor are in the churches, to be pro-poor is not a political stand, it is a pastoral stand. Let us also recognize the fact that most of the poor are not in our churches. For them, the evangelizing context is not individual encounter, being confronted with the four spiritual laws for instance; neither is it a mass rally. It is far more personal and far more corporate. Hence this plea for a missionary movement to build communities of the sinned-against among the world's poor.

Power

I would like to report that while the fact of human sinned-againstness and the Christian response must be communicated to the poor in the narrow confines of slums and factory floor, the same message must be proclaimed in the open sunshine of the market place. Jesus' command for the Christian to be both salt of the earth and light of the world means, in the case of a missionary movement among the poor, sharing the poor's struggle, being so very close to them as to feel their pulse and hear their unspeakable sigh. It also means that having understood the poor, we lift up, in community, their suffering and articulate clearly and simply their aspirations for all the world to see. In the final analysis, the authority of the Church among the poor and among the powerful comes from the same source—a clear and unhesitant proclamation of the genuine aspirations of the poor, often hidden and inarticulate. Such proclamation is both evangelistic and prophetic. Articulation of the hitherto unarticulated liberates the poor, draws them into community, and provides them with the hope to enable them to engage in struggle. And no dictatorship, whether economic or political in nature, can dare ignore the genuine aspiration of the overwhelming majority of the people, their responses, and their willingness to act.

So a missionary movement among the poor will not stop at being a concern only of the Christian community. By its involvement in the very life of the poor, it will be thrust into the heart of history, and help shape it to better conformity with the kingdom of God. By being with the powerless, the Church gains power. The powerful of the world have to listen when, through the Church, the pains and hopes of the powerless are lifted up. The closer the Church gets to the heart of the poor, the more authentic its voice will be, and more power it will be given. Could this not be an approximation of the way of our Lord Christ Jesus—the power of powerlessness? The power of self-emptying love? The power which comes from nearness with the powerless?

Good News to the Affluent

I would like to report that a missionary movement among the poor will have meaning for those who are not poor. I would like to claim that the Good News to the poor is the Good News of Jesus Christ to all, including the affluent. We must recognize that it is in the extremities, and therefore the relative simplicities, of the life of the poor, that we can better understand basic human reality and the meaning of the Gospel and its cutting edge in human lives. It is in the poor that we discover human sinned-againstness, and as we contemplate this reality, we come to realize too that the middle class is also the sinned-against. The fact of the poor as the sinned-against enables the not-so-poor to see that they too are the sinned-against. And while in their struggles against the forces of sin, the poor come to realize that they too are sinners, the middle class can also come to a similar realization, that the sinned-against is also the sinning.

On this understanding of human sinned-againstness is hope for genuine solidarity between the Church of the poor and the more affluent. Though the forces of sin which sin against them may differ in form, definitely more naked and more brutal against the poor, more illusive and complex against the middle class, they are basically the same—they create suffering, they create hunger, and they bring about hatred and despair. On the realization of their own sinned-againstness, there is hope that those in affluent suburbs who are anxious, broken, hurt and lonely will come to a better appreciation and a more profound empathy for those who live in slums, who are anxious for their next meal, broken in their body by exploiters and torturers, hurt in their pride because they cannot provide for their families, and lonely in their crowdedness for want of anyone to turn to. There is danger, however, that having said that the middle class is also the sinned-against, it becomes an excuse to dilute the Gospel's bias towards the poor and their struggles. So let me also report that the greater reality of the poor is that of sinned-againstness whereas the greater reality of the affluent is that of sinning. The suffering of the poor is real; the suffering of the middle class is also real. God has a preferential love for the poor. God also has a preferential love for the poor in spirit. But may I suggest that God accepts the poor in spirit because God has already accepted the poor? That the poor in spirit and their suffering is an approximation of the poor and their suffering? The Good News is for the poor and those who approximate the poor, i.e. the poor in spirit. The poor is the original; the poor in spirit the copy. It is silly for the copy to dismiss the original. It is presumptuous of the copy to claim it is the original. We need the original to know the Master Painter. We need the original to improve the copy. So too does the Church need the poor to know the heart and mind of the Crucified Christ. So too does the Church need the poor in order to walk the way of the cross and of the resurrection.

Finally let me report by way of recapitulation that evangelization of the poor does not begin by getting the poor to listen to God's Word. It does not begin with saturating whole cities with gospel tracts and pithy gospel melodies. It begins with God, or God's representatives, listening to the voice of the poor. The first element of the Good News is the poor and the oppressed crying out loud, "Listen to my words, O Lord, and hear my sighs. Listen to my cry for help. My God and King" (Ps. 5:1-2). "Listen, O Lord, to my plea for justice; pay attention to my cry for help" (Ps. 17:1). And the Christian response? I would like to report, and this is the other element of the Good News to the poor, that Jesus responded with *Matthew* 16:24, "If anyone wants to come with me, he must forget himself, carry his cross, and follow me. For whoever wants to save his own life will lose it; but whoever loses his life for my sake will find it." This is an extraordinary, unexpected response. To those who cry for help and for justice, Jesus Christ offered discipleship and the demands of self-sacrifice. But he offered it in the assurance of victory and the power and joy of his companionship.

Sometimes I can't help feeling with a bit of misplaced humour that the poor whom nobody bothers to listen to and who then ask God or God's representatives to hear them do not always know what they are getting into. Which factory workers would have thought that becoming a Christian implies visiting the homes of workers killed in industrial incidents, comforting the widows, demanding quick compensation and more stringent safety laws? It is awful to fall into the hands of the living God. But that is the Gospel of

Jesus Christ. He is no respector of persons. To both poor and non-poor alike, it's the same Good News. He's heard us, and he bids us to take our cross and follow him.

This then is my report to the churches, my case for a missionary movement among the world's poor.

Good News to the Poor—Its Implications for the Mission of the Church in Latin America Today
JOAQUIM BEATO*

I come from Latin America. Above all, I am a Latin American. I insist on this aspect of my personal identity in order to stress, from the beginning, the multiform nature of the reality existing under the name Latin America. I am referring to an ethnic and mutually kaleidoscopic reality which is difficult to apprehend from within and to grasp from outside with the help of simplistic and usually deforming stereotypes.

To limit more clearly the scope of my perspective I should say: I am a South American. Mexico, Central America and the Caribbean are, unfortunately, not included in this presentation. South America is a continent of 17,805,200 square kilometres with an estimated population of over 200,000,000 people. In the north and west, this population is predominantly Indian and of mixed race, with a minority of Spanish origin. In the south, beginning in Southern Brazil down to Argentina, Uruguay and Central Chile, the population is primarily European with little Indian and African influence. In the rest of the continent, European groups received in different degrees the African influence and today they coexist with a large contingency of mulattos and blacks.

In Brazil, the country from which I come, which represents half of South America both in geography and in population, blacks and mulattos represent about 40% of the population; in Colombia we are about 30% and may be a little less in Venezuela. We speak Portuguese in Brazil and Spanish is spoken in the rest of South and Latin America. The exceptions are few. We should note, however, that in some countries of the Andean region, Spanish coexists with one or more indigenous languages. Of these, the most important are Quechua, Aimara and Jibaro, which are spoken in Bolivia, Peru, Colombia and Ecuador. Also important is Gvarany which is spoken in Paraguay even by the non-indigenous population. The African languages are practically extinguished. Spanish and Portuguese spoken in Latin America incorporate into their vocabulary and pronunciation the African and indigenous influence.

---

*The Rev. Joaquim Beato is Professor of Old Testament, Episcopal Seminary, São Paulo, Brazil.

These influences are more perceptible in Portuguese which differs more from the language spoken in Portugal than South American Spanish differs from that of Spain.

We therefore have an Indian America in the north and west; a European America in the south, and a racially mixed America with a predominant African influence on the European and indigenous sector of the population. To make the picture even more complicated for those who love clichés and stereotypes, after independence, that is, from the second half of the 19th century through 1930, several Latin American countries, especially Brazil and Argentina, received between 11 and 12 million European immigrants. These were Italians, Spaniards, Portuguese and Germans.

In addition, Arabs and Japanese and, to a lesser extent, Jews, Poles, Koreans and Hungarians immigrated to Brazil. Immigration, however, has diminished considerably since 1930, to the extent that no more than 2% of the population was born outside Brazil. The impact of this post-independence immigration was more important in Argentina, Uruguay and Southern Brazil. In the rest of Brazil, however, this immigration did not affect the national identity which had already been achieved through the incorporation of the indigenous and Africans cultures into the prevailing Portuguese culture. One could say that all South American countries are nations with their own, individual characteristics, conscious of their national identity and proud of their national cultures. There are two factors which help to understand how it was possible to create from ethnically, culturally and linguistically different groups, the consciousness of belonging to a nation. These two factors are language (Spanish or Portuguese) and religion (Roman Catholic) brought from the Iberian peninsula.

The South American continent is Catholic. Until the proclamation of the Republic in Brazil, Catholicism was the official religion. It was up until Vatican II a traditional Catholicism, against Protestantism, against free-masonry, against communism, and retrograde. It was a Catholicism that was not concerned with real evangelization, but worried about maintaining its tacit alliance with the state and with the ruling classes. Since Vatican II a remarkable change has taken place within Latin American Catholicism.

The penetration of Protestant missions in Latin America was justified in face of this traditional Catholicism. These missions came during the second half of the 19th century, and coincided with the arrival of Protestant immigrants from Germany. Protestantism presented itself as a more dynamic, progressive and modernizing form of Christianity. It could show, to its credit, the predominantly Protestant Anglo-Saxon societies which were already more advanced than the Catholic societies of Southern Europe.

Today in Brazil for example, in a population of over 100 million, 18 million are estimated to be Protestant. Of these 10% are the result of Protestant missions, especially from the USA; 15% represent Protestantism which resulted from immigration, mainly Lutherans; and 75% represent Pentecostal and other groups who arrived in Brazil more than 75 years ago.

Protestantism which resulted from the missions include Baptists, Presbyterians, Methodists, Congregationalists and Episcopalians. These denominations played an important missionary role and experienced a steady growth for some time. They exercised a great deal of influence, especially in the education field, which was disproportionately high in relation to their relatively small number of members. Today these denominations are going through a period of stagnation in their growth. As a result of the upward social mobility of their members, they have become middle class churches and have lost their initial progressive and modernizing impulse, and have opted for a theological, political and socially conservative attitude. Of these denominations, only the Methodists and Episcopalians are members of the WCC. The Lutherans, it seems to me, have not yet been able to reconcile their original and historical commitment as a religion of an ethnic minority group with the challenge to put themselves at the service of all Brazilians. Pentecostalism today is, without any doubt, the most dynamic Protestant group, and it has experienced remarkable growth. In spite of signs of "aging" in some of their groups, it is the only group with close ties with the poor and the working classes, and it is the one which has absorbed the cultural characteristics of the lower classes. It does not seem to me, however, that this fact is considered by the Pentecostals as of value in itself, nor that it is the result of a conscious strategy. As far as I know, the situation I have just described is the same, *mutatis mutandis*, in the Protestantism in the hemisphere.

If we are to reflect on evangelization in Latin America, both in theological and institutional terms, in a way whereby the poor regain their position as bearer and object of the Gospel, we have to turn to what is being thought and practiced by the new Roman Catholic Church in Latin America. Beginning with Vatican II and then with the Continental Conferences in Medellin (1968) and Puebla (1978), this Church became, in the words of one of its documents:

A Church immersed in today's world; a Church amidst the deprived world of the poor; a Church obedient to the Word of God and attentive to the signs of the times; a Church that partakes in the sacrament of the poor; a Church that lends its voice to the voiceless; a prophetic Church that can say: "do not oppress your brother"; a Church that fulfils in itself the Passion of Christ; a Church that provides an institutional space for liberating practice; a Church which sees itself as the people of

God; a Church that is born amidst the people by the Holy Spirit; a Church which is more pastoral, popular and charismatic. [1]

The martyrs that this Church has produced in the past twenty years bear witness to this confession of repentance. And the serious, profound and challenging theological reflection known as Theology of Liberation attests to the fact that this is a definite, deliberate and reflected-upon option. What does it mean for Christians and their mission in the world, that Human Rights are persistently and systematically violated in a continent where about 50% of the world's Catholics live, and above all, that this violation is claimed to have religious legitimization? [2] What does it mean for Christians that a continent where about 50% of the world's Catholics live is in a situation of underdevelopment marked by huge gaps between the majority who live in poverty and a minority who possess and control abundant resources? Had these two questions been asked by an outsider they would have been taken as a condemnation of the Church and its witness. These questions, however, were asked by the Church itself, and the Church itself gave the answer in Puebla when in its theological, prophetic and pastoral response it put its "preferential option for the poor" within the context of evangelization in Latin America. [3]

More than a simple change in its missionary and pastoral strategy was involved, and whatever the historic, social and doctrinal context was that led the Catholic Church to take this position, the fact remains that the "preferential option for the poor" means a return to the Mosaic tradition of liberation and to the radical theocratic perspective of Jesus and the early Christians. [4]

It is generally recognized by scholars that in the literature of Israel there are two traditions; one derived from the pact of Moses and the other from the pact of David. The tradition related to the Mosaic pact is characterized by a protest movement of the disinherited, and its theological vision is articulated around a God who intervenes decisively in favour of the enslaved and oppressed and against the oppressive structures that are apparently unshakeable. On the other hand, the David tradition is characterized by a movement of the established groups and its theological perspective is

---

[1] *Revista Eclesiástica Brasilera* (No. 38, June 1978), 301-307.

[2] *REB* (Fasc. No. 149, March 1978), 106.

[3] *Puebla: A Evangelizaçao no presente e no futuro da America Latina* (Official Text of the CNBB, Ed. Vozes-Petrópolis, 1979), 382, 707, 733, 769, 1134, 1217, especially 27-50.

[4] Cf. Walter Brueggemann: "Trajectories in OT Literature and the Sociology of Ancient Israel", in *JBL* (vol. 98, No. 2, June 1979), 161-185, 179-180.

articulated around a God who defends and sustains the status quo.[5] A reading of the Old Testament materials of the various periods of the history of Israel, in light of the contrasts between these two perspectives, shows that this tension existed throughout the centuries covered by the Canonic literature as the two "trajectories" in the reading of history where the existence and vocation of the people of God is made explicit.

According to these two predominant theories, the conquest of Canaan by Israel was carried out either by invasion or by infiltration. A third position could be, and in fact has been, proposed.[6] Instead of invasion or infiltration, it was the "habiru", an oppressed people, who, carrying a proposal for an alternative social order, made a revolution against the tyrant kings of the city-states. Bound together by a pact with a supreme non-human "leader", and the solidarity of the newly-formed community, the "habiru" set out to form a deliberate alternative social order which became Israel. The tribes of Israel are, therefore, historical entities. They came into being through the historical process of making an option. They are international communities, deliberately defending an ideology and a social order different from those prevailing in Egypt and in Canaan.

This pact which made possible a new political experiment and which was characterized by a radical rupture with the urban culture, is much more pertinent to the situation in Israel than has been acknowledged. The Israel of this pact represented not only a theological novelty but also a novelty as a social experiment. And the "habiru" have to be understood as foreigners in relation to Canaan, not in the geographic sense, but as "outsiders" in the socio-political sense: geographically present, but without the right to participate in the decision-making process involving their own destiny. Their marginalization was more political, social and economic than geographic. The theological perspective which led them to reject the gods of the empire resulted from their rejection of the way the imperial society was organized. Either as a moving force behind the movement or as its justification, this theological perspective made possible a radical discontinuity in the social order of Israel. The gods, who were an integral part of the social system, justified a totalitarian and hierarchical social order, and were the expression of a state religion compromised by the unchangeable social order which in turn denied any space for a theological critique of itself. When the "new" God of freedom and justice was accepted in the Covenant, this social order

---

[5] Gottwald, N. K., *The Tribes of Yahweh: A Sociology of the Religion of Liberated Israel, 1250-1050 B.C.* (Ex-Orbis, Maryknoll, N.Y., 1979), 191-227, esp. 210-219.
[6] Mendenhall, G. E., *The Tenth Generation: The Origins of the Biblical Tradition* (John Hopkins, Baltimore, 1973).

became unnecessary. There is therefore a loose relationship between the theological vision and social organizations. Thus, the social order in Israel from Moses to David can be considered an experiment to determine the viability of an alternative society without the sanction of the imperial gods. The breaking away from the old theological environment, and the novelty of the Yehovism as a faith centred on justice and freedom explains the radical rupture of Israel with its political context. Yahwism is a religious movement in its deep commitment to the God of Exodus; but it is also a political movement in its rejection of the status quo.

In monarchic Israel, the social innovation of the mosaic era and its corresponding theology based on a God that took the side of the oppressed, were abandoned. The temple, the bureaucracy, the royal harem, the permanent army, the tax system, represented a conscious limitation of the imperial societies of Israel's neighbours and a rejection of the sense of liberation of the mosaic tradition. This happened 250 years after the Exodus, when the community already had the resources not only to survive, but also to dominate its context politically as during the reign of Solomon. But the tensions between the factions pro and against the monarchy, recorded in Samuel, manifest the conflict between the two "trajectories" in the struggle of Israel with its own conscience about whether it should be "like other nations" (I Sam. 8:5, 20) or a people holy to Yahweh.

The religion of God's freedom and the policy based on justice introduced to Moses and kept alive in the pre-monarchic community were abandoned. With the monarchy, Israel accepted the same principles rejected since Egypt and adopted the imperial ideology which combined the religion of the state's God with a policy of injustice and social domination.

These tensions are also present during the period of the divided monarchy. This can be better understood within the context of the general confrontation between the two "trajectories". The separation registered in *I Kings* 12 represents a split between the historical liberation community and the social order of the Davidic regime. This split is remarkable, for it happened exactly because of a concrete problem of political oppression. Rehoboam was commited to maintaining the status quo, even though injustice would be the price to pay. The Northern Kingdom also experienced similar oppression during Acabe's time, for example. But it appears that the Northern Kingdom was more open and susceptible to the transforming impact of the Mosaic tradition than the Kingdom of Judah. The continued confrontations between kings and prophets during this period show the permanent tensions between the Davidic pact with its identification with the status quo and the Mosaic pact characterized by its affirmation of freedom.

During the period of exile which begins with the tragedy of 587 A.D., the two "trajectories" are shaken at their foundations. The prophetic Mosaic pact enters a period of crisis, while the royal tradition prevails.

I agree with Hanson's suggestion[7] that dialectic relationship between vision and reality is the starting point to understand the post-exile period which is articulated in Deutero-Isaiah. After this prophet, each of the various social groups in Israel adopted one aspect of this dialectic, and made that particular aspect the basis for their faith and literature. The second Isaiah provides, therefore, the pactic and theological basis for the "pragmatic group" as well as for "visionaries". The "pragmatic group" is in power and is centred around the sacerdotal cast of Jerusalem. The "visionaries" and the groups now out of power are led to wait for a new act of God that will reverse the situation and return them to power. This group has turned to the apocalyptic and can be identified with the group of Levites who previously exercised great influence in the community but are now being increasingly marginalized. The "pragmatic group" and the "visionaries" continue, in a way appropriate to their time and place, the same confrontation we are describing between the accommodative faith of the Davidic groups and the Mosaic liberation movement. The "visionaries", the heirs to this movement, believe that the present order is being forcefully questioned by God's promises. The "pragmatic group" continues the tradition of affirming the present order as being sanctioned by God.

Brueggemann suggests the following chart as a summary of the elements that continuously appear in each "trajectory"[7a]:

A. *The Royal Trajectory*	B. *The Liberation Trajectory*
1. Prefer to speak about unity	1. Prefer to tell concrete stories of liberation
2. Speaks the language of fertility (creation) and of continuity (royal institutions)	2. Speaks the language of war and of discontinuity
3. The preferred way of perception is that of universal inclusiveness	3. The preferred way of perception is that of historical specificity
4. It appears to have been nourished and valued by the urban rich	4. It appears to have been nourished and valued by poor peasants

---

[7] Hanson, P. D., *The Dawn of Apocalyptic: The Historical and Sociological Roots of Jewish Apocalyptic Escatology* (Fortress Press, Phil., 1975).
[7a] Brueggemann, *op. cit.*, 162.

5. Tends to be socially conservative and primarily values
stability

5. Tends to be socially revolutionary and values change

6. Centred around the glory and
sanctity of God and the institutions related to this sanctity

6. Centred around the justice
and rectitude of God's will

In his sociological analysis of primitive Christianity, Gerd Theissen has reached conclusions that confirm the continuity between Jesus and his first followers and the Mosaic liberation tradition.[8] This confirmation becomes even more important when one considers the fact that Theissen has, in his studies, different objectives from those of the summary done by Brueggemann.

The tradition of Jesus' teachings are characterized by an ethical radicalism: they require leaving home, i.e., to forsake permanent residence, the family, goods and properties.[9] According to Theissen, such teachings can only be practised in extreme situations. Only outside of the establishment can such an ethos[10] be lived. And he adds that such an ethos can be practised and reached with some degree of credibility only by those who have severed their ties with the interests of the world. That, Theissen says, was the case of itinerant charismatic Christians: apostles, prophets, and missionaries. They moved from place to place and were subject to hunger[11] and to persecution.[12] If and when they found food and lodging it was from people who, like themselves, were outside of the establishment. The attention the religious and social pariahs, the prostitutes, and the publicans received in Jesus' ministry is clear evidence that those who transmitted the word belonged to the lower ranks of society. In the synoptic literature we see the world "from below".[13]

There were three types of opposition to the structures of government in Palestine in the first century: the prophetic movements who promised a miraculous divine intervention on behalf of Israel, i.e., a repetition of the salvation tradition of the past; the armed resistance movement which had as its objectives a widespread rebellion against the Romans; and the *Essenes* who were considered pacifists. But they were pacifists who dreamed of a massacre in the future when they and the angels would kill the sons of

---

[8] Cf. Theissen G., "Itinerant Radicalism" in *Radical Religion, A Quarterly Journal of Critical Opinion* (Vol. II, Nos. 2 and 3, 1975, 84-93).
[9] Idem, *The First Followers of Jesus* (SCM Press, London, 1978), 110-114.
[10] *Ibid*, 15.
[11] Mark 2:23-28.
[12] Matt. 10:23.
[13] Theissen: "Itinerant Radicalism", 89b.

darkness, which included all foreigners and apostates. All these movements intended to establish God's kingdom. All proposed an explicitly imminent eschatology in which the end of the world also meant the end of Roman domination as well as the end of the traditional society. We cannot imagine the proclamation of the kingdom of God by Jesus' movement as simply theological, for that movement was directly related to the socio-political tensions of Palestine. There would be a radical change in Palestine in the near future, and small groups of social outcasts would become the rulers of Israel.

This reading of the Scriptures, in my opinion, allows us to draw the conclusion that the Christian affirmation of the poor as the bearers and the object of the Gospel is not simply a theological thesis. It is also the result of an objective historical and sociological reading of the roots of Christianity. It characterizes the option between two different "trajectories" that are present in the history of the people of God, and it is in this history that it affirms and makes explicit the meaning of its vocation in the world.

The Roman Catholic Church, in its evangelization programme for Latin America, has made a preferential option for the poor. What position will the Protestant churches take? Our continent is characterized by a dependent, exclusivist and associated capitalism. I'm not speaking only of a state that gives preferential treatment to capital over labour as happens in any capitalism. I am also referring to the fact that the state puts all its repressive apparatus openly at the service of capital. It is what some people call savage capitalism. In addition, it is a capitalism dependent on the capitalism in the centre. This is an obstacle to the development of a national project with independent characteristics. It is an associated capitalism. For example, about 60% of all large and medium-sized companies in Brazil are owned or controlled by transnational corporations. It is an exclusivist capitalism which concentrates the benefits of development in the hands of a small minority. In Brazil, for example, the pyramids of social stratification are the following: 1) the ruling class constitutes 5% of the population with 1% being very rich and 4% rich; 2) intermediary sectors represent 15%; 3) lower classes represent 80% out of which 30% are poor (industrial workers) and 50% (unskilled workers, peasants, unemployed and marginal) live in extreme poverty. [14]

How will the Protestant churches face their evangelical mission in such a continent?

Based on what has been said above, it seems to me that a project of evangelization in Latin America that does not make a clear, decisive and

---

[14] *REB* (Fasc. No. 150, June 1978), 310-311; (Fasc. No. 151, September 1978), 388-389.

preferential option for the poor will have no future. It is necessary that Protestantism ask itself questions similar to those asked by the Roman Catholic Church. In asking those questions, the Protestant churches will have to take into consideration the fact that the rich, colonized and imperialist nations in the centre are populated primarily by Protestants. In face of the kind of capitalism we have in Latin America, we are forced to conclude that:

1. If human rights are violated in Latin America, it happens primarily to maintain a social order that benefits especially the nations of the centre who are concerned with protecting their markets and private investments of their citizens.

2. Those few who possess abundant resources in Latin America are members of the national bourgeoisies who are associated with foreign capital, i.e., the interests of the countries in the centre. If the Protestant churches are interested in having a relevant project of evangelization in Latin America, we must ask ourselves what this situation means for the Christian faith and our mission.

More than Catholicism, Protestantism has identified itself apologetically as one of the driving forces of the present development of western, i.e., European, civilization. The industrial revolution and the scientific and technological revolutions took place in Protestant countries. Protestant ethics were a necessary force, although not sufficient in itself, for the rise of capitalism. Hence the legitimization of this Eurocentric civilization and the identification of its values with Christian values, which is implicit in the statements of those who defend the present order as being western and Christian. Weber's thesis on the relation of Protestantism to wealth acquires a negative value from the perspective of the countries in the periphery. After all, the wealth of the nations in the centre is related to their domination of the under-developed nations and is therefore based on unjust relations at international level.

When we reflect upon our evangelizing mission in a world divided between a rich minority and a majority who live in poverty, it is necessary that the Protestant churches repent, and no longer legitimize and justify the success and wealth of the rich countries. It is necessary that the churches take the side of the poor to understand God's plans for them and through them. It is necessary that the churches remove themselves from the historical compromise with the wealth of the North so that they can no longer share the responsibility in the domination and exploitation of the South. It is necessary to change the social context of their exegesis and their theological reflection to a perspective that reflects the concrete historical situation and aspirations of the people in the periphery. Although it is not sufficient to add new themes to a Eurocentric theology, it should be within this *metanoia* the granting of privilege to certain biblical texts related to the Mosaic "trajectory" of liberation: in the New Testament it would be necessary to move from Paul to the Synoptics, from post-Paulist to Apocalypse; in the Old Testament, it would be necessary to turn from David to the Mosaic revolution, from worship to prophecy, from the *sapiential* literature to Apocalypse. It is necessary to make an effort to let the poor of the Bible speak, because their message will certainly be heard by today's poor. The oppressed and marginalized form a fellowship which transcends national, cultural, linguistic and time barriers.

If it is necessary that Protestantism participate in the evangelization of Latin America, world Protestantism cannot forget the churches that are already present in Latin America. They can provide the necessary link between the Protestant message and the Latin-American reality. They speak the language and reflect, at different degrees, the different national cultures in Latin America. Without their help, the evangelization of Latin America would not be viable. In order for the churches in Latin America to participate in the liberation and redemption of the continent, they will have to become Latin American churches in Latin America and for Latin America. Through the example of world Protestantism and in permanent dialogue with it at the pastoral, missionary and theological levels, they will be able to translate at the regional level their true universality. And it is important to stress that when I say Latin American churches, I am referring to the grass-roots and not exclusively to the intellectuals of Latin American Protestantism.

Good News to the Poor
CANAAN BANANA*

The spirit of the Lord has been given to me
for he has annointed me. He has sent me to
bring the good news to the poor

(Luke 4:18)

I have come
so that they may have life and have it to the full

(John 10:10)

He remembered us when we were down.
His love is everlasting!
And snatched us from our oppressors.
His love is everlasting!

(Psalm 136:23, 24)

The twentieth century will be known in history books as the century of revolts against "the entrenched positions of the establishment"[1] and against poverty. The most bitter struggles that have paved the path of mankind through this century originated in situations of despair, when men chose to lay down their lives instead of continuing to live under conditions of hunger, poverty, marginalization and exploitation.

Still there will be many who will ask whether man has gained anything in these bitter struggles. Has he changed the situation? Had he any hope that this world was going to be different? They go on answering their own question by taking a defeatist attitude and by defending it with this kind of slogan: man achieves nothing by revolting; revolution engenders bitterness, hatred and division; revolution will always leave man where he was before, without any hope of changing a world which will always be as it is.

---

* The Rev. Canaan Banana, President of Zimbabwe, prepared this paper for Section I, but official duties prevented his attendance at the Melbourne Conference.
[1] J. Woddis, *New Theories of Revolution* (Lawrence and Wishart, London, 1972), 9.

The Christian message contains a completely different answer, because its answer is that of the poor, "the only ones who can understand it", as E. Cardinal has said.[2] It is in the middle of their struggle that they discover the meaning of life and history. They never knew what liberation was until they became involved in their own liberation. It is then that the Good News turns to be news and to be good. It is then that the poor of the world will repeat with those of Emmaus: "Did not our heart burn within us as he talked to us on the road?" (Luke 24:32).

In this paper the connection between the struggle of liberation from poverty and the proclamation of the Good News will be investigated. In order to appreciate the significance of the subject under discussion, we need to define what is meant by "Good News" and by "the poor".

Poverty and Expectations

The background against which any news can be received as good news is important for our definition of "the poor" and "the Good News". We must have in mind a situation where life has been mutilated in a variety of ways, where there is more expectation than fulfilment. It is a state of things which has turned people into refugees in their own homes and within themselves.[3] Self-confidence and self-reliance is superseded by anxiety and a sense of insecurity. The agonized yearnings of the human soul go unmet indefinitely. In short a gross dehumanization of persons has taken place. Man has dehumanized man. He has certainly replenished the earth to a great extent, but he has used his brothers as instruments and has prevented them from using the surplus wealth they have created. "If capitalism" said Professor Birch "was the engine that lifted man to new levels of economic and technological progress, it was equally the burial ground of his moral integrity."[4] With this background in mind it will not be difficult to understand the full extent of poverty in the world today.

Who are the Poor?

To be poor is to have not, to experience lack and deficiency. In Jesus' words the poor are the "little ones" (Matt. 11:25), the insignificant people of no consequence. They are powerless, voiceless and at the mercy of the powerful. The powerful are the oppressors and the powerless poor are the oppressed. The methods of keeping the poor perpetually in their place are

---

[2] E. Cardenal, *The Gospel in Solentiname* (Orbis, New York, 1976), 133.
[3] C. Banana, "The Biblical Basis for Liberation Struggles", *International Review of Mission* (Geneva, LXVIII, No. 272, October 1979).
[4] D. M. Paton, *Breaking Barriers: Nairobi 1975* (SPCK, London, 1975), 22.

oppressive social, political and economic structures. Oppression is always marked by the suffering of the oppressed.

The dynamics of being poor are such that the oppressed poor finally accept the inhumanity and humiliation of their situation; they accept the status quo as the normal course of life. Thus, to be poor becomes both a state of things and an attitude to life, an outlook, even a worldview. The vicious circle is completed when the oppressor, in turn, internalizes an attitude of permanent supremacy and paternalism towards the poor, and undertakes to speak, think and act for the poor. The poor are thus made dependent and made to feel dependent on the rich.

Superficial Explanations of Poverty

It is important at this point that we try to delineate the concept of poverty in order to differentiate it from other vague connotations. We want to keep clear from such notions as the "idealized poverty" attributed to the words of Jesus: "How happy are you who are poor" (Luke 6:20). Similarly the concept of "necessary poverty" has to be corrected. The meaning of the words of Jesus is grossly twisted, as if he would be condemning the poor to some kind of fatality: "You will have the poor with you always" (John 12:8). Poverty and discrimination in South Africa have been justified in similar terms by the leadership of the Dutch Reformed Church: "This happened not through ill-will towards the non-whites, nor with the approval of the official leadership of the Church, but must be seen as the result of *uncontrollable* circumstances and of general *human weakness*" [5] (my emphases).

Poverty cannot be explained either by resorting to race, culture and progress as if some people would be classified as poor and others would qualify to be rich merely by the circumstances of their birth. Duncan Clarke has reacted very strongly against what he called the "market mentality" of the white settlers in Zimbabwe. According to this mentality the causes of poverty "are predominantly internal to the psyche, make up, ways, behaviour, traditions and culture of the African". [6] Obviously the colonist does not need to excuse himself once this explanation is accepted. He, belonging to a superior race, is endowed with the necessary qualities to direct and structure the forces of the market, and every economic success will be due to his initiative, enterprising spirit and skills which the "native" lacks. At the same time he has to keep the "native" in his own place, thankful for being allowed to "par-

---

[5] Idem, *Church and Race in South Africa* (SCM, London, 1958), 99.
[6] D. Clarke, "Settlers' Ideology and African Underdevelopment in Post War Rhodesia", *The Rhodesian Journal of Economics* (VIII, No. 1, March 1974), 53.

ticipate" in the abundance created by the master. Of course, if he remains poor, that is due to his inferiority. He has many roads open to become as rich as the master, but he will have to imitate the master's abilities and achieve his high degree of education. But that is an impossible dream because the "natives" are so irresponsible and handicapped by their own culture.

This settler's mentality indicates that poverty is a human creation. When it is internalized by the poor it becomes one of the ingredients used to control the masses through a set of principles known as "the moral basis of backward societies".[7] These are some of the current rationalizations about poverty common among those who have not experienced it. The poor of the world know better. Let us see now what the experience of poverty implies, looking at it from the side of those who suffer it.

Poverty as a Consequence of Dependence

Poverty is not a necessity but a consequence of present structural arrangements. Avila, writing from South America, has said. "The riches of the developed countries should be explained in terms of the poverty of the underdeveloped."[8]

This description coincides with that which the World Council of Churches used in Nairobi in 1975: "Underdevelopment is essentially a state of dependency and domination."[9]

Another South American writer looks at it from the point of view of domination when this is internalized by the dominated population: "The system of external domination from one country to another cuts through the dependent country and interpenetrates it. To the extent that it does, the external structure is experienced as internal."[10]

Seen in this context poverty becomes part of the daily existence of people. It cannot be done away with if the system of dependence stays, because this system affects the roots of the economic and social structure. Escape from poverty is thus blocked. The only way out would be to break away from the "net" formed by the relationships of dependence.

Political independence in Africa has not been able to overcome the poverty of the people because poverty has been accepted and has been internalized together with the system that produced it. Due to migrant labour arrangements introduced in most colonies "the population of the rural areas is

---

[7] E. C. Banfield, *The Moral Basis of A Backward Society* (Macmillan, New York, 1967), 83.
[8] R. Avila (197), 12.
[9] D. Johnson, *Uppsala to Nairobi* (SPCK, London, 1975), 143.
[10] Cardoso (1969), 24.
[11] G. Gutierrez, *A Theology of Liberation* (Orbis, New York, 1973), 84.

heavily weighted by women, children and males over 35 years of age"[12] living at the level of mere subsistence.[13] Consequently what little voice the poor possessed is taken away together with their capacity to think through the problems of their situation and to act in an attempt to better themselves, and to develop their God-endowed potential. We can say that the poor are those who can no longer hear, speak or act for themselves. It is possible that they are living, that they live at the periphery of life. What can be said with certainty is that they just exist. The poor are those who exist more than they live. The quality of their lives has been eroded by the dehumanizing forces of all kinds of oppression.

The sad thing, indeed shocking and frightening thing, about the world situation is that the poor form the majority of our population. This is a universal threat: a dispossessed majority flanking a privileged minority. It is as if the world was sitting on a powder keg. The explosion when it takes place (as it surely always does) is what is known as revolution.

Bishop Reeves was much aware of these realities when he wrote in 1955: "Much that is now happening is fertilizing the soil of African life in such a way that it will be all too easy for the seeds of conflict to grow and flourish in the coming days."[14]

He went on to compare the universal threat of the conflict between poverty and wealth with the conflict between East and West. An adequate redistribution of riches all over the world and a new set of economic structures to regulate them was "a better solution against war than piling up greater and greater stocks of atomic weapons".[15]

The pleasantly surprising thing about the poor is that no matter how serious their dehumanization is, there remains an indestructible element within their personality. There is an inner kernel, linked perhaps with the image of God in man, which is very difficult, if not impossible, to crack. This is the capacity to be human still. The recognition of this capacity is at the centre of the Good News. The poor need not remain poor, lying in the dust, being trampled under the feet of the oppressor. God calls the poor up and out from his sad plight. He has the capacity to stand on his own feet and say: "I will leave this place and go to my father" (Luke 15:18). Coupled with the capacity to be human in dehumanization and to be noble in indignity is the poor's inherent capacity to fight for their own liberation and to think for themselves.

---

[12] M. Yudelman, *Africans on The Land* (Harvard, Cambridge, 1964), 132.
[13] I. I. Potekhin, *African Problems* (Moscow, 1968), 59.
[14] Bishop Reeves, quoted in Paton, *Church and Race in South Africa* (SCM, London, 1958), 24.
[15] Ibid.

The last two decades of the history of Zimbabwe have been a clear confirmation of this capacity that the poor have, to overcome their own destruction and to triumph in every adversity. It seems incredible that more than five million Zimbabweans, who have lived in the rural areas during all these years, have suffered the consequences of the war so valiantly, without losing any of their fine qualities. In a book written in Zimbabwe during the war and banned in 1977 on account of the denunciations made against the security forces, many missed the clear signs of hope and courage present in every account as they concentrated their attention only on the negative aspects of the conflict (*Civil War in Rhodesia:* 1976).

The same capacity to overcome their difficulties and to fight for their liberation can be found today in Palestine, Western Sahara, Namibia, Azania and Central America.

Poverty and Plenitude

There is very little doubt that our description of poverty will cause some discomfort, or be dismissed as an economic explanation, irrelevant as far as the spiritual meaning of the text of *Luke* 4 is concerned. Certainly one cannot ignore the spiritual meaning attributed to this text, but at the same time, we continue to think that Jesus was talking about the material relief of poverty. Most comments contain essentially something like this: The poor about whom Jesus spoke are those who come to him spiritually disposed and free from material wants. The reason why these authors wish to keep clear from temporal connotations is to preserve Jesus from becoming a political leader, and nothing else.

Gutierrez reacts very strongly against such spiritualization of the Gospel simply because the only way to the spiritual is God's material creation, [16] the temporal, secular reality. By refusing to enter into the spiritual realm through the only available gate—historical, temporal encounter—one risks remaining outside forever in an imaginary spirituality. Jesus is the gate (John 10:7). His presence in this world, the historical Jesus, has to be accepted first in its historical dimension in order to discover in him the plenitude promised to the poor: "The hungry he has filled with good things" (Luke 1:53).

The need of facing this issue in dualistic terms is typically western: What is not totally spiritual must be totally material. This is not a problem for most of the peoples of Asia and Africa who possess a different concept of man, as John Mbiti has indicated. [17]

---

[16] Gutierrez, *op. cit.*, 166.
[17] J. S. Mbiti, *New Testament Eschatology in An African Background* (OUP, London, 1971), 132.

If western theologians are unable to see that the spiritual message of the Gospel is contained in the historical temporal realities by which Jesus was surrounded, that is their problem, not ours. The poor of the world know very well what Jesus is saying. That is why they find in him the plenitude they are looking for. They will never accept any longer the disincarnate "spirituality" of western Christianity, "scornfully superior to all earthly realities". [18]

Dr. Allan Boesak said what Jesus brings to the poor is "a fulfilment through liberating historical events which in turn are new promises marking new roads towards total fulfilment". [19]

Christ does not spiritualize human realities. He gives them meaning and fulfilment today. And this brings us to the next point in our discussion.

What is Good News?

Good News then is the fulfilment of legitimate human expectations and the realization of dreams. It is that which releases and liberates the poor and enables him to define, analyse and come to grips with his situation. It is the arm that rescues humanity out of the great moral avalanche set in motion by evil and oppressive structures.

Good News and Bad News

Reference to good news presupposes the presence of bad news or a state of hopelessness. The background against which any news can be received as good news is important for our definition of Good News. We have to imagine a situation where life has been mutilated in a variety of ways, a state of affairs where there is more expectation than fulfilment. Self-confidence and self-reliance are replaced by anxiety and a sense of insecurity. The agonizing yearnings of the human soul go unmet indefinitely. The social, economic and political inequalities caused by the selfishness of the few leave scars that can only be redressed by a tornado or force greater than the forces of negation and deprivation. In short, it is a situation where a gross dehumanization of person has taken place.

Where the Good News has been proclaimed, restoration of the dignity and personality of man must be clearly evident; restoration to wholeness, to humanness. This is healing in the true sense of the word. It signals the banishment of anxiety and insecurity. In a nutshell, Good News is that which humanizes the whole of life all of the time.

Good News as Liberation

The poverty and marginalization of millions cannot be considered as a mere sociological fact. It must be seen in historical terms, as a result of

---

[18] Gutierrez, *op. cit.*, 166.
[19] A. Boesak, *Farewell to Innocence* (Raven, Johannesburg, 1978), 23.

human intervention, therefore as the embodiment of human decadence. Like the traveller of the parable "left half dead" (Luke 29:37) by the roadside, mankind is seen today left badly hit by its own socio-economic and cultural system. Drastic measures are to be taken because it is a matter of life and death. In the same way as Jesus was involved with the poor of his time, many men today try to liberate themselves. Boff has suggested this can only be done by complete political participation following scientific analysis of reality. [20] Only then will the Christian understand the full meaning of poverty, the meaning of the Good News and the meaning of liberation. He will be taking part in the history of man, the locus for any possible encounter between God and man.

The Historical Context

When Jesus was speaking of the kingdom he was using a concept familiar to his hearers. Israel had reached her historical climax as a nation during the era of the monarchy. The national decline had catapulted them into a succession of imperialist bondages: the Assyrian, the Babylonian, the Persian, the Seleucid, and now the Romans were about to quell Jewish nationhood. Jesus taught about the kingdom of God in an imperialist context. That is why he said: "The kingdom of God has been subjected to violence and violent men are seizing it" (Matt. 11:12).

The same forces that operated in Palestine during the times of Jesus are present among us today.

The Forces of Oppression: Imperialism and Capitalism

Imperialism is as old as the emergence of organized society. And Roman imperialism, as Jesus knew it, was not going to be the last. Imperialism is built on power, power to impose and subjugate, power to oppress. This power is vested in an elaborate machinery consisting of the army, the police, the government, the prison service. Nationalism is nipped in the bud and a public example is made of dissidents.

National aspirations were suppressed during the Roman empire as they are suppressed by imperialist regimes today. The imperialist state does not serve the nation but the interests of the small minority which controls the means of production and which subjugates the nation to its brand of economic system.

The kind of poverty engendered by economic, authoritarian imperialism is manifold. It is much more than lack of material possessions. It is full-scale dehumanization; it is outright exploitation and consummate degradation.

---

[20] L. Boff, *Liberating Grace* (Orbis, New York, 1979), 79.

The poor, who in this case are the workers, receive an inequitable proportion of the profits from organized production. They lack the power to redress the situation. The majority poor must live by the decisions of the minority capital holders. From the point of view of the imperialist, good management actually means ingenuity in exploiting the poor more subtly and more effectively.

Racism

A phenomenon integral to both imperialism and capitalism is the myth of master races created, as it were, by some divinity to rule over other races. Curiously enough this divinity is very often the God of the Christians. This is the phenomenon of racism by which one's racial stock, the colour of one's skin and eyes, and one's mother tongue determines one's social status, political rights and economic worth. Needless to say this has generated formidable tension between the master races and the oppressed peoples, tensions that have to be defused in one way or another or disaster would be imminent.

This tension and the dangers inherent in it have become an international issue these days. In the General Assembly of the WCC in Nairobi it was stated: "Racism can be seen today in every part of the world. No nation is totally free of it. Its victims cross the path of most of us daily. Yet it is obvious that some of our countries are more visibly plagued than others, e.g. where racism is legally enforced."[21]

It was in the same conference in Nairobi that racism was called "a litany of shame of the whole human family",[22] and it was described as a plague which "destroys the human dignity of both the racist and the victim".[23]

Racism is so closely connected with the structures of exploitation that it breeds all kinds of injustices and violations of human rights.

Elitism

The oppressor, in a desperate bid to maintain the status quo, resorts to unrestrained guile and craft to frighten, demoralize, divide and confuse the oppressed. He will ensure the obliteration of all vestiges of self-confidence in the spirit of the oppressed poor, resulting in the latter's succumbing to a defeatism that shies away from any conflict, verbal or physical, with the oppressor. As the poor, nearly exploding with tension, seek to ventilate their frustration, the oppressor deflects the wrath from himself by sponsoring what Franz Fanon calls "horizontal violence"—studiously stage-managed violence between the oppressed themselves. He will foster ugly divisions and

---

[21] In Paton, *Breaking Barriers*, 61.
[22] Ibid, 61.
[23] Ibid, 57.

splits against the people's unity of purpose. More and more the leaders of the poor will be tempted by the prospect of immediate personal gain at the expense of the people.

This is the problem of elitism. An elite is created on the basis of education and economic considerations, and used as a buffer between the oppressor and the oppressed. The legitimate aspirations of the poor remain unsatisfied. No change has taken place except in the oppressing family which has become an extended family.

Elitism has been substituted for racism. But the tragic effects on the poor are the same if not worse.

When the new elite is admitted into the oppressing family and gains power, the reformist character of the struggle tends to prevent the attainment of genuine national liberation, in the place of which there will be "an empty shell, a crude and fragile travesty of what might have been" as Fanon has pointed out. [24]

Nyerere has also denounced elitism as a new obstacle in the liberation process: "We have got rid of the foreign government, but we have not yet rid ourselves of the individualistic social attitudes which they represented and taught." [25]

Despite the red herrings that are ceaselessly drawn across the path of redress of evil structures, the question remains that of the necessity, indeed the imperative, of change. Change must take place.

The Response of the Poor

In the final analysis it is not so much a social struggle as a class struggle: poor against rich, oppressed against oppressor. But a struggle for what? For power. What they lack, however, and strive to acquire are the actual instruments of power, the ability to influence and control the structures and institutions of power. Each historical situation will determine the choice of the method the poor will use to achieve their ultimate goal of changing the system and building socialism. It is for this reason that the working class requires its own political movement as Woddis has suggested. [26]

But the poor do not always muster a positive response to oppression. Sometimes their response is marked by apathy, acquiescence and a perverted enjoyment of suffering. They grow into what Felipe E. Maglaya calls "a

---

[24] F. Fanon, *The Damned* (Paris, 1963), 21.
[25] J. K. Nyerere, *Freedom and Development: Uhurn na Maendeles* (Government Printers, Dar es Salaam, 1968), 341.
[26] Woddis, *op. cit.*, 21.

culture of silence".[27] Sociologists believe that the passive attitude which affects most societies in the Third World reflects a specific way of relating to
the environment at a specific point in time. The relationship of man with his
environment is essentially dialectical. At a first stage, man sees himself as
part of the environment and therefore unable to extricate himself from it. He
is dominated by insecurity and fear. This stage can last until new
developments in the environment force man to take the necessary steps to
cope with them. It is then that a more dynamic attitude appears in social
groups. Changes occur rapidly and they are accepted easily: new methods are
introduced to till the earth, fashions in dress appear, new styles in buildings,
new trends in education. Because the relationship between these two
moments is dialectical, they may occur simultaneously and create tensions. A
dormant population like the one described by Maglaya is not completely dormant. The seeds of revolution are to be awakened. It may be necessary to
take advantage of external events which will help ignite the fire.

It is very easy to understand that a certain population can be kept in a
period of dormancy by controlling key elements in the environment. When
an economic situation has the character of permanency and is seen as wanted
by God, who ordains everything, even our misery and deprivation, for our
own eternal salvation, poverty is then seen as something natural and all one
can do is to endure it patiently.

The connection between passive social attitudes and religion is not inciden-
tal. When people are forced to live for a long time under conditions of mere
subsistence, human groups usually have to resort to religious beliefs to make
their daily existence more bearable. As Mol has said, the precariousness of
human identity has led man repeatedly to wrap it in "don't touch" senti-
ment.[28]

People living in these situations are to be put through a process of
liberating their consciousness to enable them to identify and interpret their
situation and ultimately to rise above their problems: "Poverty by itself does
not produce militancy or revolutionary understanding."[29]

The Response of the Church

The same religious force which can be used to stabilize human activity and
render entire human groups into dormant communities has the capability of
stimulating them into action, giving a new meaning.

---

[27] F. E. Maglaya, *Organizing People for Power* (Asian Committee for People's
Organization, Tokyo, 1978), 4.
[28] H. Mol, *Identity and The Sacred* (Blackwell, Oxford, 1976), 54.
[29] Woddis, *op. cit.*, 55.

The imperialistic forces of the Roman Empire, served by the religious leaders of Israel, had turned the compatriots of Jesus into a very subversive population. Different revolutionary movements were active in open confrontation with the Roman Empire. The attitude of Jesus as a religious leader at this moment is very important to the Church today. But the historical link between imperialism and the evangelical mission of the Church continues to be a thorn in the Church's flesh. In some cases it was the Church that was brought to mission fronts on the back of imperialism. In others it was the reverse, imperialism riding comfortably on the back of the Church. On the mission field the Church had a chequered career, sometimes as champion of the poor (Arthur Shirley Cripps and John White of Mashonaland in Zimbabwe) or as unblushing collaborators with the forces of oppression. At times the Church has wished for a twilight zone existence when she was neither this nor that—not champion of the poor for fear of falling out of grace with the powers of State, and not collaborating with the state in order to retain her prophetic credibility with the faithful as well as her critics.

When the history of the Church is examined it appears that western civilization and Christianity have blended in such a way that "civil power and ecclesiastical authority were closely linked".[30] It is considered that the Edict of Milan in A.D. 313 was the beginning of this period of connivance. Recent studies on the sociology of religion have shown how this marriage of convenience was contracted. The consortium between religion and society is effected when groups of people living together and facing a common situation construct their universe of meaning. Religion has then a sociological function as Berger has explained. Continuity between society and nature is established through religion and it is a well-known fact that prevailing inequalities of power and privilege are explained and justified in that way.[31]

This ambiguity between a religion of legitimation and the religion of liberation represented by the Good News announced to the poor explains the chequered career observed among the religious leaders of our time and their followers.

On one side we have seen the Christian churches of Zimbabwe closely united in condemning "the assaults upon innocent people by members of the investigating authorities" during our recent war (*An appeal to conscience by Christian leaders:* 1974). On the other we find Christians belonging to these churches perpetrating those atrocities as members of the Special Branch, soldiers of the regular army, or condoning them as Members of Parliament

---

[30] A. Fierro, *The Militant Gospel* (SCM, London, 1977), 48.
[31] P. L. Berger and T. Luckmann, *The Social Construction of Reality* (Penguin, New York, 1976), 67.

or Ministers of the Government. In many of these cases the whole Christian community has accepted the responsibility of those crimes by its silence.

Today it is not enough for our leaders to condemn a few isolated incidents. This attitude can be compared with the few charities of the past, while doing nothing to change the situation that produced the misery of the poor.

What is wanted today is an outright clear denunciation of capitalistic exploitation and dynamic action to overthrow it. It seems that institutionalized religion is not capable of effecting this. Sipo Mzimela has expressed this forcibly: "Why does the western Church confine itself to platitudes today? When the oppressed are fighting to throw off their yoke and their struggle is belittled and scorned, and all manner of insults are hurled at them in the western media, does the western Church speak up for people who cannot speak for themselves?"

The sad thing is that the concern of the western Church centres around its own economic interests. There is concern about the safety of pension funds. There is no concern for the black lives it costs to guarantee the safety of pension funds. [32]

But while the Christian faith strongly resists being cast in the either/or mould, its Leader and Lord decreed and demonstrated a clear bias in favour of the poor. About the poor Jesus did not mince his words. God is on the side of the poor. Jesus was one of them, worked with them, and struggled for their liberation, giving his life for them: "the greatest love a person can have for his friends is to give his life for them" (John 15:13).

The issue of the Church involvement or participation in action for social change is at the centre of the vertical/horizontal dichotomy or the evangelical/ecumenical debate. We cannot go into detail in this regard here.

All we can say in passing is that the either/or model is not an appropriate key with which to unlock the problem of the Church and social change. God is dynamic, not static. No single dimension, therefore, is capable of capturing the total spectrum of his activity. An eclectic approach would be more in line with the variety and richness of God's ways and resources.

Besides, enlisting as a collaborator in oppression or attempting clumsily to take a stance of neutrality, the Church has suffered setbacks in its mission to the poor owing to hindrances deriving from its image and life-style. Church government is a case in point. This can be democratic or autocratic. It can be liberating and conducive to development or repressive, oppressive and blocking to development.

---

[32] S. E. Mzimela, *The Western Church and The Liberation of Southern Africa* (South Africa Freedom Committee, New York, 1978), 14.

Theological imperialism is another sore thumb. While the Gospel breaks across the frontiers and either fulfils or judges cultures, each people must be able to formulate an indigenous response to God's invitation through the Gospel. This indigenous response can be reflected in theological formulations of the Christian witness and in celebrations of the liturgy.

Even small things such as the architecture of Church buildings, liturgical instruments and ecclesiastical vestments are important in determining the image and lifestyle of the Church.

The Power to Effect Change

Before the power to effect change is theirs, a resurrection of the self must take place within the personhood of the poor. By transcending their neurotic self-hatred they can re-affirm themselves and re-assert their crestfallen self-esteem. As a liberation redemptive movement gets off to its start, the goals ahead of it have to be clear and focus maintained on these from moment to moment. What such a movement would need to take cognisance of is the phenomenal responsibility that devolves upon it. This liberation model can serve to maintain the focus on goals, but it has the danger of producing wrong, ideological connotations. It tends to give a wrong picture of what liberation is all about. The oppressor and the oppressed are the only elements taken into consideration. What really matters, the relationship of exploitation, is not sufficiently stressed.

Several pitfalls lurk in such a simplistic view of the problem of oppression and its redress, the most serious, perhaps, being that liberation may be aimed at a simple reversal of the roles in the vicious relationship of oppressor and oppressed. As a goal of liberation, simple reversal of roles is self-defeating, counter-productive and unredemptive. Distasteful as it might be to victims of oppression, the oppressor has to be liberated along with the oppressed. As it is expressed in a very impressive document of the World Council of Churches during the Nairobi Conference, "when the exploited confess Christ, the rich should be enabled to hear in such confession their own freedom announced".[33]

Sources of Liberation

This, however, is where many, if not most, liberation movements fail with serious consequences not only for the one-time oppressor but just as seriously for the latter-day oppressor. The question may be posed at this point: Is it possible to achieve total liberation of the whole person of the whole of society without recourse to theological or religious resources? Can man transcend himself and his limitations by drawing upon his internal capacities alone,

---

[33] M. Paton, *Breaking Barriers*, 48.

without reference to a reality that is greater, outside of and beyond himself?

This is where the Gospel in general and the concept of Good News to the poor in particular, comes in quite usefully. Here is the reality that is outside of and beyond man to which he can refer in seeking direction for his liberation programme. Jesus, the man who could love through anger, who loved all the way to suffering and through suffering to victory, addresses all liberation movements from the vantage point of an accomplished liberated liberator. Jesus was internally liberated. That is why he could liberate others. And that is the crux of the matter: liberators of mankind must be integrated and liberated within their own personalities.

The Death of Christ as Liberation of the Poor

On the cross, Christ identified himself with the poor, the oppressed and the captives of all times, "Today you will be with me" (Luke 23:43), he said to one of the prisoners crucified with him.

He was so involved in the struggle that the Pharisees started to panic: "If we let him go on in this way everybody will believe in him and the Romans will come and destroy the Holy Place, and our nation" (John 11:48).

He was suspected, intimidated, falsely accused, prosecuted as are all those who are a menace to the established order. He was expelled from the synagogue (John 2:22), and there were several attempts to imprison him (Mark 11:18). Twice he risked stoning (John 8:59; 10:31). He was condemned as a freedom fighter: handed over (Mark 14:10, 42) and crucified for his political activities. He opposed the Pharisees who represented the religious support of the political system and that could not be tolerated. How many religious traditions were used to achieve political goals can be seen in the circumstances of the birth of Jesus. In order to facilitate the census and to condition everyone to move to important centres, towns of religious significance were chosen (Luke 2:1). Jesus died in the process of exposing those who enslaved the human person in the name of the law. "The sabbath was made for man, and not man for the sabbath" (Mark 2:27).

The death of Jesus does not need to be spiritualized in order to make it redemptive. It only needs to be given additional, external meanings by those who have not experienced personally "the agonies of the oppressed" (Banana, 1979). The poor, only the poor, can understand the full meaning of the death of Christ. He saves them by giving them the certainty of future fulfilment when they are engaged in their struggle against the oppressor. The forces of oppression were completely defeated as they collided against the cross of Christ. Liberation became possible when somebody much stronger than the powers of this world overcame death through the power of the resurrection. Recent theological studies have projected new light on the permanent relevancy of the death of Christ:

The universal meaning of the life and death of Christ is that he sustained the fundamental conflict of human existence to the end: He wanted to realize the absolute meaning of this world before God in spite of hate, incomprehension, betrayal and condemnation to death.[34]

Conclusion

Good News to the poor is an announcement, a proclamation in the present of God's victory through Jesus and through human agents over all forms of oppression. As a signal from out there, beyond man and his limitations and capabilities, it is a promise of the eschatological potential of man, a guarantee of the restoration of the ideal man, the man who was good and free at the beginning. Good News to the poor is a pronouncement of judgement on all oppressive structures, actions, as well as thoughts and intentions, regardless of who the perpetrator might be. It is a judge of the wretched blocks that separate man from God and man from man. It is a rebuke of everything that stunts the growth and hampers the development of man into the full stature of Jesus Christ. Good News to the poor is a celebration and enactment of the classic and normative liberation struggle in which Jesus defeated all human and spiritual forces of oppression.

---

[34] Boff, *Jesus Christ Liberator* (Orbis, New York, 1978), 119.

The Kingdom of God and Human Struggles
DANIEL VON ALLMEN *

When I think about "The Kingdom of God and Human Struggles", my thoughts go far back to those early days in which I learned Latin. One of the first sentences that we had to learn was a Latin tag "Vita perpetuum proelium est": Life is a perpetual battle. Others of you will think of Darwin who in his teaching about evolution in nature saw the struggle for life as its highest principle, as the motor of evolution as a whole. Not so different from these slogans is the proverb of African wisdom which can be found on many Mammy trucks, those lorries that are used in Ghana as popular taxis: "life is war".

At once I realize that this struggle has many layers.

First is the struggle for life itself. We who come from the northern hemisphere and from the middle class probably forget all too often that contest of our fellow human beings who are struggling not for an improvement in their conditions of life or for any social progress, but purely and simply for life itself. They are deprived of their basic rights—of their right to sufficient and appropriate nourishment, of their right to clothing and housing, but also often of their right to love, to warmth and to a human environment in which they can grow and develop as persons.

It is, however, also a fact of experience that a person finds himself struggling against others. Here I do not mean to ask so much why this is so but rather simply to state the fact that it is so. This I can do through the words of the Swiss sociologist Jean Ziegler: "Despite his utopian ideas, man has not, in a history which stretches over a million and more years, succeeded in being reconciled with himself, and with his neighbour. In other words, nowhere on this planet, and at no time in history has any human group yet succeeded in building a truly peaceful society. Conflict seems to be a permanent truth—perhaps the deepest of them—about human life" (*Retournez les fusils! Manuel de sociologie d'opposition*, Paris 1980, page 52, quoted from "Domaine public" No. 541 of 17.4.1980). So that conflicts between human groups are not necessarily to be seen immediately in negative terms. It is probably one of the mistakes of traditional Christianity that we have put much energy into trying to avoid conflicts in the church. It would have been wiser

---

* The Rev. Daniel von Allmen is President of the Basel Mission, Switzerland.

to learn how, in the spirit of the Gospel, we could face up to conflicts and cope with them. Yet we must also not deny that among human beings there are enmities, hatreds, envies, individual and collective egoisms and all too many other forces which lead people again and again into struggles against one another.

We need also to talk about a struggle which reaches still further, which I shall call the struggle against the powers. Today we would probably speak about the structures, yet as I do so I must immediately add that human life without structures would quite simply be impossible. There are, then, two sides to this struggle: the struggle against structures of oppression, and also the struggle for better and more just structures.

If we believe in the Lordship of God, and if we hope for the coming of his kingdom, what are we to think of the struggles and conflicts in our world?

Our situation in the struggles of humanity

It strikes me as impossible to say anything generally valid about our topic if we refuse to consider where we personally stand in these struggles of humanity. I must therefore begin by a description of my situation, but you, too, will not be able to avoid describing your own situations. In this we must take account of two aspects: on the one hand, the aspect of personal commitment, but on the other, the aspect of our position in a given society. We cannot ignore this second aspect, since whether we wish it or not our participation in our own society is a fact of life that we cannot ignore. It gives us a quite particular solidarity which has both positive and negative sides to it. Even if we forget this solidarity with our own society, others will soon remind us of it.

To take the second aspect first, I must recognize that I am a man from the West or from the North. The preparatory documents of our section have already clearly shown us the perplexity and indeed the division in which we find ourselves. A large majority of our population feels threatened, dismayed by today's situation. We in the West have put much effort into the welfare and the prosperity of our people, out of which values and structures have arisen which we would be unhappy to give up. Yet quite suddenly all these values are called in question, and these structures which are so advantageous for us are shown to be threatening to others. Are we to admit that those structures which ensure a good standard of living for us are seen by others to be structures of exploitation?

Can we struggle to the understanding that our emphasis on the nuclear family and our development of provisions for the care of individual and old people has had to be paid for by the increasing isolation of the unmarried and the old as well as by the destruction of any sense of the extended family, which still existed in many cases among us thirty or forty years ago? More and more people are now pointing to the fact that the technological progress that we rate so highly has brought with it a loss of human values and that the very technology which was expected to liberate humanity is gradually oppressing and enslaving us. Our problem is now, how to be human? How to come back to a true humanity? "Come back": in this expression we have to see an exact translation of the Hebrew word for "repentance" or "conversion"!

Many people, older ones as well as younger, have come to the view that we don't need only an individual repentance, but that a deep transformation is now necessary in our society. They have often come to this commitment through their contacts with other cultures or through participating in the human struggles of the so-called third world. They are struggling for a new style of life, for new possibilities of being human even in our highly technological society. But how is their witness and their struggle seen by others? For the most part, they are labelled as bothersome leftists and pushed to the margin. All too often, out of their hasty rejection of our society, they even allow themselves to be pushed out to the margins. On the one side, fear rules when our values are questioned. On the other, there is a strange balance between a desperate search for new paths and resignation before a task which is too difficult for our strength.

This leads me to the other aspect of my situation. My job is in the leadership of one of the largest missionary societies in Switzerland. Where does my society stand in the struggles of humanity? Our traditional past has been geared to overseas countries, and there are plenty of people both in the churches at large and in our own immediate committees who ask for a strict division of labour: our task is not at home but overseas. Yet to this I would like to put the question: "Why do we send people overseas? Who offers today for service in the third world?" Precisely those people who have critical questions about our own society. Do they leave because they no longer feel at ease among us or because they have given up? What will be their aims when they are overseas? Will they be trying to bring about there the utopias that have not proved successful at home? In the group with which I prepared this talk, someone put it vividly: "When something is wrong in my life I go and knock at my neighbour's door and offer him my help." Here I am not pleading for any moratorium, for the call for a moratorium should not come from our side. Yet I do see that a substantial part of our task in the missionary societies consists in awakening people in the so-called West to the awareness that we too need help and that it is precisely our brothers and sisters from other cultures who are the most appropriate people to bring us that help. The presupposition for this would of course be that we avoid the danger of taking them captive in our structures when they come to help us. We must find ways of making it possible for them to be themselves also within our society.

Thus as I approach our topic I cannot avoid wondering where I stand in the struggles of humanity. You will perhaps also be asking what have human struggles to do with the kingdom of God? Does our church or missionary work only deal with the kingdom of God in that sense in which we spoke until a few decades ago of missionary work as "the work of the kingdom"? This is the question to which I now turn.

Your kingdom come or God's struggle for Lordship

In the preparatory documents much has been written about the biblical theology of the kingdom of God. I shall thus restrict my biblical, theological remarks to two trains of thoughts, namely the perspective of the kingdom of God, or rather of the sovereignty of God, and the perspective of messianic expectation in the Old Testament and the fulfilling in the New Testament.

Now it is of course impossible to talk of the Lordship of God in any absolute sense. If there is sovereignty it is sovereignty over something. And this something is closely linked with God by the fact that God has claimed sovereignty over it. In the Old Testament this something is in the first place the people of Israel. Historically we can only begin to grasp this as the people begin to settle in Palestine, the land of promise. Here we see a first important aspect of God's struggle for Lordship. God is not simply the God who brought Israel from Egypt into the Promised Land. He is not simply a tribal god. By his achievement in bringing Israel through to the land of Canaan with his strong right arm he has shown that he is LORD; Israel misunderstood the sovereignty of this God whenever it supposed that alongside God there are other Lords—as we must no doubt translate the name of the canaanite "baals". Prophets like Hosea raised their voice in the name of God: "Plead with your mother, my children, though she is no longer a wife to me and I am no longer her husband. Plead with her to stop her adultery and prostitution" (Hos. 2:2). God is the Lord, the one whose wife, the people of Israel, has become unfaithful.

Israel supposed that God was only the god of nomadic people and that now they were in Canaan they must also worship those other gods who make agricultural land fruitful. Thus God complains through the mouth of Hosea: "She would never acknowledge that I am the one who gave her the corn, the wine, the olive oil, and all the silver and gold that she used in the worship of Baal" (Hos. 2:8).

Israel gradually discovers that their God is not one god among others, but the LORD who is creator. Yet if God is the Lord of creation, he has the right to expect that humanity shall treat his creation properly. For their tendency—our tendency—is to exploit creation; whoever has the greater power becomes rich and oppresses the weak. So God speaks through the mouth of Amos: "Listen to this, you that trample on the needy and try to destroy the poor of the country. You say to yourselves 'we can hardly wait for the holy days to be over so that we can sell our corn. When will the Sabbaths end so that we can start selling again? Then we can overcharge, use false measures, and tamper with the scales to cheat our customers. We can sell worthless wheat at a high price. We'll find a poor man who can't pay his debts, not even the price of a pair of sandals, and we will buy him as a slave.' The Lord, the God of Israel, has sworn: 'I will never forget their evil deeds. The earth will quake and everyone in the land will be in distress. The whole country will be shaken; it will rise and fall like the river Nile'" (Amos 8:4-8).

The Lordship of God is thus closely bound up with justice. God the Lord is also the judge, i.e. the person who creates justice. He leads his people towards justice, and when they do not let themselves be led, they will be judged. Yet in this sense God is judge, not only as Lord of Israel but as LORD of the world. We hear the demand of Psalm 96: "Say to all the nations 'the Lord is King! The earth is set firmly in place and cannot be moved: He will judge the peoples with justice. Be glad, earth and sky! Roar, sea, and every creature in you; be glad, fields, and everything in you! The trees in the woods will shout for joy when the LORD comes to rule the earth. He will rule the peoples of the world with justice and fairness" (verses 10-13).

In what sense is God LORD? How are we to understand the justice which he demands of us? At the end of the day we can see it, in all its depth, in Jesus' proclamation of the kingdom of God: "Only if you are more faithful than the teachers of the Law and the Pharisees in doing what God requires ("what God requires" = literally: "justice") will you be able to enter the kingdom of Heaven" (Matt. 5-20). Justice is neither a religiosity nor the following of commandments. Justice is only truly fulfilled in love, for love has to do with the human being as a whole and with all human beings: "You have heard that it was said, 'love your friends and hate your enemies' but now I tell you: Love your enemies and pray for those who persecute you"—and then comes the decisive saying in which we discover in what ways God the Lord is sovereign—"so that you may become the sons of your Father in Heaven. For he makes his sun to shine on bad and good people alike and lets the rain fall alike on those who do good and those who do evil" (Matt. 5:43-45).

We recognize God the Lord as the Father who embraces all humanity in his love and his care. Yet this means that we cannot separate the Lordship of

God from his fatherhood, and that we can only see humanity as a single brotherhood.

From this starting point we could and should discover afresh all the dimensions of the kingdom of God. Here I should like to emphasize one single aspect. In the parables of Jesus a very large role is played by creation, the natural world. It cannot be merely by chance that in Jesus' preaching nature is taken as an image of the kingdom of God. We have to ask what this means for us. For he is talking about that creation which in the poem of *Genesis* I is seen as the good creation. Jesus is talking about this good creation rather than about the chaos which God overcame, yet which is always threatening the creative order.

God is Lord. God is "Our father in heaven". We can pray "your kingdom come", for his kingdom is coming, and he is spreading his fatherhood over the whole world. Yet he does not do this from a great distance ("our father *in Heaven*"), which leads me to the other aspect that I should like to emphasize, the dimension of messianic expectation.

In his relations to mankind, as in those with his own people, God never acts, according to the witness of the entire Bible, from a great distance. He appears personally to Abraham, or—as is in fact the same thing—in the form of his angel, his messenger (Gen. 18:1 16 etc.). The whole history of Israel is the history of God's care for his people through a series of mediators, whether the great prophet Moses, the line of judges or indeed the charismatic King Saul. It belongs to the faith and to the fixed expectation of Israel that God gives and will give to his people those who speak, rule and judge in his name. This faith is concentrated in the messianic faith and in the messianic expectation. David is the anointed of Jahweh. Just as Moses was God's agent in liberating the people from Egypt, from the house of slavery, so David is the one who liberates the united tribes of Israel, after the settlement in Palestine, from the pressure of the surrounding peoples and who establishes them as one people in one kingdom. Yet this golden age did not last long. All too soon the people of God fell once more under the pressure of the Egyptians or of the Assyrian-Babylonians. Yet believers will never give up the hope that the cause of God and of his people will win through and that God will give them another liberator. Is there a contradiction between this messianic hope and the hope for the kingdom of God? I believe not. This is precisely the witness of the history of kingship in Israel. The king rules in the name of God and not out of his own power or right. As soon as he forgets this he loses those powers and God's free people fall back into slavery. God is not limited by the institution of the monarchy, and when it is appropriate he can use the king of the Persians as his anointed, can hail him as his Messiah and can use him to liberate his people (Isa. 45:1ff). I believe it to be extreme-

ly important that in all these texts and situations we should see the relation
between God's intervention in human history by means of his messenger, his
Messiah, and the liberation of the people from slavery. The passage I have
just referred to speaks, however, less about the liberation of Israel than
about the freedom of God. God does not let himself be tied to institutions,
not even to those which he brought into being for the liberation of his people.
Human structures and institutions, including those of God's people, have no
permanent or final value.

At their best they are provisional. What is permanent and final is the
sovereignty of God.

God's nearness in his relationship to humanity is, however, to be experienced above all in the sending of his Son. In the time of Jesus, messianic
expectation had become a rather exclusive and nationalist political affair.
Jesus does not let himself be trapped by this dimension, yet still sees liberation as central to his task. In the interpretation of his mission a text such as
Isaiah 61:1-2 plays a role of the highest importance: "The sovereign Lord has
filled me with his spirit. He has chosen me and sent me to bring good news to
the poor, to heal the broken-hearted, to announce release to captives and
freedom to those in prison. He has sent me to proclaim that the time has
come when the Lord will save his people and comfort all who mourn." You
know the much-quoted story in *Luke* 4 in which Jesus uses this passage about
himself. In Matthew's Gospel the same passage plays a comparable role in
Jesus' response to the question from the disciples of John the Baptist: "Are
you he who should come, or should we expect someone else?" (Matt. 11:1-6).
I know that in certain circles people would prefer not to notice that liberation
is a favourite biblical concept, since all of a sudden it has taken on a large
and, in the eyes of many people, far too political a meaning. I doubt that in
Paul's writings the concept of liberation plays any smaller part than the concept of justification. This could be proved by statistics, yet of course it is far
more a matter of the intrinsic weight of what is said. Here I should simply
like to point to one passage, namely *Galatians* 4:1-7: "In the same way, we
too were slaves of the ruling spirits of the universe before we reached spiritual
maturity. But when the right time finally came, God sent his only Son. He
came as the Son of a human mother and lived under the Jewish law in order
to redeem those who were under the law, so that we might become the sons of
God." And, later on, "so then you are no longer a slave but a son" (see also
Rom. 8:3-4, 15).

This is a way of suffering. To name but one example in the whole New
Testament literature: this is precisely the meaning of the so-called messianic
secret in Mark's Gospel. Jesus is indeed King and Messiah, but this must not
be spoken abroad before it is clear *how*. He is a messiah by being the suffer-

ing servant. It is on a donkey that the prince of peace makes his entry into Jerusalem. It is on a cross that he is enthroned as king (Mark 15: 26). I believe it would have been appropriate to give these remarks the title that Professor Jan Milic Lochman took for his lecture at our mission anniversary in Basel (20-22.6.1980): "Hope well founded; God's suffering in human struggles." By this title he was trying to give expression to a crucial insight of Asian and particularly of Korean theology. Here we touch the centre of our faith, and here both aspects we mentioned became one: justice and liberation. On the cross, Jesus broke the power of sin and guilt and made us the gift of God's justice (see II Cor. 5:21). Since the incarnation, the struggles of humankind in this world can no longer be a matter of indifference for us. For in Jesus Christ God has made common cause with humanity, and his suffering struggle for the liberation of humanity will last till the end of the world. This is what Blaise Pascal saw long ago: "Jésus est en agonie jusqu'à la fin du monde." It will be our task to recognize where God is at work in the struggles of our fellow human being.

Human struggles in the light of the kingdom of God

Again and again it is emphasized that our hope for the coming of God's kingdom has an influence on the way in which we judge human realities. In face of the coming of the kingdom all the realities of human history become relative, indeed downgraded. Even at its best, human struggles in this world have no more than penultimate status. Yet if it is true, must we not necessarily draw the conclusion that we all, Christians and non-Christians alike, have been made equal? For even the historical reality of the Church at its highest and best has no more than penultimate status. We are all in the same boat. Yet are we convinced about this? This is of course a huge question.

May I suggest for discussion the thesis: In their struggles all human beings are basically in a common solidarity. In reflecting on the concept of solidarity I am reminded of an image from the world of climbers. If you are making a dangerous climb in the Alps or the Andes or the Himalaya, you must be roped together. All human beings in the community of the rope depend on each other.

The rope ties them, and when one falls, only two things can happen: the one who falls may be held by the others, or else the whole community will fall into the chasm. Theoretically, there would be a third possibility, namely that the ones who didn't fall cut off the rope. But in reality, it is an illusion to believe that one part of humankind could reach safely the goal of prosperity and happiness at the cost of the other part, "cutting off" the rope of solidarity. In this sense, all human beings stand in solidarity. Even the most bitter conflicts cannot do away with this solidarity. In one way or another we all depend on each other in the human family. The only question is whether we intend to kill each other by pulling on the rope in opposite directions, or whether we will find more constructive means of expressing this given solidarity. Christian faith does not dissolve this solidarity but confirms it. For it is not the case that we Christians are already at that peak where no rope is now needed. In faith we look to that peak, see in it a reason and goal for our solidarity, and can help to lead our whole company towards that goal. That is my thesis. Perhaps it sounds good. Yet you know that for many Christians, especially in the so-called western churches, it is by no means acceptable. It presupposes an awareness toward which we still have to struggle. Our natural tendency would rather be to look away from this basic solidarity and withdraw into the protected space of the church. We suppose that we can remain neutral, i.e. that we can be absolved from any responsibility for pulling on the rope. Yet this image of the rope shows us that any such neutrality is nothing but illusion. He who does not pull on the rope has given support to whoever is the strongest. He justifies the ironic aphorism of the French poet Jean de la Fontaine: "La raison du plus fort est toujours la meilleure." Yet in which direction are we to pull? This is the question at which we are to work in this section, and I hardly dare to answer it here. I shall simply try to give a few pointers, which make no claim to cover the ground completely.

We should start, I believe, from that saying of Jesus which is often mentioned in the context of mission and the recruitment of missionaries: the harvest is great, but the labourers are few (Matt. 9:37). The task of Christians in what we call mission is not that of sowing but of reaping. It is God who through his spirit sows the seed, and we cannot prescribe for him where he is to sow it. Our only task is to recognize where the seed is growing and where there is a harvest to be brought in.

How then are we to recognize the seed of the spirit in our human reality? For it is surely clear that we never come across those values which belong to the Lordship of God in a pure form. We are not yet in heaven. We still have to struggle for those values. While we are on pilgrimage, these values will always stand in the ambiguity of human reality. Yet the very fact that we struggle for them points to the goal. We must let ourselves be surprised by the way in which God's light encounters our struggles, purifies them and puts them to use for his purposes. We shall, during our work, be telling each other how this happens. We shall learn from one another to recognize God's work in human struggles. Here are simply one or two headings.

Today, no less than ten or twenty years ago, people throughout the world, are struggling for their *freedom*. I simply raise the question: Is it possible for a war of liberation to end in any other way than with the introduction of new structures of oppression? I am not trying by this question to seduce anyone into resignation or retreat. But we shall perhaps discover that it is simply not possible to liberate oneself. Liberation is a gift. Only those who have been freed can lead others to freedom, without this liberation bringing with it new dependencies and slaveries. We often conveniently draw a clear distinction between liberation from sin and liberation in a social or political sense. In his essay "Evangelism Today" (*Monthly Letter on Evangelism,* July/August 1979), Raymond Fung has convincingly shown that this distinction cannot be supported theologically, for "if the proclamation of the gospel is to reach the heart of the human being, we must take account of the fact, for our evangelism, that the human being is both subject as well as the object of sin". We are to see our fellow man not only as a sinner but also as the victim of sin. We cannot preach the liberation of human beings from the sins they commit unless we believe that the spirit of God is stronger than the power of sin. The power of sin has two consequences: on the one hand that men and women sin, and on the other that they are the victims of sin, i.e. that they are sinned against. The failure of our evangelism in the poorer classes is largely to be attributed to the fact that we have been challenging these people to accept the gospel as a liberating power over those sins which they commit while expecting them to accept as their fate the sins from which they suffer.

Hardly less important than the struggle for freedom is the human struggle for *justice.* Evil is to be found in the way in which our horizon is always horribly limited. All too often my struggle for justice is limited to the defence of my own rights. In social and political matters this tendency leads to the rights of the powerful being made into law which all, including the weaker and the oppressed, must accept as right. This is not so much justice as solidified injustice. Any genuine struggle for justice will begin at the point where such limits are called in question and where the rights of the one are seen also as valid for the other. We have sent missionaries into all the world because we believed that the gospel we have received is also good for humanity beyond all frontiers. Will we now—and I am speaking as a man from the West—passionately defend the frontiers when it is a question of a better sharing of the riches of creation throughout the world? Will we claim that the struggle for a more just international economic order has nothing to do with mission?

We could readily add other things to the list of points at which the struggle of humanity in this world has meaning for the kingdom of God. Yet we must gradually draw to a close, and I want to bring out one last point: the struggle of man and woman for the *truth.* Are we in this case, too, in the same boat with the rest of humanity? Many people will dispute that, for in comparison to all other faiths is our faith not the true faith? Must we Christians not lay claim to truth for ourselves and for our faith? This is said as a question but it comes very near to being an assertion. In the Bible Jesus says "I am the way, the truth and the life" (John 14:6). Yet this means that the truth is a living person who cannot be taken captive by words. This in turn means that I cannot say: my faith is truth or that I possess the truth. I can only say that the truth (i.e. Jesus Christ, my Lord) possesses me. My faith has of course to do with truth inasmuch as it brings me into relationship with the living truth—-Jesus Christ—and brings me life. But as soon as I try to express this truth with my words it is inextricably caught up in the weakness of all human activity, loses all absoluteness and can only be treated as human. Until the kingdom of God has fully arrived, until we see God face to face, our awareness of truth can be at best partial (cf. I Cor. 13:12).

Every pronouncement about our faith results not only from a struggle with the stubbornness of our inability to express the truth, but also from a struggle with God and with the truth which is always running way ahead of us. Seen in this way we are on the same footing with all those who sincerely struggle for truth. This struggle for truth takes place in dialogue. We need to have no fear of this word "dialogue" and of the reality hidden behind it, for we human beings can only reach out for truth in a process of dialogue. This is particularly the case when it is a matter of proclaiming the truth, for I must be able to test that *that* which *I* know and try to express as truth, can also be received and understood by my partner as truth. Here it seems to me to be crucial that precisely those speeches in the fourth gospel, in which Jesus most clearly announces "I am the truth", are built up in a scheme of dialogue. The "truth" which Jesus proclaims runs in the first place into total incomprehension among the Jews or even among the disciples. This in turn becomes the reason for Jesus to go into further explanations, further nuances, etc. For me this means that dialogue is a basic structure of Christian witness, and therefore quite naturally of all missionary witness, while we remain on this earthly pilgrimage.

The way of discipleship under the sign of the coming Lordship of God

It was not myself who chose the title of this address—the topic of this section. I noticed that this title has only two parts. First the kingdom of God, and second the human struggles. It does not have three parts: the kingdom of God, the church of Christians, and the human struggles. Yet I must here add a few thoughts about the task of Christians in the midst of human struggles.

I have already suggested that the history of God's relationship with humankind is to be seen in the light of mission. Yet this dimension of God's activity does not end with the sending of his Son. In the fourth Gospel, the risen Christ says to his disciples: "Peace be with you! As the Father has sent me, so I send you" (John 20:21).

We shall never be able to say that God works exclusively through those of us who call ourselves disciples of Christ, since God's sovereignty and kingdom can never be simply identified with the Church. Yet we have to take our mission seriously. That which God accomplished in Jesus Christ on the cross—it is indeed accomplished (cf. John 19:30) and does not need to be in any way completed—that must now be taken out into the whole wide world. This taking out belongs to God's struggle for Lordship.

You will not expect me to offer you a complete theology of mission in this short section. May I simply bring out two aspects which seem important:

First and foremost it is the spirit who liberates us from all fear in making us sons of God (cf. Rom. 8:15): "For the spirit does not make you slaves and cause you to be afraid; instead, the spirit makes you God's children." The power which now drives us is the power of love and not of fear. If only it were so! For how often does fear still gain the upper hand? If we look back over our mission reaction we should remind ourselves that in at least two ways fear can be reflected in our attitudes and in our activities: on the one hand as a brake—how much do we omit out of fear!—but on the other hand as a motor. What is the motor-force of our development aid? Love or cold calculation? Love or fear that our brothers and sisters in the third world might take their revenge when they come to power?

I mention the second aspect with trepidation for I have by no means finished thinking through what it implies. If we are called to take the love of God out into the world, then the basic characteristic of our commitment will not be pity but compassion. For in the word pity there is always a sense of condescension or at least of distance. One can feel pity without really being deeply and directly struck. Yet this is not how God acted in Jesus Christ. God did not help us from a distance—as it were from heaven. He came to us in his Son, who identified himself fully with us. God suffered with us and for us. If we are to be his disciples we can only choose to meet our fellow human beings on the path of fellow-suffering. I realize that what I am here saying raises great problems. If we were to take it seriously we should have to transform all our policies in church and mission, and I do not know if we would be ready—if I would be ready—to begin on that transformation. This is why I prefer to quote a passage from an article by a man who knows what fellow-suffering means, a theologian from South Africa—and this quotation should be my conclusion:

> By way of compassion it becomes possible to be generous in forgiveness, when we see hatred in the eyes of people, or hear bitterness flow from their mouths. Compassion tells us that when they distance themselves with a hateful glance or kill with a sharp tongue, we could have done the same. For a compassionate person nothing human is alien: no joy or sorrow, no way of living and no way of dying.

We need to re-establish the basic principle that nobody can help anyone without becoming involved, without entering with one's whole person into the painful situation, including the risk of becoming hurt, wounded or even destroyed in the process. This is the way that the Incarnation took, and what other more worthy example does the Church and its ministry have than He who took precisely that way? No God could save other than a suffering God—that is his example and supreme lesson. No suffering can be taken away without entering into it. No minister can lead mankind from sin and evil to life and freedom, other than he/she who has been crushed by his/her own sinfulness, but who has been given grace to rise from the burden in absolution, and who sees beyond death a vision of that which has no end (A.-I. Berglund, "New Patterns of Ministry", in *Ecunews*, Johannesburg, 29.9.1978).

The Church Witnesses to the Kingdom
JOHN V. TAYLOR*

Living the future now, or making the dream come true

The kingdom of God is "at hand", although it is "not yet". The kingdom does not lie within the span of world history; it belongs to another dimension. Yet it is so near at hand that it throws its light ahead of its arrival, and those who respond to its promise and invitation live in that light. Jesus called men to live the life of the kingdom in anticipation of its arrival. The sick did not have to wait for the consummation of the kingdom before God's victory over disease could be manifested in them. "If I by the finger of God drive out the demons, know for sure that the kingdom of God has already come upon you" (Luke 11:20). So neither should those who have responded to the announcement of that kingdom's arrival wait any longer before beginning to live its life. The Sermon on the Mount does not add to the regulations and precepts of the former Law nor set before us a stricter ethic, but it places us in the path of the approaching God himself and demands that we be like him so that our ordinary relationships reflect his nature. "Be compassionate as your Father is compassionate. Love your enemies and pray for your persecutors; only so can you be children of your heavenly father who makes his sun rise on good and bad alike. There must be no limit to your goodness, as your heavenly Father's goodness knows no bounds" (Luke 36; Matt. 5:44, 45, 48.)

We cannot eliminate the historical fact that Jesus saw himself as the one in whom the kingdom was already being realized. His task was not simply to announce its arrival but actually to inaugurate it. Most of our dreams of a better world are no more than airy longings, but Jesus made his dream solid by actually living it here and now. And he demanded that all who were moved to put their trust in him should do the same. The Church is called into being in order to live the life of the kingdom in anticipation of its arrival. The Church is meant to be shaped by its certainty about the future which God is giving. That certainty throws its light upon everything in the present. The future, in which everything will find fulfilment in accordance with the will and nature

---

*The Right Rev. John V. Taylor is Bishop of Winchester, Great Britain.

of God, is already pressing itself into the present world order to question and to change it. The kingdom arrives from beyond, yet it is this-worldly through and through. It is the Father's will and the Father's rule on earth as in heaven. Therefore what the Church offers mankind is an alternative lifeview and an alternative lifestyle. As Jürgen Moltmann said in *Theology of Hope*, "Mission means not merely propagation of faith and hope, but also historic transformation of life... Not to be conformed to this world does not mean merely to be transformed in oneself, but to transform in opposition and creative expectation the face of the world in the midst of which one believes, hopes and loves."

But the heirs of the kingdom act in this way upon the world they live in, not by calculation and policy, as though they were inspired by another of the world's ideologies, but simply out of the intensity of their awareness of the closeness of God, and their response to his nature. Their challenge to the world, like that of Jesus himself, must always be an amazed cry: "How can we act like this if God is what he is? For the honour of God this must be changed."

The kingdom reflects the God who is known to all men, yet known to Jesus alone

If the Church is to live the life of the kingdom which reflects the nature of God, it must expose itself to the reality of God himself, not to an image of its own making. Psalms and hymns which are the songs of the ghetto and the captivity are not to be despised for their tone of self-preservation, self-pity and longing for comfort, but we must not define God in these narrow ecclesial terms. In order to know the true pattern of the kingdom, the Church must accept the God to whom all men cry and, at the same time, seek for the God who is hidden from all except Jesus.

In order to explain the first point, let me give a rather long quotation from Martin Buber concerning the word "God".

It is the most heavily laden of all human words. None has become so soiled, so mutilated. Just for this reason I may not abandon it. Generations of men have laid the burden of their anxious lives upon this word and weighed it to the ground; it lies in the dust and bears their whole burden. The races of men with their religious actions have torn the word to pieces; they have killed for it and died for it, and it bears their fingermarks and their blood. Where might I find a word like it to describe the highest? If I took the purest, most sparkling concept from the inner treasure-chamber of the philosophers, I could only capture thereby an unbending product of thought. I could not capture the presence of Him whom the generations of men have honoured and degraded with their awesome living and dying. I do indeed mean Him whom the hell-tormented and heaven-storming generations of men mean.

Certainly they draw caricatures and write "God" underneath; they murder one another and say, "in God's name". But when all madness and delusion fall to dust, when they stand over against Him in the Loneliest darkness, and no longer say "He", but rather sigh "Thou", shout "Thou", all of them the one word, and when they then add "God", is it not the real God whom they all implore, the One Living God, the God of the children of men?

We need that magnificent quotation to remind us that when Jesus used the phrase "the kingdom of God" he was deliberately using second-hand words, words already weighted, soiled and twisted with many meanings. He took up the hungers and needs and prayers of mankind just as he took their loaves and fishes, their bread and wine. He took up the cry of the ancient prophets and the common folk for enlightenment and liberation, the cry of the poor for food and justice, the cry of the diseased and possessed for healing, the cry of women for dignity and value, the cry of the outsiders for acceptance. And he never denied that the kingdom he was talking about was the kingdom of their dream. "He has sent me to announce good news to the poor, to proclaim release for prisoners, and recovery of sight for the blind, to let the broken victims go free, to proclaim the year of the Lord's favour" (Luke 4:18, 19). So the lifestyle of the kingdom which the Church is called to live may never be disengaged from the dusty struggles and ambiguous aspirations of humanity.

Yet those struggles and aspirations may never by themselves dictate the lifestyle of the true Church. For the God whom the kingdom reflects is the Father whom no one knows but the Son and those to whom the Son may choose to reveal him (Matt. 11:27). As his hearers found themselves unexpectedly trapped by his parables and shocked by his attitudes towards people of all sorts, they were slowly compelled to recognize that he was filling the word "God" with an entirely new meaning. The God whom Jesus evidently experienced with such intensity and intimacy was one who was ready to give unconditionally and without limit, to forgive, to heal, to create new chances for anyone without asking what sort of person he was. This God was recognizably on the side of the poor and outcast, yet his mercy was more fundamental even than his justice, and his incomprehensible goodness fitted none of the existing ideas of righteousness. Most astonishingly of all, this God of Jesus was as vulnerable, as weak and as much at risk as love itself.

There is no witness to the kingdom without cross and resurrection

Very early in his ministry Jesus had to come to terms with the resistance and hardness of heart with which his preaching was met. People in power, people supported by tradition, and people who were insecure and envious, were not going to be changed cheaply. And so, having seen that he himself was to be the inaugurator of the kingdom which he proclaimed, he came to see that it was going to be fully inaugurated only through his suffering and death. The idea that the kingdom of the future is to be inaugurated by the suffering and death of God's faithful servant is summed up in the special title which Jesus seems to have chosen for himself, "the Son of Man". The phrase is best translated, "*that* Son of Man", referring back to the earlier use of the title in the vision of Daniel, where "One like a Son of Man" is presented before the Ancient of Days as an image representing not a single individual, but God's loyal people, vindicated in the heavenly kingdom after much tribulation. "The Son of Man", therefore, means the agent and inaugurator of the coming kingdom who will enable others to share with him his special relationship with God through a voluntary acceptance of death.

Whenever we think about the Church, therefore, we must never forget that when Jesus chose the title of "Son of Man" he was using a figure with a *plural* meaning. He called others to be with him in living the life of the kingdom, with him also in dying the necessary death for the kingdom. There are indications in the Gospels that Jesus expected, almost to the end, that in doing what had to be done to enable people to trust themselves to the coming kingdom and let it transform them, he would not be alone, but his chosen companions would share the task with him. It had been his confident hope that those who chose to walk with him would literally take up their crosses and follow him through sacrificial death into resurrection on behalf of the world. The twelve were selected by Jesus as representatives of the tribes of Israel in order to constitute the faithful remnant in its final manifestation as the suffering and dying Servant. As it became clear to him that the twelve were not ready to go through with it, Jesus seems to have set his hopes upon the three, clinging to the possibility that they would at the end drink the cup that he had to drink and be baptised with his baptism. In the event, Jesus had to go forward and make the sacrifice entirely on his own. But the Apostolic Church realized that the invitation to share this with him was renewed by the Risen Christ. This became for them the main significance of baptism. "If we have become incorporate with him in a death like his, we shall also be one with him in a resurrection like his" (Rom. 6:5). And the sharing of the broken bread and the poured-out wine was the symbol he gave them to show that they were still included in his own vocation to be the Son of

Man. The koinonia of the Church is nothing less than the most literal partaking in the sufferings and the resurrection of Christ in order to make up the balance of what has still to be endured in order to unlock the kingdom for others to enter in (II Cor. 1:7; I Peter 4:13; Col. 1:24).

The Church which shares with Jesus in being the Son of Man will expose itself to the same humiliation and derision: "He saved others, himself he cannot save." For striving to save others from exploitation, the Church will itself be persecuted. For opening prison doors and setting people free, the Church will lose its freedom. For living the lifestyle of the kingdom, the Church will be condemned to death. This is actually happening in parts of the world. But many of us do not often see either a Church that unlocks the kingdom for others or a Church that is crucified. Yet those two aims, which are one aim, should be always before our eyes and, at this time especially, need to be brought into sharper focus than ever before.

Those who are called to live the life of the kingdom in anticipation of its arrival commit themselves to the pattern of cross and resurrection. If we live by any other pattern we are not preaching the Gospel Jesus preached. This is not the same as a neurotic search for suffering. The gospel of the kingdom is life-affirming, and when Christians accept for themselves the formula of life-through-death, this is simply because they recognize the life-giving power of him who opened the kingdom that way.

It is, however, a formula that opposes absolutely the way of the world, and this opposition is all the more bitter because it was a distorted Christianity which once gave such strong endorsement to the world's values. I refer to the two doctrines of achievement and militarism. The doctrine of achievement has produced our modern efficiency-oriented society in which people are constrained to make progress and be successful in order to justify themselves. In the process their real selves and, what is worse, the real selves of their children, disappear under their heap of achievements, or their heap of failures. Then a Church which is witnessing to the kingdom must cry: "How can we do things this way if God is what he is?" The doctrine of militarism trusts in superior force as the final solution. It confesses that there is no stronger persuader than the fear of death and destruction. In the past this doctrine has appeared so realistic as to confuse and divide the Church. But now the strategy of nuclear threat is so contrary to realism as to raise a huge new questionmark against the doctrine of militarism and compel all Christians to look again at the pacifist alternative. The Church which is witnessing to the kingdom must cry again: "How can we do things this way if God is what he is?"

The Context of the Church's witness is the local human situation

It is in this world that the lifestyle of the kingdom has to be lived in anticipation of its arrival. That lifestyle cannot be lived in a religious enclave constructed to provide favourable conditions. Christians live the life of the kingdom not as members of a sect, but as parents, as neighbours, as workers, as citizens, as people of a particular race, as members of privileged or deprived groups. Witnessing to the kingdom means enabling people in each particular situation to see the nature of God truly reflected in the mirror of their own culture, their own institutions and their own conflicts.

This is the strength of the genuine parish church, the congregation of which is drawn from the neighbourhood, and knows it is sent to serve and witness in the whole life of that community. It is almost impossible for the eclectic church congregations of a fragmented, mobile society to have any sense of responsible mission unless they deliberately form themselves into smaller groups related either to their residential neighbourhood or work situations. Clergy also must learn to see themselves less as the necessary leaders of worship in these gathered congregations and more as the enablers and coordinators of the smaller groups, making them aware of one another and uniting them in a common witness through their own mobile ministry. Clergy should also become much more aware of, and supportive to, those other groups of Christians who choose to live together in some form of experimental community in order to experience and express the lifestyle of the kingdom and make their homes available to some of the damaged victims of society.

The ministers of the Church are the guardians of its evangelical truth and continuity but they must learn to be less concerned with its uniformity. They must not turn the *depositio fidei* into an *impositio*. The use Jesus made of his parables shows that he understood that a vision of the kingdom is not something which can be given by one person to others; it can only be discovered. When we say, rightly, that the Church must everywhere be indigenous we are thinking too much of national characteristics and not enough of the cultural differences between people in different economic and social situations. Those who take responsibility for guiding the growth of the Church should be more ready to trust local groups, especially among the poor, uneducated and struggling people, to respond in their own way to the story of Jesus, like those factory workers in Raymond Fung's account of his Bible study group in Hong Kong. They should be more ready to entrust the discovery of the Gospel to groups which contain people of other faiths as well as Christians. They should be more ready to entrust the formulation of theology to teams which include serious seekers after truth from other disciplines as well as biblical and dogmatic studies—especially from the physical and human sciences. Only in such ways will the kingdom that is to come throw its light on the realities in which people actually live. Then the hope of the kingdom will be seen to be related to the hopes of Asia, South America and South Africa, and the word "God" will be filled with new meaning for those who are captives in the deadlock of western industrialism or those in the underdeveloped world who are consumed by the present moment and conditioned by its violence. We need to hear the "Our Father" spoken in their voices as well as our own if we are to recover its full meaning.

The kingdom of God should be central in all of the five basic activities of the Church

The Church, then, consists of those members of the human family who share with Jesus Christ the belief that the kingdom of God is so near at hand that they already begin to live its life, and who are confirmed in that hope by the knowledge of his resurrection. This should give shape and direction to the five basic activities of the Church, which must also be the activities of every local church—worship, fellowship, learning, service and witness. These are the five basic elements in the life of the first Christian communities as described in the Acts of the Apostles: the breaking of bread and prayers; fellowship; the Apostles' teaching; daily ministry and distribution; witness (Acts 2:42; 4:33, 35; 6:1).

Worship is central to the lifestyle of the kingdom because the certainty that the kingdom is on its way is derived from an intense awareness of the reality and nearness of God. This was the case with Jesus, and it must be the case with those who follow him. "You have received the Spirit that makes us sons, enabling us to cry, Abba, Father" (Rom. 8:15). It is through worship that we constantly renew, by the activity of the Holy Spirit, our Abba-relationship with the God of Jesus Christ. By recovering this sense of God's closeness to our life in this world, we renew the connection, the ladder, between his true nature and the situations in which our lives and struggles take place. Worship is the recognition of that which is worth most. To worship God is to recognize that he is worth more than all else to ourselves and to the whole creation. To worship is to feel that he is worthy of a greater love than we can either give or understand. To worship is to realize afresh that his greatness belongs to dimensions we cannot begin to comprehend, yet his nearness is familiar and open to our utmost simplicity, and we depend on him for everything. Even the most homely and informal act of worship, if it is true, can never be casual. It is always accompanied by the inward imperative: "Take off thy shoes from off thy feet, for the place whereon thou standest is holy ground."

Moses was an activist. That is why he had had to get out of Egypt. The plight of his people in slavery still preyed on his mind. But instead of plotting and scheming like an exiled revolutionary, he was overtaken by this experience of the absolute priority of God. He heard the voice of the Lord, saying: "I have seen the misery; I have heard the outcry; I have taken heed of the sufferings and have come down to rescue." Real worship takes place when the people who see and care and are active on behalf of the needy *recognize* that God sees more and cares more and is more active than they can ever be. They wait in silence before him, knowing their dependence and letting him fill their vision. Then, having fully realized that it is God's action that is righting the wrong rather than men's, they may hear him say: "Come now, I will send you to Pharoah."

Human beings live in a to-and-fro rhythm, alternating between responsibility and dependence. In his book *The Dynamics of Religion*, Bruce Reed calls this rhythm "oscillation" which he likens to the movement of very young children whom he saw playing in a public park. "After a while, they would use up their store of courage and confidence, and run back to their mothers' sides and cling there for a while, as if to recharge their batteries. After a moment or two of this they were ready for more exploring, and so they went out, then came back, and then ventured out again." Christians who respond to the needs of the world with immediate and unbroken activity become spent, nervy and indisciplined. Christians who cling to God without ever having heard, seen or cared for the cry of the world, grow childish and fussy. True worship is that which, in responsible awareness of the struggle for righteousness in the world, turns back to God as the supreme source of confidence and meaning. If this is true, we must seek for forms of worship which are not in themselves totally "busy" with words or demonstrations which merely reflect our neurotic activism in the world outside. We must make more spaces for silence, wordless communion, reverence and thankfulness. As wonder and thanksgiving deepen in our relationship towards God we shall find that it is more natural for us to look on every human being with reverence and with gratitude, and this will cleanse our service to others from all condescension.

Fellowship in the Christian community is more than friendliness and natural amiability. It is human relationship being redeemed from fear, inhibition, pretence or pride. It is a deep companionship which the followers of Jesus Christ share not only with one another but always with their Master as well. We have seen that, at its deepest, it means partaking in the death and resurrection of Jesus.

We are all made for mutuality, interdependence and love. But our hidden guilt, anger and dread of rejection make us unable to expose ourselves, trust ourselves or give ourselves to others. All this merely reflect our broken relationship with God. But as we begin to take in the astonishing fact of Jesus' acceptance of us as we are, and his total forgiveness and trust, we can begin to dare to make ourselves available and vulnerable. We can give love without fear of being consumed, and take love without fear of being smothered. It may not happen all at once, because old habits and fears live on after the cause for them has been taken away. But in any truly Christian community our mutual trust should be growing deeper all the time, like cripples whose limbs have been healed and are learning to walk again.

The dynamic and demanding nature of Christian fellowship is very clearly seen, strangely enough, in the description that Father Aelred Stubbs has given of his friendship with Steve Biko. He writes of "this amazing man, whose gift of leadership consisted pre-eminently in discerning the capacities of those whose trust he had gained, and enabling them to realize them to the full. I would have to go back to Jesus himself to find a parallel to this extraordinary pastoral care which Steve had for his own. I suppose this is why I was prepared to commit myself so wholeheartedly to the care of his leadership. And then, there was the new quality that life in his company took on. It was like the kingdom. The impossible became possible. Sometimes indeed it became actual" (Steve Biko, *I write what I like*, p. 192f). We must not be content with less than that within the Church in our caring for one another and for one another's potentiality. This is the quality of fellowship which heals the disturbed and depressed, the victims of evil and the broken in spirit, and those in the grip of sin. This is the quality of fellowship that will send its members triumphantly into the fight against the machine-like institutions. This is the quality of fellowship that will draw the outsider into the Christian circle.

The followers who attached themselves to Jesus during his earthly ministry formed a "school" around a new teacher. After his death and resurrection, the Apostolic Church, while not expecting its members to be intellectuals, did demand that they should make over their minds as well as their souls and bodies to the service of God (Rom. 12:1, 2). Why has the Church in our day gone soft on this aspect of its responsibilities? I think it is partly because we have allowed the world as a whole to persuade us that religion is an essentially private affair. That is an idea that suits a materialistic world very well, since it excludes Christian thought and Christian questions from the spheres of politics and business. But no local church can flourish, still less can it challenge its society with the lifestyle of the kingdom, unless Christians *together* are searching their Scriptures, making themselves informed about the situation in which their human community is placed, asking themselves how the nature of God would be more truly reflected in that situation, and interpreting these insights to their neighbours and fellow-workers. It is through such corporate learning that the Good News of the kingdom is seen to be relevant to the context in which it is lived and proclaimed.

To put it into such words makes it sound like a very academic exercise. But in practice it can be as simple as the parables of Jesus, and no less disturbing than they were.

In recent years the Church has started to talk a great deal about its diakonia. This is bearing fruit, thank God, in a new sense of social responsibility in a vast number of local congregations. Are we, perhaps, in danger of losing the simplicity, spontaneity and deep love which ought to be characteristic of all Christian service? The lifestyle of the kingdom must reflect the nature of a God who appears to be almost naïve in the disposal of his love. The parables of the workers and their wages, the prodigal son and the unmerciful servant reveal a God who gives solely because there is a need, and not because his gift is deserved or even just. Jesus revealed the same God in his treatment of men and women, welcoming their company without discriminating between good and bad, rich and poor, citizens and foreigners. People were excluded from his circle only by their self-righteousness and rejection of others. This totally radical acceptance and trust must be the keynote of all Christian service, and it should be seen in the Church's attitude towards people of other races, or tribes, or faiths; people with a different economic or educational standard; people of dubious reliability, like vagrants or ex-prisoners; and people from the other side of the political fence. Their need, whatever it is, lays claim to our love and service.

But, while it must maintain this radical simplicity, the Church must not continue in the error of supposing that Christian service can only be given by individuals to individuals. It should always remain personal, but it must often move beyond the person-to-person level. It is the impersonal, corporate structures that do most violence to people, and they can achieve liberation and personal meaning only through corporate action. Healing and reconciliation cannot be got on the cheap. Some evil powers cannot be cast out except with prayer and fasting; there are others that require organization and confrontation as well.

The worship and the fellowship, the learning and the serving, are all part of the witness which the Church bears to the coming kingdom. But we witness supremely by living the life and telling the story. The Bible makes it clear that the people of God are his witnesses in two senses. Like someone in the witness box, they are called to say what they have seen and heard and experienced. But they are also, in themselves, by the lives they lead, the exhibits which the counsel for the defence will produce as evidence before the eyes of the court. What we are, as well as what we say, speaks either for the God of Jesus Christ or against him. The aim of all Christian witness is to persuade people whose minds are not yet made up to decide *for* God, to believe and trust in the God whom Jesus knew as his Father, and to experience the reality of that God for themselves. I have already said a good deal about living the life of the kingdom in anticipation of its arrival, and what this may mean for us.

But the case has to be stated in court. The story has to be told. The Gospel is not an idea about God which might have cropped up anywhere; it is news of an event. A report presented by its Board of Mission and Unity to the Church of England last summer contained these words: "The story of God in Christ is the essential kernel which lies at the heart of all evangelism and at the centre of every activity of mission. A major problem is to tell that story in such a way that people hear it as contemporary and relevant."

Those last words remind us sharply that we are up against some very great difficulties of communication. Our Christian conviction and commitment contain features that are completely against the grain of modern thought These stumbling blocks are inherent in our faith; we cannot get rid of them, we can only help people to get over them.

We shall never do that so long as we remain inside our own cultural stockades. Genuine outsiders can only be reached outside. We shall not communicate with them through anything we do inside the church buildings or even in public rallies. They can, however, be met in the places where they gather and devote time to their own concerns. If we do not naturally belong to the world of the particular "outsiders" we want to reach, some of us must take the trouble to cross over and learn to be at home in that alien territory. The Christian group, therefore, which can best witness to the youth culture is one which is already familiar and sympathetic with the values and concerns of the young. And no one will be a very effective witness to those who are being dehumanized by the violence done to them and the violence aroused within them unless he is ready to enter that vicious circle himself and be at risk amid all its pressures and threats.

Advance by assessment, planning and action

It is all very well to talk in these large, universal terms, but too many conferences and assemblies leave us up in the clouds. Local congregations and Christian groups need to see the next, practical steps which they may realistically hope to take. We should be humble enough to set out sights in the same way that any good business firm might do. Renewal, renovation, repentance, call it what you will, advances by three steps: *assessment* of our present situation and our present performance; *planning* the position at which we wish to arrive, the stages by which we might get there, and the people who will be responsible for particular action; *action* to carry out the plan;

and then back to assessment again to judge honestly how we have done and why we made mistakes. So the process starts all over again, and renewal is a continual going forward.

So with regard to each of the five elements of the Church's activities which we have just considered, we should begin by asking ourselves in every local Christian community such questions as these. Where do we actually stand at the moment with regard to this aspect of our church life? In order to move further towards the ideal, what might we change or achieve within the next twelve months? What factors are hindering us and what might help us? Are there resources we are not yet using? Are all our members able to understand what is happening, and if not, why not? Which of us feel responsible, and why not others? What shall we actually do, and who will do it? And will they be left to do it in their own way?

These are disturbing questions but they may be life-giving.

Yet, as we go forward with this degree of humble obedience, we shall recognize more and more that it is not we who either make or mar the future. The kingdom is being given to us. The penultimate reality in which we live and struggle is not the road by which we reach the ultimate. It is the other way round. The ultimate which lies beyond our sight is shaping the penultimate in which we live, through the power of faith, hope and love. In his *Ethics*, Bonhoeffer made this comment on the text, "Prepare ye the way of the Lord": "It is not our way to him, but his way to us that has to be prepared... Preparation of the way is a way from the ultimate to the penultimate. Christ is coming, of his own will."

The Church—Sign of the Kingdom
HALINA BORTNOWSKA*

I was asked to talk to the Melbourne Conference on the Church as the sign of the kingdom, and to do so within the context of the life of my country, Poland. This is difficult because this context is largely unknown to my listeners. We live immersed in this context: to notice it as a "context", as something special, peculiar, not self-evident, we must take distance—and this rarely happens. Now it has happened: I face a foreign audience. It is easier to communicate with such an audience if it consists of visitors, if you come to my country and you look around, not just listen to me. But here we are and we must try to communicate.

It is bad philosophy, bad theology and generally bad didactic method to think within just one context. A hermeneutical exercise imposes a step beyond one's own world, and a *comparison* of this world with something more familiar to the audience. This is why I am going to talk about *two* contexts: one is my own, the country where I grew up, where I live, to which I return from all my travels. The other context which I will try to describe and use as reference may happen to be one which you will be able to identify. I discovered it in western Europe. The interpretation of this context is not just my own. It was suggested to me in many ecumenical encounters.

My own context is often called "socialist". I do not think that this is a good name for it. There are many reasons why I prefer to call it simply "Polish". One of the reasons is that "socialism" is not responsible for all distinctive features of this context; our history is much longer than the 35 years since the end of World War II. Similarly, I do not want to talk about "the capitalist context". Let us call it "affluent atlantic".

The two contexts have many features in common. They also differ—profoundly.

I shall try to explain certain differences and affinities—relevant to the function of the Church as sign—using a graphic model. It will be a very simplified schematic explanation—as we only have minutes for this purpose, I can only give a rough outline of a reflection.

---

*Halina Bortnowska, Poland, is a Roman Catholic pastoral worker in Krakow.

I believe that the method must reflect the message; in a sense I agree that the method is the message. As a pastoral worker in an urban parish I work daily with people who come to think and talk about their life and their faith in the evenings after hard work in a foundry or at home. Many are not young any more; many have little experience of intellectual work. All are certainly too tired to listen to long lectures. The members of our community—you can call it a "basic group" if you like—are very serious people, and we talk about serious problems, but our method cannot be scholarly. We often use very non-scholarly visual aids. I hope that you are also a little tired after reading and drafting so many serious papers so you will enjoy this rather nursery-style presentation.

The first thing I want you to look at is the symbol of certain experiences that we all share. The blank space around the symbol is intended to remind us of the fact of *indifference*, of lifestyle which avoids deeper problems and meanings. We all live in a diaspora among people of this lifestyle. In my country atheism is rare, but even people who believe—who "in principle believe"—often act as if they don't believe. We act like that, too. We shut our eyes because we do not want to see and experience the challenging fact of *suffering*, oppression, loneliness, alienation. This figure is the symbol of various evils. It may be a burden, a stone which crushes and cripples a man working in a quarry. It may also suggest the evil of isolation, of being abandoned in an impersonal institution, of imprisonment, physical or mental handicap, dire poverty, rejection, exile...

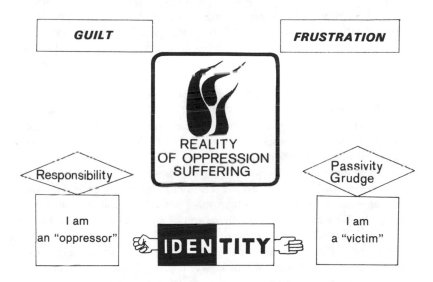

Suffering is a fact which we *all* face. I believe that our *identity* takes a more definite shape, if and when we dare to confront the fact of suffering as a constant background and accompanying tune of existence, a *continuo* of every melody of life. We see that there is suffering in the world, some of which cannot be blamed on anybody. *It is just there.* Only some of the suffering can be blamed on us.

And a great measure can be blamed on others, who inflict it on the world—and on ourselves. It is a question of proportion and of dominant feelings, of a certain very basic mood which is a result of accumulating experiences.

In my native context, when I face the fact of suffering in the world, I most often feel that my identity is the identity of a *victim*. In my country people have had to go through many different frustrations. Our history abounds in situations of oppression. Many wounds from the past, from long periods of misery and humiliation, are still open. The grandchildren of poor landless peasants, now second generation city dwellers in an industrial environment, still bear the scars, traces of attitudes so deeply ingrained that people seem to inherit them—together with the whole deposit of culture transferred from generation to generation. The same applies to more recent instances of great collective and individual suffering during and also after the second World War. Polish refugees and displaced persons on all continents are eye witnesses to this difficult chapter of our history. These memories are still very much a part of our life at home. During the war we were sustained by a very strong, "self-evident" hope for the future. Many, perhaps most of those too optimistic dreams of a future Poland—free, independent, peaceful and just—were frustrated. For example so many families dispersed by the war were not reassembled due to death, continuing political emigration or estrangement. Europe has not become a place where all war-weary people could begin reconstruction of their disturbed and destroyed life in peace and according to their own choice of social system. Very many people at various stages had a deep experience of nearly total failure of all that they strived for, of all their initiatives and loyalties. This was extended over many years and hardly anybody was spared. Some of the causes were in ourselves but on the whole the burden was put on us; the tragedies happened by or with international agreement, by the will of other, more powerful peoples pursuing their own goals. We were deprived of choice and of a normal democratic way of exercising responsibility for public affairs.

All this contributed to the fact that we live *with a victim mentality*. And what we must overcome in order to survive is precisely the frustration which makes people resign and all too often live a lie, repress the dictates of conscience, live day by day seeking small satisfactions. Who cares for great issues, if so many great concerns have failed and are bound to fail again and again? The "victim" is not responsible, the "victim" is excused from participation (and so complicity with evil is seen as the fault of others, of the oppressors—"we are not guilty").

In the other context—affluent atlantic—which I visit occasionally, many people tell me how they themselves feel that they are *oppressors*.

I do not like this word "oppressor". In Polish in the Lord's prayer we have another word: *winowajca*—this is somebody who is both guilty and in debt. That would be the meaning which I give here to the word "oppressor". A person realizes: "I live at the cost of others"; "I have plenty, because some do not have enough and are forced to live in misery"; "Somebody pays for my affluent life; somebody pays for all that I have and consume". This identity has its roots in a history of colonial empires, of exploitation of others. Of course it is not just past history: the sources of guilt feelings are still open: they consist in the continuing existence of disparities between the "central" countries and the poor "periphery" and in the continuing exploitation. Intelligent westerners know that realistically they cannot avoid complicity: just by living "normally" they participate in the spoils. Therefore the guilt feelings are justified and should be a more common experience than they are now.

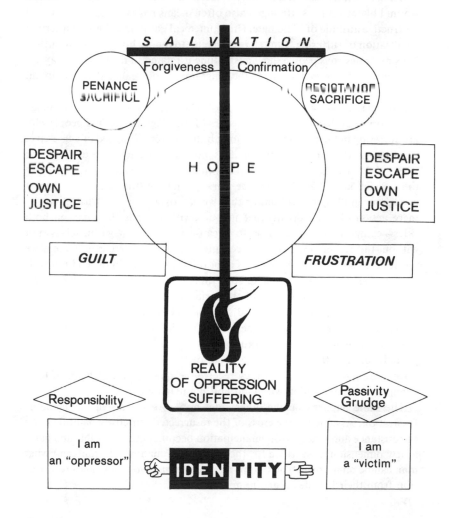

Of course the problem of suffering is not exclusive to Christians—all people with their eyes open face it. As Christians we can confront the fact of suffering in the light of the faith and of the kingdom. Or rather: as Christians we are called to see, to discover our identity in this light but we accept this vocation and learn to live up to it only step by step, slowly, not even very consequently, by a series of repeated and gradual conversions.

The cross has its roots in our suffering. The cross makes us reflect on our identity in a different way. If my identity is that of a *victim* it does not make me immediately and necessarily a holy person.

Being a victim means frustrations, it means a certain grudge against others, whom I blame for my suffering; it also often means passivity, depression, or a destructive attitude of blind hate. (In ecumenical gatherings I notice a certain idealization of suffering. Church people tend to ignore how often real suffering simply destroys people, how misfortune is related to death and decay.)

Now turn to the other side of the diagram: if you realize that you are an oppressor—you feel a responsibility, and this is a positive fact, but responsible people often fall into the trap of helpless desperate guilt feelings. Therefore in both contexts, on both sides of the diagram, we find people who are suffering in their identity, becoming bitter, bitterly resigned or aggressive.

Although the cross is there, it does not immediately save us from the worst—which is the same on both sides. In both we can easily be trapped into the conviction that justice must be our own justice, that we can and must cancel our guilt by restitution, or that we can overcome our frustrations by mere action. The result of belief in our own justice is the same on both sides—escape and despair. It is so because we cannot save ourselves, not without the acceptance of the gift coming from God. There is no hope if we see Jesus as somebody who gave us a moral example but in the end failed, if his resurrection is either fiction or something very remote, a mere theological thesis. If the cross is the cross of the resurrected, then it can give us hope.

The prime object of hope is God's victory, God's kingdom—his reality in us. Hope challenges our helplessness. In our union with God we become able to see and live our efforts at restitution and reparation as supplemented, supported, surpassed, *assumed* in the Cross of the resurrected, in this way our efforts are more than efforts, they receive the quality of *metanoia*, of total change, reversal, reunion with God and the neighbours.

The same happens on the other side: hope breaks the vicious circle of frustration. Assumed in the cross of the resurrected our costly painful action of resistance and struggle for emancipation becomes more possible and gains a new dimension of sacrifice for these values of man which transcend what man can be on his own. The victims also need a *metanoia*, a kind of resurrection from their half-death and humiliation.

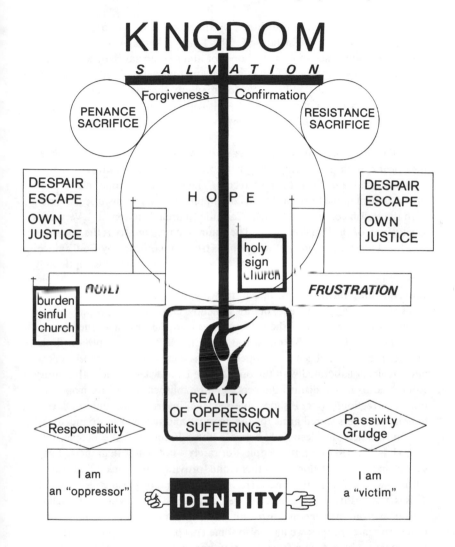

What is the function of the Church in this whole process? My title says: "Church as Sign of the Kingdom". In order to function as a sign of the kingdom the Church has to be situated at the level of hope. This is where it ought to be according to God's plan, according to his economy. In a sense the Church *is* always a sign of hope, by the strength of its vocation, by its *nature*: the bond of Christ himself. The Lord makes us one by this faith which is the substance of what we hope for and the substance of what makes us able to hope—the reality of our participation in God's life, in his all-powerful and delicate selfless love for man for the sake of man. This is something very real, not in the clouds, it is truly "a substance", tangible, experienced in everyday life. There is worship in the Spirit; there are saints, people who are signs of the sign.

At the same time the concrete pastoral work, the presence of a given historical church community, may be more or less apt to convey this hope coming from the cross of the resurrected. The message of hope can be more or less evident in the life of a church community, of a local, historical church.

In the Polish context the Roman Catholic Church functions as a very convincing sign of the kingdom hope. The Church in my country is the one thing which did not fail, did not betray people's trust. It happened by God's grace, not by our own virtue, certainly not because our clergy were exceptionally wise or heroic. Polish priests and bishops are not exceptional in their personal qualities, intellectual or moral: they are like everybody else, some with great gifts, some just average, but all somehow close to their people; there is a unity which transcends the differences in education, in economic and marital status. The Polish Roman Catholic Church has always been with the people, it has never been the property of the rich nor of the foreigners, it never really collaborated with the oppressors. Even when in the 19th century Rome told us not to disturb the peace and established order in Europe with our insurrections, our Bishops blessed the insurrections and our contemplative orders stored arms for the guerillas and nursed the wounded. All this maintained the deep link between the Church and the people. The Church is not wiser than the people—or rarely—nor better than them, but it surely and deeply belongs to them and provides a means of access to Christ—who is seen as the One suffering with us and promising resurrection. This is why in Poland the Church is seen as a sign of hope, why it is somehow exempted from the general frustration. This does not mean that the Church never frustrates people: we have also some lazy priests, given only to routine functions, we have even a few who may shock people by their immoral conduct. But now this does not really matter much.

What makes the Church holy and a real sign of the kingdom is not the personal moral virtue of church members and their priests. The Church is holy by virtue of its bond with Christ, and by this alone. *Christ* makes us one in the Church—so far as we permit it—because all too often we do not accept this gift or if so only in very small measure. This is a basic fact of theological nature. The Church teaches it everywhere—all Christian Churches are aware of it. But it is also true that the results of this teaching and the clarity of awareness depend on the situation. For instance, if the teaching clergy does not fully share the problems and sufferings of the people, the message is hampered, then miracles are needed to get through to the people over the gap in existential contact.

There are many ways of being in such existential contact yet a certain solidarity is a precondition of them all. And individual solidarity of some pastors is not enough: the whole complex works if and when the local Church—or even Church group—is seen as "our own", something which is "of us", "in us". This is how the Church is experienced in Poland, and this feeling grows and becomes very intense in crucial moments of history, when both the awareness of danger and the elation of hope move the people to lift their eyes, to be more aware of the values they choose.

When we enter the Church we are in the zone of light, we are in a sanctuary where we dare to be ourselves, where we feel accepted. This is the only place where there is no waiting line to get what we need, where we are not told to come next day because the service is over for today (as we are likely to be told in all secular "service stations"...). Jesus is always there and accessible to all, Jesus, the Advocate, Healer, Friend and Saviour, Son of Mary who intercedes for those who pray. This image of the Church is the most important feature of our religious life. And if it is so, if the Church is there as a holy sign of the kingdom, then the Church can also in some way lift up peoples' hearts, sustain them so that they become more able to get out of frustration in a spirit of sacrifice. This spirit for us means to be involved in some kind of resistance against corruption, against universal frustration and negligence, against giving up. It encourages people to engage in action for survival as a community, for defence of dignity and identity—to be subjects and not mere objects of historical processes. Instead of suffering it all for nothing, we take responsibility for the direction of the life of our community. This is painful and costly and risky but immensely different from submission which breaks the spirit and deprives life of meaning.

In drawing this image of the Church in my country I have tried to give you an idea of its basic function, of its place in our awareness. Of course, in everyday life the Church people fail each other; they—*we*—do not always live up to this vocation. The Church dominates for one hour on Sunday, perhaps also on certain very important moments in personal and community life. It provides a measure for the consciences, inspiration to those willing to accept it... otherwise we are morally still very far from being entirely faithful or saved from frustration and resignation. In all this usual human mess the Church continues to be a sign—the Church, by the grace of God comforts and challenges people to raise up.

We have been looking mainly at the right side of this diagram. Let us look now at the function of the Church in a western affluent context, among the people with the guilt-identity. I have spent some time in this world. Let us take, as a very typical example, Holland. My impression of the Dutch Church—the Roman Catholic one—is that it is not seen at the level of hope. People place it rather at the level of guilt feelings. The society is guilty and the Church is guilty. In fact, this guilty Church constantly teaches you how guilty you are. The Church proclaims the duty of restitution of the cost of suffering inflicted on the exploited and oppressed: to be morally okay we must repair the wrongs. Yet there is a question whether this message is rightly understood, and whether the proclamation of guilt is not degenerating into promotion of the vain hope of working one's own justice. Can we really repair the immeasurable wrong of the destruction of human substance, of true misfortune, of killing people and killing whole human cultures?

Penance is more than restitution. The idea of restitution is unrealistic: man is meant to be in debt to his neighbours. And there are wrongs which cannot be repaid, there is irreparable destruction. If the Church does not proclaim God's pardon and mutual reconciliation as free gift, as grace, then it is bound to hold people (or at least to let them stay) at the level of helpless guilt and helpless, hopeless remorse. The message of reconciliation must come through loud and clear. And a given historical situation—unless it is changed and transcended—can obscure it.

Let us look at the diagram again. In the end the differences converge: we need the same thing, we need forgiveness. The victims need forgiveness for giving up too easily, for living a lie, for co-operating with destructive decisions, for selfish and short-sighted lack of solidarity with other victims, for building a system of mutual self-help which so often excludes the innocent weak. It is a system of exchange: "I can provide eggs and you can provide meat"; "I shall sell you a pair of good shoes but next day you will help my son to pass an examination". And so on... But if you have nothing to contribute, if you are a retired person with no resources and no influence, then you are left out of the system of mutual aid and your life becomes very hard. We need forgiveness for such neglect of the weakest, for wrong priorities. We need it in the same way as the other side, the "oppressors", need it for giving up the effort to live less at the cost of others.

To victims and oppressors God's promise gives a realistic hope that we can raise up: forgive and be forgiven. We need forgiveness and also something which I call "confirmation". God gives us power to do more than we can do; one aspect is healing. God heals the soul so that man can forgive. God's forgiveness is a seed of mutual reconciliation. For me reconciliation is the soul of the spirituality which sustains people in situations of oppression, danger, frustration. The victims need the healing of a reconciling act no less than those who oppress them.

On both sides, in both contexts, God's confirmation brings a correction of the position of the Church. Perhaps the position of our Church just on the level of hope is too angelic. Perhaps we overlook how often the Church needs forgiveness for its contribution to the frustration of certain people. Only by God's grace the Church in my country has been until now prevented from participating in the system of mutual help which excludes the weak. The Church has spoken for the weak and does not discard them. But it needs to be brought closer to the people in their frustration and desperation. Closer to full understanding, closer to witness on moral matters in the context of everyday life.

At the same time I believe that the Church of guilt feelings should be lifted up more to the level of hope, so that its people will not continue to feel like unredeemed sinners. It is very depressing and even boring to be blamed all the time. Some people revolt against this and impress with feelings. Everywhere there is need for more realistic hope, a hope that in the end we are all to come to the Father and everything will be restored by his overpowering goodness. The churches must also teach more boldly that the victims can even forgive those who are their own direct oppressors. We have a very convincing example of such forgiveness between the people of Poland and Germany. The beginnings of reconciliation we owe to the initiative of the German Protestant churches and of groups consciously seeking contact and understanding, like *Aktion Suehnezeichen*. These people first addressed us and asked for forgiveness. They worked for it and prayed for it for a long time without response. In the end we had an exchange of letters between bishops, and more initiatives came. We can say that what there is of reconciliation, of truly, healing reconciliation, came by Christian mediation. We dared to trust each other again because of Christ and because of shared faith. In this also the Church is a sign of hope.

Just one more remark. When you try to understand my former bishop and the present bishop of Rome you must remember that he was born and brought up here, that he was a choir boy in this Church of hope, this Church was his sanctuary, his shelter and his treasure. It is very difficult for him to see the Church at the guilt level. Jesus who links people together in the Church is so brilliant in his eyes that this bright vision obscures the very real guilt of the churches—the fact that churches as human institutions are also responsible for quite a lot of innocent suffering. Pope John Paul II proclaims the Church of Christ which *is* a sign of the kingdom. No sign is identical with the reality to which it points, but the main, essential and indefectible function of the Church is to be such a sign and no amount of moral failure can really destroy this fact. The Church is the place where we receive forgiveness and confirmation from God in Jesus. This is how John Paul sees it and I think that this is a message not only for Roman Catholics. It is a message of joy for everybody. Please, remember this when you are confronted and even shocked by his other messages. He speaks from the context of the Church seen as a sign of hope. This largely forgotten context has something to say to the world.

The Crucified Christ Challenges Human Power
KOSUKE KOYAMA *

Behold, the Lamb of God who takes away
the sin of the world! (John 1:29)

With his mutilated hands he builds his world community; he challenges the power of efficiency-mindedness towards neighbours.

He exposes human deception

The crucified Christ exposes the deception of those who "have healed the wound of the people lightly, saying 'Peace, peace' when there is no peace" (Jer. 6:14). He exposes human deception, not from the luxury of an arm chair, but by abandoning himself to human dominance, even to crucifixion. What a painful and inefficient way to expose human deception. This inefficient way is the secret of his power that confronts human power. It is the secret of his love.

No one now can mutilate him, because he is already mutilated. No one can crucify him. He is already crucified. No one can add or substract anything from him. Jesus Christ is not "Yes and No" (II Cor. 1:19). Because he—the crucified Christ—is the ultimate sincerity (*emeth*, "steadfastness"). In the crucified Christ we are confronted by the ultimate sincerity of God.

The sincerity of the crucified Christ was expressed in the taunting words of the people who were passing by the cross: "He saved others. He cannot save himself." Perhaps only taunts can reveal the depth of such sincerity! Normal avenues of theology are closed. All the world *becomes* silent and all human powers *are* challenged by the profound sincerity of the crucified Christ.

It is true that he saved others. He commanded the lame to walk. He gave sight to the blind. He cast out demons from the demon-possessed. He was, let me expand the Apostles Creed by four words, "born of the Virgin Mary, *cast out the demons*, suffered under Pontius Pilate". The demons were cast out. The reign of God came. "... If it is by the finger of God that I cast out

---

*Dr. Kosuke Koyama, a Japanese theologian, is Professor of Ecumenics and World Christianity at Union Theological Seminary in New York City.

demons then the kingdom of God has come upon you" (Luke 11:20). He shared his life with the poor and the needy, giving them hope. He was an other-oriented person. His sincerity was identical with this orientation. But this amazing power of healing rooted in the other-oriented sincerity he did not apply to himself. He saved others from humiliation. He himself went to the depths of humiliation. He saved others through not saving himself. He affirmed his lordship by giving it up. By healing others and not himself, he established his authority.

The mutilated hands of Christ and technology-bureaucracy

The mutilated hands of Christ represent the sincerity of God towards all humanity. Today hands are a symbol of technology. Are not our hands reaching the moon and beyond by our science and technology? Are not our hands changing our living environment to suit our liking? Do not powerful engines obey the signals we give by our fingers? Are they not capable of sending lethal bombs to destroy our enemies? Our hands are powerful. Ours are not mutilated at all.

Look at the disfigured and mutilated hands of Christ!

Technology is an efficient arrangement to "duplicate" things. By the printing press, newspapers can be duplicated by the thousands. By motors, distance can be rapidly duplicated under the rotation of the wheel. The ability to duplicate is today dangerously divorced from the discussion of the meaning of such ability. Efficiency is suffocating meaning. The good is impoverishing the best. The fertility god Baal is becoming stronger than the Covenant God Yahweh. Meaning is subordinated to efficiency. When meaning is subordinated to efficiency the attractive hands appear. The attractive hands often direct our minds to the fascination of idolatry. Who will make an idol out of the mutilated hands?

We appreciate technology. How could we do so many good things in the sight of the God of the Bible today without the help of technology. Technology may be permitted to duplicate anything, but not human beings. The machine must be switched off when it begins to duplicate the image of God in humans. It must not desacralize the holy in people. The world of efficiency—the world of attractive hands—must be watched by the world of meaning—the world of mutilated hands. What does it mean to duplicate human beings? Today perhaps one could speak of the duplication of the human in the sense of biological science. But I am thinking at this moment of the surrendering of human space and human time to the efficient technological space and technological time. When the human environment is thus technologized, the uniqueness of the person will eventually suffer, and there may appear a faceless mass of people. The crucified Christ challenges such a technologically efficient way of dealing with people. Technology must serve the maintenance and development of human values, the values of sincerity and reliability in the human community. The lifestyle of the Atlantic world is not the standard for all humanity. It must be judged together with other lifestyles under the light of the crucified Lord.

Bureaucracy is a world of filing cabinets and endless classification. It can reduce a living person into the set of numbers one sees on his or her passport. Information is stored in the cabinet alphabetically. The infinite amount of information about people can be used for the welfare of the people. Then bureaucracy is practising the mind of the reign of God. But it can also use the information in order to destroy people. Both the Nazi and the Japanese bureaucracies operated with remarkable efficiency to destroy the lives of the peoples of Asia and Europe. Without bureaucratic systems both militarism and racism cannot work.

We appreciate bureaucracy. But it must be in the hands of the responsible king *(melek)* and not in the hands of the irresponsible king *(mulek)* who seeks human sacrifice (Jer. 32:35). Bureaucracy must be judged in the light of the sincerity of the crucified Christ. Both technology and bureaucracy are subject to the danger of efficiency which suffocates meaning. The most extreme example of the triumph of meaning over the idolatry of efficiency is the crucifixion of Christ. There Christ demonstrates the depth of his sincerity in the most painful and "inefficient" way. It takes suffering to expose idolatry. Technology and bureaucracy tell us today "peace, peace". Is there peace? Have they not become the tools of militarism and racism?

Who says it to whom?

The sincerity and reliability of the crucified Lord exposes human deception. If someone, quoting from the Bible, says "Blessed are you poor, for yours is the kingdom of God" (Luke 6:20), let us ask, who is this person who is saying this, and to whom? Is a wealthy man saying this to a famished man? The rich to the poor? Literate person to the illiterate? Well-fed to the starved? If someone quoting from the Bible, says "Man does not live by bread alone, but by everything that proceeds out of the mouth of the Lord", let us ask again who is saying it and to whom? I am not saying that no rich man can say, "Blessed are you poor, for yours is the kingdom of God." Indeed, he may say this *to himself*. Then it will become an extremely embarrassing and painful thought. It will become a call to surrender wealth to God and to work towards a more just society. The passage, "Man does not live by bread alone, but by everything that proceeds out of the mouth of the Lord" does not idealize poverty. It plainly tells us that humanity needs both bread *and* the word of God. It does not say that the word of God is more important than bread, or vice versa. We cannot live by bread alone. We cannot live by the word of God alone. We need both. This must be the charter of the Christian commitment towards a more just society. Often, however, the well-fed tend to preach to the hungry people that all they need is the word of God.

The hungry do not recognize sincerity in these words of the well-fed people. It is therefore difficult for the missionaries sent by the rich and mighty nation to preach the word of God in the poor and starved nations. Not impossible, but difficult. Poverty and hunger are not something the God of the Bible is happy about. They must be eliminated. Poverty-stricken people cannot and do not idealize poverty. The rich can afford to idealize it.

If a rich man says to the poor "Blessed are you poor, for yours is the kingdom of God", he is gossiping. Gossip is irresponsible talk. It does not heal. It causes a dangerous inflation in human spirituality, which makes us believe that this gossip is the word of God. Idealization of poverty by the rich is just such an arrogant bit of gossip, and not theology. Behind such gossip there must be a "duplication" and "filing cabinet" way of looking at people. The poor are quickly classified and labelled. But when living persons are reduced to sets of numbers, someone begins to have demonic power over them. Such a destructive force ignores the living context in which we all find ourselves. "Blessed are you poor, for yours is the kingdom of God"—even this becomes a detached, classified statement which can be applied, and is indeed applied, in order to enhance the prestige of those who are technologically and bureaucratically in power.

There is a difference between gossip and theology. The presence of the "contrite heart" (Ps. 51:17) makes the distinction between gossip and theology. Contrite heart? Yes. It is the heart shaken by the sincerity and reliability of the crucified Lord. When the one who "saved others but cannot save himself" touches us, the necessity of repentance comes to us. The crucified Christ judges our technological and bureaucratic gossips. With his mutilated hands he disapproves of our gossips. A theology which is not rooted in the contrite heart is gossip. It is irresponsible talk. It may be an impressive theological system with tremendous intellectual cohesion and abundant relevant information. Yet it may be a gossip and not a theology. Our world conferences of Christian churches are impressive, yet it is possible that what is said there may be a gossip and not a theology.

One of the prevalent gossips is a talk of ascribing all good things to us Christians and bad things to others. "Behold, I send you out as sheep in the midst of wolves..." (Matt. 10:16). Immediately we think that we are sheep and the other people are wolves. We seldom stop and think that we can be rapacious wolves eating up sheep. Do we know how the Christians destroyed the Jewish people, for instance, through the centuries? Have you thought how the Christians looked down on the people of other great faiths? When we look down on something, we will soon find ourselves planning to destroy it.

Will not action save us from gossip? Yes, if it is action which is touched by the crucified Christ. When his mutilated hands hold us, we are delivered from the deception.

Then we begin to see the difference between *"he saved others*—he cannot save himself" and *"he saves himself*—he cannot save others". Deception takes place when we think we are other-oriented, while in truth we are self-oriented. The mutilated hands of Christ are sincere and reliable. "For the foolishness of God is wiser than men, and the weakness of God is stronger than men" (I Cor. 1:25).

Is the church performing the mission and evangelism of God with the mutilated hands? Are the resources of the church managed by attractive hands or by mutilated hands? Are we free from "teachers' complex"? Do we have a crusading mind or a crucified mind? Are not the mutilated hands themselves the resource that is given to the church by her head, the crucified Lord?

Beware lest you say in your heart, "My power and the might of my hand have gotten me this wealth, you shall remember the Lord your God for it is he who gives you power to get wealth; that he may confirm his covenant which he swore to your fathers, as at this day" (Deut. 8:17, 18).

The crucified Christ who is the centre is always in motion towards the periphery; he challenges the power of religious and political idolatry.

"My God, my God, why hast thou forsaken me?"

"Centre" is a fascinating subject to think about. Many cities have their centres. The palace sits at the centre of Tokyo. I can make the same observation of Bangkok. I have difficulty, however, to find the centre in New York. It is in that sense that New York is a psychologically unsettling city in which to live. I lived in a small university city in New Zealand for five years. The city is located near the southern tip of the South Island. In this end-of-the-world city there is a beautiful centre area called the Octagon. The Octagon is the centre of the whole city and of the countryside beyond. There one finds shopping complexes, post office, court, city hall, church and so on. To make contact with the centre is to come into contact with salvation. The centre is the point of salvation. It is there that the confusing reality of life finds a point of integration and meaning.

The church believes that Jesus Christ is the centre of all peoples and all things. "He was in the beginning with God; all things were made through him, and without him was not anything made that was made" (John 1:2, 3).

But he is the centre who is always in motion towards the periphery. In this he reveals the mind of God who is concerned about the people on the periphery.

"When you make your neighbour a loan of any sort, you shall not go into his house to fetch his pledge. You shall stand outside, and the man to whom you make the loan shall bring the pledge out to you. And if he is a poor man, you shall not sleep in his pledge; when the sun goes down, you shall restore to him the pledge that he may sleep in his cloak and bless you; and it shall be righteousness to you before the Lord your God" (Deut. 24:10-13).

Jesus was the centre person laid in a manger "because there was no place for them in the inn" (Luke 2:7). He "came not to call the righteous [respectable] but sinners [outcasts]" (Mark 2:17). Jesus Christ is the centre becoming periphery. He affirms his centrality by giving it up. That is what this designation "crucified Lord" means. The Lord is supposed to be at the centre. But he is now affirming his lordship by being crucified! "Jesus also suffered outside the gate" (Heb. 13:12).

His life moves towards the periphery. He expresses his centrality in the periphery by reaching the extreme periphery. Finally on the cross, he stops this movement. There he cannot move. He is nailed down. This is the point of ultimate periphery. "My God, my God, why hast thou forsaken me?" (Mark 15:34). He is the crucified Lord. "Though he was in the form of God, he did not count equality with God a thing to be grasped, but emptied himself" (Phil. 2:6-7). From this uttermost point of periphery he establishes his authority. This movement towards the periphery is called the love of God in Christ. In the periphery his authority and love meet. They are one. His authority is substantiated by love. His love is authoritative. In the periphery this has taken place, as in the periphery the sincerity and reliability of Christ were demonstrated.

In the sixth century B.C. the people of Judah were threatened by the invading army of Babylonia. This pagan army, the people thought, could not touch the holy city of God. In this centre city is the temple of God, the sacred centre of all the traditions of Israel. Jerusalem is therefore safe. It is the divinely protected centre. It is the seat of "religion" and the kings. "This is the temple of the Lord, the temple of the Lord, the temple of the Lord." "Do not trust these deceptive words" says Jeremiah. Jerusalem was destroyed in 587 B.C. The people of Tokyo in the twentieth century recited "This is the palace of the sacred emperor, the palace of the sacred emperor, the palace of the sacred emperor" in the face of the powerful American army. "Do not trust in these deceptive words." Tokyo was destroyed in 1945.

The altar and the throne have been related to each other far more intimately than we may admit. Common to both of them is the feature of centrality. In the map of religion an altar stands at the centre. In the map of politics the throne occupies the centre point of power. From these centres both exercise power and authority. But the mere recitation of the power of the altar and the throne is, according to Jeremiah, a deception. In religion we say that altar will automatically protect us. In politics we say that throne will automatically protect us. They do not! Look at Jerusalem of B.C. 587 and Tokyo of A.D. 1945!

Until 1945 the imperial throne was called "the throne coeternal with the universe". In what is termed the "Treaty", promulgated on August 22, 1910, on Japan's relationship with Korea, Article 1 has this to say:

His Majesty the Emperor of Korea makes the complete and permanent cession to His Majesty the Emperor of Japan of all rights of sovereignty over the whole of Korea.

By the time this "complete and permanent cession" came to an end in 1945(!), the fanatic Japanese emperor worship cult had become the centre of the Japanese people's life. This cult placed the emperor at the centre of the whole universe and asked that all who are on the periphery bow before this central personage of the imperial glory. For the sake of the glory of the centre it demanded sacrifice from the periphery. The 35 years of colonial history of Korea under Japan were marked by brutal exploitation and destruction. In this politics of the emperor worship, the periphery was there only to be sacrificed. The centre maintained its centrality by affirming centrality and staying at the centre. The centre engaged in self-idolatry. The Japanese emperor up to 1945 was thought to be the highest person in both religious (he was a god manifest) and political (he had absolute power) worlds. This imperial centrism is in rapid resurgence today!

Over against such destructive centrism in the world of religion and politics, the crucified Christ affirms his centrality by giving it up for the sake of the periphery. This is his way to *shalom*. Jesus Christ is not "imperial". His kingdom does not work in the way that the Japanese empire worked and destroyed itself. "My kingship is not from the world" (John 18:36).

Theological education

Jesus Christ moves towards the periphery. He thus bestows his authority upon the periphery. With the presence of the centre at the periphery the periphery becomes dynamic. Our thoughts on mission, evangelism and theological education must be examined in the light of the periphery-oriented authority of Jesus Christ. Historically the West has been the centre of theological education, mission and evangelism. Jesus Christ has been mostly presented to the wider world in the mould of the mind of the West. Languages such as Spanish, French, English and German are the centre languages in this Christian enterprise. Cultural and religious zones which are outside of these languages have been asked to adjust themselves to the image of Jesus Christ presented in these languages. These "centre-theologies" (of the "blond Jesus") have had more than one hundred years of painful irrelevance to the world outside of the West, and most likely to the West itself. Even today most of the world's Christians, including their theologians, believe that somehow Jesus Christ is more present in America than in Bangladesh, and therefore America is the centre and Bangladesh is a periphery. By thus thinking, they unwittingly entertain the idea that in all our Christian mission, evangelism and theological education, America is the standard for all. Such centre-complex, coupled with teacher-complex, must be judged in the light of the periphery-oriented authority of Jesus Christ. Christians have only one centre. He is Jesus Christ, who affirmed his centrality by giving it up! It is he who stands at the centre of our obedience and worship. As we worship him, we are taken into his centrality which he gave up.

There is an important stream of Christian literature coming from the innumerable competent theologians today. But the authors of these important works are doing their best to discourage *people* from reading them. These books are replete with the most difficult theological words and concepts. It takes a Ph.D. in theology to digest them. The theme of the periphery is discussed with the full-blown centre-language. In general the sin of theologians is that they write books for fellow theologians and thus they build up a special circle in which they admire each other. So, too, far too many students from the world outside of the West come to the West to receive their theological education. But the majority of theological schools in the West are still dreaming a happy dream of centre-complex. Such a dream is not innocent. It is harmful to the living reality of the Church Universal. It is idolatrous because it is elevating the tribal to the universal. The crucified Lord is as much present in Jakarta as in Jerusalem, in Rangoon as in London. The dynamism of the periphery judges our centre-complex.

In the light of the periphery-oriented authority of the crucified Lord, how do we see the people who are living in the prosperous sections of this world today?

"People are wasted"

Affluence and an inhuman level of poverty are coexisting side by side in this world. One section of humanity is dying from overeating and the other from starvation. This global tragedy is reflected often within the nations. The Philippines have a tiny minority of Filipinos who are enjoying enormous wealth while the absolute majority of the people are struggling in despairing poverty. In Thailand, Thai people exploit most brutally their fellow Thais, exhibiting a kind of internal exploitation which came to be known as

"Herodianism", some Filipinos have named it. These exploitative systems are all supported by the guns of the military. Even in so-called democratic countries there exists an impoverished class "colonized" by the affluent.

The Sixth Assembly of the Christian Conference of Asia, in June 1977, describes "The Asian Situation":

The dominant reality of Asian suffering is that people are wasted:

Wasted by hunger, torture, deprivation of rights.

Wasted by economic exploitation, racial and ethnic discrimination, sexual suppression.

Wasted by loneliness, nonrelation, noncommunity.

The conference focused its attention on the people. All other kinds of wastes in this world contribute to this chilling result: *the people are wasted*. That "people are wasted" is, according to this Asian conference, the fundamental pain of Asia. There are multiple reasons for the wasting of people. All these reasons point to the economic exploitation which is going on in our world on both the local and international levels. There is no doubt that those who are starved because of poverty are persons wasted. The conference report continues to say, "In this situation we begin by stating that people are not to be wasted, people are valuable, made in God's image..." If a person is starved, the living image of God is wasted. There is a difference between a hungry dog and a hungry man. The hungry man feels an assault upon his human dignity; the dog does not. For the human person, physical humiliation means spiritual humiliation. The empty stomach means an insult to the image of God.

After this fundamental observation, we are invited to take a second look at the focus point of the Asian conference: "People are wasted". There are people who, in their own economic zone, are neither poor nor rich. They have something to eat, somewhere to sleep and something to wear, and they may have more in addition to these. But it is obviously possible that their lives also can be wasted. They are not starved. But they can be wasted. Physical comfort does not necessarily mean spiritual fulfilment. Then there are those who are rich. Ordinarily we think that the lives of rich people are not wasted. But this point cannot be made so easily. Wealth enslaves man and woman. I am not prepared to say that the enslavement by wealth and enslavement by poverty are identical. They are not. We all desire to be enslaved by wealth but we do not want to be enslaved by poverty. The former is a sweet enslavement; the latter is a bitter enslavement. But enslavement is enslavement. The image of God suffers from different reasons. The people who are poor must be emancipated from their grinding poverty. The people who are neither poor nor rich must be emancipated from their "wasting life". The people who are rich must be emancipated from their enslavement to wealth. Life must not be wasted.

Behold, Lord, the half of my goods I give to the poor; and if I have defrauded anyone of anything, I restore it fourfold. And Jesus said to him, "Today salvation has come to this house" (Luke 19:9).

People who are wasted are on the periphery. The poor are periphery. Jesus moves towards them. People who are not poor can be at the periphery if their lives are wasted. Jesus moves towards them. But often people who are not poor do not think that they are at the periphery. Then the irony of *Mark* 2:17 is applied:

Those who are well have no need of a physician, but those who are sick; I came not to call the righteous, but sinners.

Indiscriminate God

Jesus Christ, who has travelled to the extreme periphery, has authority to speak to and heal those who are "wasting their lives" under many types of enslavement. "The Word became flesh and dwelt among us" (John 1:14) to show the supreme importance of people in the mind of God. The name of Jesus Christ represents more than an economic analysis of society by Karl Marx. "The Word became flesh and dwelt among us" does not specify that he dwelt among the poor, or among those who are neither poor nor rich, or among the rich. He dwelt among *people* to save them from wasting life. When we say that God has opted for the poor—he has taken the side of the poor—in Jesus Christ, we must not mean that all others have become the enemies of God. "The Word dwelt among us" points to the mysterious dimension of the "indiscriminateness" of the mercy of God for all. "For God has consigned all men to disobedience, that he may have mercy upon all" (Rom. 11:32). "All men" ("all humanity" in nonsexist language) here I understand to be indiscriminately the poor, those who are neither poor nor rich, and the rich. Here is the depth of God's mercy. It is so deep. It goes beyond any calculation and prudence. It touches upon a risky quality of indiscriminateness. "He makes his sun rise on the evil and on the good, and sends rain on the just and on the unjust" (Matt. 5:45). He shows his mercy upon all, the rich and the poor. God moves towards the poor; he is concerned about their empty stomach and cold nights. God must tell us who is "in his view" his enemy. There are millions of "pious Christians" throughout the world who benefit from the status quo of the repressive regimes and merciless exploitation. All American educational systems, including theological seminaries, are entrapped in the capitalistic system by receiving capitalist interest for their endowment funds. Shall we just call military juntas, capitalists and exploiters "enemies" of God? How about other millions who accept the fruits of such unjust social systems? What kind of money is it that brought us to Melbourne from the four corners of the world? Pure uncontaminated money? Is there such money in this world today? The overwhelming majority of "good Christians" are busy living a kind of Christian spirituality which does not demand social justice. Isn't it true that Christians are, in fact, supporting the oppressive regimes? "For the time has come for judgement to begin with the household of God" (I Pet. 4:17).

Even the most careful theological language about the poor is paternalistic. Paternalism often breeds idolatry. When the poor are elevated to the height of history, when all humanity is centred by the presence of the poor, when the poor are the only mediators through whom we can come to God in Christ, a new idolatry has been created of which the poor themselves are unaware. Then humanity is divided into two faceless sections: the rich and the poor. Faceless divisions are highly dangerous. One side is "absolutized" against the other. "The Word became flesh and dwelt among us" means that the coming of Jesus Christ eliminates this freelanming, He means a community rather than mass. He is against "wasting life" in *all* life contexts. In the parable of the Pharisees and the publican in the temple (Luke 18:9-14) it is possible that the religious Pharisee is far poorer than the secular businessman tax-collector who said, "God, be merciful to me, a sinner".

Jesus, in this particular parable, does not touch on the economic background of these two spiritually contrasting people. Again, in the parable of the Good Samaritan (Luke 10:25-37) one can imagine—and certainly it is possible—that the Samaritan who was able to pay medical expenses for the man beaten on the highway is perhaps economically a little stronger than the religious persons who passed by. Our world is full of confusing and complex social situations, and it is there "the Word became flesh and dwelt among us".

"The Word became flesh and dwelt among us." He "pitched his tent" among us. He did not live in the "big house" (*pharaoh* means "the great house"). He lived his life as a "periphery man". As the periphery man he challenged the idolatry in religion and politics and confirmed the deeper tradition of "God, be merciful to me, a sinner" in the life of the synagogue and the church. When these words are said by someone, whether he or she, rich or poor, they can challenge the existing unjust social order, because such souls are free from idolatry. They do not try to be peaceful when there is no peace. They are "broken souls" (Psalm 51:17). The broken souls can become community-minded souls. They are equipped with keen perception on the whereabout and works of social injustice. We must not understand these words of humble cry to God only as personalistic, spiritual words which do not have much to do with the world's reality. These words of the tax-collector can challenge human religious and political power. The idolatry-free dynamism of periphery is at work in these words. They point to the authority of Jesus Christ.

In the crucified Christ the reign of God has come: the *scars of Jesus* challenge the power of the good that suffocates the best.

The scars of Jesus

The Apostle Paul concludes his Letter to the Galatians with these words:
For neither circumcision counts for anything, nor uncircumcision, but a new creation... Henceforth let no man trouble me; for I bear on my body the marks of Jesus (Gal. 6:15, 17).

"The marks" *(stigmata)* means brands stamped on slaves. It must mean the scars Paul received from beatings as narrated in II Corinthians 11:23-28. "Five times I have received at the hands of the Jews the forty lashes less one. Three times I have been beaten with rods; once I was stoned." These scars he carried on his body were a symbol of communion between Paul and the crucified Christ. It was as if they were the scars of "a new creation". With these scars he was freed from the need for circumcision or uncircumcision. He speaks then unusual words about this most honoured institution of all, circumcision. Not scars of circumcision but scars of Jesus are now the central reality for him.

The Christian church is an institution. Life is never free from institution. Vitality which rejects institutional form is a wild vitality. Where there is life there is institution. Then the question is, what kind of institution is it that expresses the power of life and the imagination of life? Creative institution? Destructive institution? Lively one? Petrified one? In the face of the approaching army of Babylonia, the people of Judah recited the name of the most sacred institution, the temple of the Lord. Jerusalem could not be destroyed by the pagan army, they thought, because it had the most sacred institution in it. But it was destroyed. Jeremiah gave the reason for the destruction of Jerusalem:
If you truly execute justice one with another, if you do not oppress the alien, the fatherless or the widow, or shed innocent blood in this place, and if you do not go after other gods to your own hurt, then I will let you dwell in this place, in the land that I gave of old to your fathers for ever (Jer. 7:6-7).

Even the most sacred institution cannot protect the nation if the life that began the institution is not faithfully demonstrated. In other words, the temple of the Lord will protect the population if they practice the inner message of the institution: "Execute justice one with another". Institutional power is rooted in the ethical responsibility of that institution. "Do not oppress the alien, the fatherless or the widow." Then the institution of the temple of God becomes meaningful to the people of Judah. Jesus stands in this tradition.

Come to the altar twice

So if you are offering your gift at the altar, and there remember that your brother has something against you, leave your gift there before the altar and go; first be reconciled to your brother, and then come and offer your gift (Matt. 5:23-24).

You must come to the altar "twice". The first time you come, the living spirit for which the altar is an institutional expression will make you aware of what this "coming to the altar" means. There you will remember that "your brother has something against you", not that you have something against your brother, because the altar stands for the judgement upon egocentric perspective. Then you must take a side trip, as it were. "First be reconciled to your brother." Then come back and continue your act of offering your gift at the altar. Practise what the altar stands for. Practise what the temple of the Lord stands for. If the scars of Jesus, and not the circumcision, are the fundamental symbol for the Church, the Church must express the meaning of those scars in the way it exists and acts. The Church must show this original quality through its institutional life. Bad institution is that which muffles the meaning of the temple of the Lord. Good institution is then the opposite of this, namely, that in which the original intention of the temple of the Lord will come out clearly to the hearing and seeing of the people.

Where there is life there is institution. But the Church is a strange institution created by the crucified Lord. It is this image of the crucified Lord that must come out through the life of the institutional church. It is the life that accepts humiliation in order to save others from humiliation. That life must be seen in the life of the institutional church. The crucified Christ cannot be easily institutionalized. He cannot be tamed so easily. He is always able to crucify the institution built in his name. He visits his Church as the crucified Lord. He asks his Church to have a crucified mind rather than a crusading mind. The crucified mind is not a neurotic mind. It is a mind ready to accept humiliation in order to save others from humiliation. It is a strongly community-directed mind. It is a healthy mind. The Church is inspired to come to the people with the crucified mind, not with the crusading mind. It is asked to follow the crucified Lord instead of running ahead of him.

But the power of the crucified Christ expresses itself in its own way of "crusading". It is a "crusade" deeply rooted in the crucified Lord. Such a "crusade" is different from the ordinary crusade. It is a crusade staged by the mind that accepts humiliation in order to save others from humiliation! It does not bulldoze others. It takes the way of suffering. "Your kingdom come!" has a history of suffering.

In our world today, "good Christian people" are those who distanced themselves from the suffering of the world. They talk about the suffering and give some charity to alleviate inhuman conditions of life. They are upright, honest, hard-working and church-going. They are good people. But it is these "good people" who innocently support the oppressive global system of exploitation. They live in "cruel innocence", as Michael Harrington says. They are concerned about their Christian spirituality. They live a "rich internal life" with Jesus Christ. But their goodness is that of the bystanders. Millions of times the prayer "Your kingdom come!" is said by these good people who live in "cruel innocence". This is perhaps one of the greatest visible and invisible institutions of Christianity. These good Christians are bulldozing others!

This prayer, "Your kingdom come!", does not originate in the Christian Church. The Church inherited it from Israel. The Jews prayed, "Your kingdom come". They prayed this prayer through the catastrophe of the holocaust in recent history. It was not a cheap prayer. Today when we pray this prayer we must know that we are saying it after Auschwitz and the Cambodian genocide. The world is replete with hideous lethal weapons. It is in this world that we pray this prayer. We must know the tragic brokenness of the world when we say this prayer. With the scars of Jesus that heal the wounds of the world, we say "Your kingdom come".

MELBOURNE CONFERENCE SECTION REPORTS

SECTION I

Good News to the Poor

The Poor and the Rich and the Coming of the Kingdom

1. The kingdom of God which was inaugurated in Jesus Christ brings justice, love, peace and joy, and freedom from the grasp of principalities and powers, those demonic forces which place human lives and institutions in bondage and infiltrate their very textures. God's judgement is revealed as an overturning of the values and structures of this world. In the perspective of the kingdom, God has a preference for the poor.

Jesus announced at the beginning of his ministry, drawing upon the Word given to the prophet Isaiah, "The Spirit of the Lord is upon me, because he has anointed me to preach good news to the poor..." (Luke 4:18). This announcement was not new; God had shown his preference for the poor throughout the history of Israel. When Israel was a slave in Egypt, God sent Moses to lead the people out to the land which he had promised, where they established a society according to God's revelation given through Moses, a society in which all were to share equally. After they had come into the land, God required them to remember that they had once been slaves. Therefore, they should care for the widow, the fatherless, the sojourner within their gates, their debtors, their children, their servants and even their animals (Deut. 5:13-15, 15:1-18). Time and again the prophets had to remind Israel of the need to stand for the poor and oppressed and to work for God's justice.

God identified with the poor and oppressed by sending his Son Jesus to live and serve as a Galilean speaking directly to the common people; promising to bless those who met the needs of the hungry, the thirsty, the stranger, the naked, the sick and the prisoner; and finally meeting death on a cross as a political offender. The good news handed on to the Church is that God's grace was in Jesus Christ, who "though he was rich, yet for your sake he became poor, so that by his poverty you might become rich" (II Cor. 8:9).

2. Poverty in the Scriptures is affliction, deprivation and oppression. But it can also include abundant joy and overflow in liberality (II Cor. 8:1f). The Gospel which has been given to the Christian Church must express this continuing concern of God for the poor to whom Jesus has granted the blessing of the kingdom.

Jesus' option for the poor challenges everyone and shows how the kingdom of God is to be received. The poor are "blessed" because of their longing for justice and their hope for liberation. They accept the promise that God has come to their rescue, and so discover in his promise their hopes for liberation and a life of human dignity.

3. The Good News to the rich affirms what Jesus proclaims as the Gospel for the poor, that is, a calling to trust in God and his abundant mercy. This is a call to repentance:

— to renounce the security of wealth and material possessions which is, in fact, idolatry;

— to give up the exploiting power which is the demonic feature of wealth; and

— to turn away from indifference and enmity toward the poor and toward solidarity with the oppressed.

4. The coming of the kingdom as hope for the poor is thus a time of judgement for the rich. In the light of this judgement and this hope, all human beings are shown to be less than human. The very identification of people as either rich or poor is now seen to be a symptom of this dehumanization. The poor who are sinned against are rendered less human by being deprived. The rich are rendered less human by the sinful act of depriving others.

The judgement of God thus comes as a verdict in favour of the poor. This verdict enables the poor to struggle to overthrow the powers that bind them, which then releases the rich from the necessity to dominate. Once this has happened, it is possible for both the humbled rich and the poor to become human, capable of response to the challenge of the kingdom.

To the poor this challenge means the profound assurance that God is with them and for them. To the rich it means a profound repentance and renunciation. To all who yearn for justice and forgiveness Jesus Christ offers discipleship and the demand of service. But he offers this in the assurance of victory and in sharing the power of his risen life. As the kingdom in its fulness is solely the gift of God himself, any human achievement in history can only be approximate and relative to the ultimate goal—that promised new heaven and new earth in which justice abides. Yet that kingdom is the inspiration and constant challenge in all our struggles.

Who are the Poor Today?

5. Poverty is an obvious fact in the world today. The majority of the nations are poor by comparison with the few countries that hoard the wealth and resources of the whole earth. And even within the rich nations there are large segments of the population that are poor by comparison with their fellow citizens. Yet we have had great difficulty in arriving at a common

understanding of who the people are who should be identified as "the poor" today.

Part of our difficulty comes from the fact that, although we live on the same globe, we come from different situations and speak of different realities which, although clearly related to one another, have quite different characteristics (context). Part of our difficulty comes from the fact that, although we serve a common Lord and share a common faith, we read the Scriptures in different ways and emphasize different aspects of our understanding of the kingdom of God (content). We have struggled long with this question and hope that further prayer and study and engagement in mission will bring us closer together.

6. We have been helped by a simple definition given to us in one of the papers: "To be poor is to have not, to experience lack and deficiency... the poor are the 'little ones' (Matt. 11:25), the insignificant people of no consequence. They are powerless, voiceless and at the mercy of the powerful... The dynamics of being poor are such that the oppressed and poor finally accept the inhumanity and humiliation of their situation; in other words, they accept the status quo as the normal course of life. Thus, to be poor becomes both a state of things and an attitude to life, an outlook, even a worldview" (Canaan Banana, "Good News to the Poor", Melbourne Conf. doc. No. 1.04, p. 3f).

Although at times we have been tempted to contrast "material" poverty and "spiritual" poverty, we have found that an inadequate way to understand the situation. Humanity has been created by God as "living souls", and lack of food and shelter and clothing produces anguish and misery, while lack of identity and love and fulfilment can make even the most affluent circumstances unbearable. The Gospel of the kingdom is addressed to whole people in all of their life relationships. God is working for the total liberation of the whole of human life—indeed, for the redemption of the cosmos.

7. We have not agreed on where to place the emphasis, but we have used several ways to identify the poor in the world today:

a) *Poverty in the Necessities of Life* — Those who have been deprived of material and cultural riches. In some situations, this poverty is a result of environmental scarcity, lack of adequate technology and of economies and policies that have been imposed from outside. In most cases, the necessities of life have been expropriated by others in an unjust accumulation of wealth by the few.

b) *Poverty amid Material Wealth* — Those who, possessing material and cultural riches, still do not live in a state of well-being. In both capitalist and socialist states among persons who have enough—and more than enough—of the necessities of life, there is malaise, anomie and self-destructive behaviour that has both social and personal causes. Not all of these poor can be described as the result of unjust exploitation. Some would say that these should not be called "poor", although they are in a situation of need.

c) *Voluntary Poverty* — Those who, possessing the possibility of having material riches, are prepared to live a life of frugality or self-denial, in order to make responsible use of those riches. For some this goes as far as solidarity with the poor in which they voluntarily give up their wealth and security to join themselves with the poor in order to struggle against the poverty produced by injustice.

8. We share a common conviction that God intends all humanity to have the necessities of life and to enjoy a personal and a social state of well-being. We feel that this is what our Lord meant when he said: "I came that they may have life, and have it abundantly" (John 10:10) (fulness of life). They are to have life and to share in his life.

Stories of the Poor

9. We have heard from Guatemala of a campesino (peasant) who in a Bible study in his rural village interpreted Isaiah 40:3-5 in this way: The Lord is already near. He comes, but not even the poor are able to recognize him because they are at the bottom of a pit (barrancos = deep canyons), the pit of hunger, exploitation, sickness, poverty and injustice. The wealthy exploiters cannot see him either, because their sight is obstructed by their mountains of money, bank accounts and business.

We have heard from several nations in Africa that some of the African independent churches are churches of the poor that were started because people preferred to worship in a church where they could feel at home as Africans.

10. We have also heard from an ancient church how it has been possible to live for centuries as a church of the poor, being a persecuted and oppressed minority in a hostile environment. This church has sought to maintain the distinctive spirit of Jesus and not to bypass the way of the cross. Its response in the face of violence has been the way of constant love and peace in Christ. The mission of their church, they believe, is to demonstrate the kingdom and to call others to share in its life with the poor.

11. We have heard from Europe and North America many stories of the ways in which a rich society that has provided all or most of its citizens with enough of the necessities of life still has many persons who are needy—where the human condition of loneliness has driven older women and men to alcoholism, where the human condition of lovelessness has caused many to depend on drugs for solace, where the human condition of despair over the direction of society has made young people choose suicide.

12. We have heard from places in Asia as varied as the factories of Hong

Kong, the villages of Philippines, the teeming neighbourhoods of Bombay and the coastal fishing fleets of India, Sri Lanka and Japan how the decision of some of the churches through the Christian Conference of Asia to be "with the people in their struggles" has resulted in the formation of peoples' organizations that fight concretely for justice and dignity against employers, land owners, government bodies and the far-flung transnational corporations. When the people are organized, they have much to say and their voices can be heard very clearly. In Asia too, revival movements within Islam and Buddhism have reinterpreted their tradition to favour the poor and oppressed.

13. We have heard of the great suffering of innumerable refugees throughout the world. There has been a tremendous increase in refugees in recent years. Many of these are found in refugee camps, where disease and inhuman conditions are rampant. Many others are living in marginalized situations—isolated, lonely, without resources and often without citizenship. Many churches are aware of these persons and join with other groups in various forms of assistance and advocacy.

14. We have heard from Latin America of base Christian communities *(communidades de base)* which have been organized inside the Roman Catholic Church among the poor, both in the large cities and in the countryside. Led by lay catechists and priests who have determined to live among the poor, these groups are able to study the Bible together, share the Eucharist, develop common actions and strengthen the people of their communities in the struggle against injustice. They have become real churches of the poor. They assume the role of active subject inside the church, revitalizing the spirit of community and of participation, and become the leaven of faith in the wider people's movements.

15. We have been shocked to hear during our time together at this Conference of new assaults against the workers and staff of Urban Industrial Mission in the Republic of Korea—including a large number of women workers—in their continuing struggle for sufficient wages, decent working conditions, freedom to organize and to speak out, and the dignity which God has promised to every human being. In this case those in the church who have chosen to be with the poor in their poverty and in their struggle have found themselves the object of opposition from conservatives in the church and from the government. But the more ruthless the persecution, the more the people who come to join them.

The Churches and the Poor

16. The Church of Jesus Christ is called to preach Good News to the poor, even as its Lord has in his ministry announced the kingdom of God to them.

The churches cannot neglect this evangelistic task. Most of the world's people are poor and they wait for a witness to the Gospel that will really be "Good News". The Church of Jesus Christ is commissioned to disciple the nations, so that others may know that the kingdom of God has already drawn near and that its signs and first fruits can be seen in the world around the churches, as well as in their own life. Mission that is conscious of the kingdom will be concerned for liberation, not oppression; justice, not exploitation; fulness, not deprivation; freedom, not slavery; health, not disease; life, not death. No matter how the poor may be identified, this mission is for them.

17. As we look at the churches in the world today, we find some places where a new era of evangelization is dawning, where the poor are proclaiming the Good News. We find other places where the churches understand the situation of the poor and have begun to witness in ways that are Good News. Some of the stories we have mentioned above show the possibilities for a witness with and on behalf of the poor. The base communities in Latin America are churches of the poor that have been willing to share in their poverty and oppression, so that they can struggle to reach a just society and the end of exploitation. Some local churches and church organizations have been willing to redistribute their wealth for the benefit of the self-development of the poor. Some church leaders and denominational groups have been working to challenge the transnational corporations at their business meetings and in their board rooms. Through ecumenical bodies, churches have joined in the search for a new social, political and economic order, and committed themselves to support those organizations, churches and national leaders that share this vision.

18. We have heard of more places where the churches are indifferent to the situation of the poor or—far worse—actively allied with those forces which have made them poor, while enjoying the fruits of riches that have been accumulated at the expense of the poor. All over the world in many countries with a capitalist system, the churches are part of the establishment, assisting in the maintenance of a status quo that exploits not only nations and nature but the poor of their own country. The churches are alienated from the poor by their middle-class values. Whereas Jesus identified with the poor in his life and ministry, the churches today are full of satisfied, complacent people who are not willing to look at the Lazarus on their doorstep. In some socialist countries, although a measure of economic equality has been achieved, the churches have yet to recognize their responsibility toward the kinds of poverty that still exist among the people. And in developing countries, where poverty is the inescapable lot of the overwhelming majority of the population, some churches have been content to make ways for a limited number of

the poor to join the elite without working to overcome injustice. We have also heard many stories of ways in which the missionary enterprise of the churches, both overseas and in their own countries, has been financed with the fruits of exploitation, conducted in league with oppressive forces, and has failed to join the struggle of the poor and oppressed against injustice. We need to become more aware of these shortcomings and sins, to repent genuinely and find ways to act that will be Good News to the world's poor.

19. The message which the churches proclaim is not only what they preach and write and teach. If they are to preach Good News, their own lifestyle and what they do—or fail to do—will also carry a message. In his earthly ministry, Jesus Christ was consistent in proclaiming Good News by what he said, what he did and what he was. If the churches are to be faithful disciples and living members of the Body of Christ, they too must be consistent in what they say, what they do and what they are.

20. We wish to *recommend* the following to the churches:

a) *Become more in solidarity with the struggles of the poor.* The poor are already in mission to change their own situation. What is required from the churches is a missionary movement that supports what they have already begun, and that focuses on building evangelizing and witnessing communities of the poor that will discover and live out expressions of faith among the masses of the poor and oppressed.

The churches will have to surrender their attitudes of benevolence and charity by which they have condescended to the poor; in many cases this will mean a radical change in the institutional life of the missionary movement. The churches must be ready to listen to the poor, to hear the Gospel from the poor, to learn about the ways in which they have helped to make them poor.

Ways of expressing this solidarity are several, but each must be fitted to the situation of the poor and respect their leadership in the work of evangelization and mission. There is the call to act in support of the struggles of the poor against oppression. This means support across national boundaries and between continents, without neglecting the struggles within their own societies. There is the call to participate in the struggle themselves. To free others of poverty and oppression is also to release the bonds that entangle the churches in the web of international exploitation. There is the call to become churches of the poor. Although not all will accept the call to strip themselves of riches, the voluntary joining in the community of the poor of the earth could be the most telling witness to the Good News.

b) *Join the struggle against the powers of exploitation and impoverishment.* Poverty, injustice and oppression do not voluntarily release their grip on the lives of the poor. Therefore, the struggle against the powers that create and maintain the present situation must be actively entered. These powers in-

clude the transnational corporations, governments and the churches
themselves and their missionary organizations where they have joined in exploitation and impoverishment. In increasing numbers, those who will claim
the rewards that Jesus promised to those who are persecuted or the martyr's
crown of victory in today's world are those who join the struggle against
these powers at the side of the poor.

c) *Establish a new relationship with the poor inside the churches.* Many of
the poor belong to the churches, but only the voices of a few are heard or
their influence felt. The New Testament churches were taught not to be
respecters of persons but many churches today have built the structures of
status, class, sexual and racial division into their fellowship and organization.
The churches should be open to the presence and voice of the poor in their
own life. The structures of mission and church life still must be changed to
patterns of partnership and servanthood. This will require a more unified
mission outreach that does not perpetuate the wastefulness and confusion of
denominational divisions. The lifestyles of both clergy and lay leaders need to
be changed to come closer to the poor. The churches, which now exploit
women and youth, will need to create opportunities for them to participate in
leadership and decision-making.

d) *Pray and work for the kingdom of God.* When the churches emphasize
their own life, their eyes are diverted from the kingdom of God, the heart of
our Lord's message and the hope of the poor. To pray for the kingdom is to
concentrate the church's attention on that which God is trying to give to his
whole creation. To pray for the kingdom will enable the churches to work
more earnestly for its development, to look more eagerly for its signs in
human history and to await more patiently its final consummation.

The Kingdom of God and Human Struggles

I. Human Struggles, the Churches and the Kingdom of God
The many struggles in the many places
1. During the course of the CWME conference at Melbourne on the theme "Your kingdom come", we listened to and reflected upon many testimonies on human struggles. We heard voices of people involved in such struggles during workship sessions, in plenary addresses, prayer intercessions and Bible study groups. We made use of our experiences during the weekend visits to congregations in Australian churches. For the section work on the theme "kingdom of God and human struggles", we had an introductory presentation and panel presentation from five different areas of human struggles—relating to the sub-themes of our section. We listened to action reports from local situations, where people are concerned about finding the points of contact and relation between the kingdom of God and ongoing human struggles.

In certain areas the churches are confident about the immediate future. They feel that they have come to a "kairos", a God-given time, in which they can join the struggles for a dignified and meaningful life for all human beings. In other areas the churches seem to be at a loss as to what their specific witness should be. In still others they feel overwhelmed by powers working in opposition to the kingdom of God. They see attempts at individual and communal self-preservation at the cost of others and the setting of far too limited goals for communities and societies as well as for humankind and the world at large. In all these situations the churches must continue to evangelize themselves in order to become ready instruments for the kingdom of God.

In the ongoing struggles we hear the groans of the whole creation in all its parts as if in the pain of childbirth. And we who have the Spirit as the first of God's gifts groan within ourselves as we wait for God to make us his children and set our whole being free (Rom. 8:22, 23).

The ambiguity of the ongoing process of struggles
2. In view of the ambiguity of what is going on in the struggles, the task of the Christian churches, therefore, will be to discern in each place and context

the various tools—outside and inside the churches—that God might use for his purposes.

He has used and uses various cultural and historical, as well as religious and ideological means, for the service of his kingdom.

There is a need for the churches to awaken to their prophetic task in the many human struggles—to say "yes" to that which conforms to the kingdom of God as revealed to humankind in the life of Jesus Christ, and say "no" to that which distorts the dignity and the freedom of human beings and all that is alive.

The churches' calling to live in the midst of human struggles

3. There is a temptation for the established leadership in the churches to avoid confrontation with the struggles of this world on the grounds that the kingdom of God is not "of this world". It is true that it is not of this world but it is "at hand" precisely in a confrontation with principalities and powers as has been clearly revealed to the churches in the life of Jesus Christ. It is our conviction that the churches are called to return to and renew the hope they have in Jesus Christ, instead of succumbing to despair and passivity, so as to be able to join forces with all those who hope.

In the churches' participation in the salvation of God in Jesus Christ through the Holy Spirit, in the sacramental realities of the divine Word, prayers and the Eucharist, they are called to remember and present to God the struggles of this world and intercede on behalf of the world.

4. This should lead the churches to be more sharply aware of their real relationship to the ongoing struggles of humankind and to examine their own structural relations and ideological conformity to the principalities and powers of this world. They should be open to self-criticism and willing to enter into a dialogue with people of other convictions, faiths and ideologies about their own involvement in their common situation. The churches can become aware of what precisely is their witness as those entrusted with the revelation in Jesus Christ, and of where they can, in his name, join forces with other people of good will.

In their witness to the kingdom of God in words and deeds the churches must dare to be present at the bleeding points of humanity and thus near those who suffer evil, even taking the risk of being counted among the wicked. The royal reign of God appears on earth as the kingdom of the crucified Jesus, which places his disciples with him under the cross. Without losing sight of the ultimate hope of the kingdom of God or giving up their critical attitude, the churches must dare to be present in the midst of human struggles for penultimate solutions.

5. The specific task of the churches is to disclose the final revelation of God himself in Jesus Christ, and by the assistance of the Holy Spirit establish such visible signs of the kingdom of God as offer new hope to all who long for a more human world. Among many young people, in particular, there is a search for reconciliation in the world today. As Christ has come not for a part but for the whole of humanity, the churches must be a means of reconciliation in the midst of human struggles; this will make it necessary to take very specific stands in struggles and conflicts.

Above all the churches have the privilege of witnessing to common hope for humankind and for the whole of creation in the life and death, resurrection and ascension of the Son of God, and that the coming of the kingdom of God is linked with the turning of human minds to Christ as Lord of the kingdom.

II. The human struggles facing the churches today

6. In the five subsections, the areas we have concentrated on and the way we have dealt with the problems involved vary a great deal. In order not to lose the concreteness of our reflections and suggestions, however, we present each area of concern under its own heading.

A. *The kingdom of God and the struggles of people in countries searching for liberation and self-determination*

7. We find ourselves as churches and individual Christians involved in and a part of peoples' struggles for liberation and self-determination in our own countries. This means that we and the churches we belong to must awaken to the role we are playing in these struggles and be ready to look for God's presence in what is happening, even when he surprises us.

The liberating Gospel in the life of the churches

8. It is always necessary for the churches to return to a full understanding of the Gospel as a proclamation of a message to the world and, at the same time, a proclamation of a way of life. The churches are true to their common missionary task of bringing the Gospel to the world when they let that Gospel be a challenge to their own styles of life and the structures by which they appear to the world.

We recognize that some Christians may feel that they cannot identify themselves with their churches or their own local congregations as being signs of the kingdom because the churches or their established leadership are not willing to evangelize themselves. When people feel that they have to identify themselves with groups outside the church in order to be a sign of the kingdom, there is a great need for the churches to rediscover their own spiritual resources and to care for those who have joined forces with other people of good will.

We are aware of the fact that there are Christians who despair about the possibility of evangelizing their local churches to respond to the Gospel they are entrusted with. A proverb from Ghana says: "It is impossible to awaken anybody who pretends to be sleeping!"

9. We believe that the churches have frequently supported the establishment in order to preserve their own traditional identity and so have ceased to be authentic signs of the kingdom of God. In many countries the struggles for liberation and self-determination have taken place outside the churches and even in spite of the churches.

In a changing world a church that does not respond to the changes is an anomaly. A church that lives in a situation of injustice but is not able to discover in the light of the Gospel entrusted to it the injustices within its own fellowship is no longer an authentic sign of the kingdom of God. The churches in many places have to discover anew and more deeply what the Gospel as a message in words and deeds means amidst human struggles, and what the role of a church as a servant to the Gospel in a concrete situation implies.

10. Again in some countries where independence or liberating revolution has been achieved, the churches cannot withdraw from the urgent task of reconstruction that these societies must face. The Christians are called to participate actively in the process of building the new society. Nevertheless, the churches, conscious of the eschatological dimension of the kingdom that they proclaim, should reject the temptation to develop an uncritical relationship to the governments of their countries. A church which becomes part of the establishment in a settled society is an anomaly. Church leaders in particular must be constantly challenged by the warnings of Jesus himself of the temptation to use authority indiscriminately.

The role of the churches in the ongoing search for cultural identity

11. The previous conference of the Commission on World Mission and Evangelism in Bangkok urged the churches to formulate their own responses to God's calling, that is liturgies, styles of involvement and forms of community which are rooted in their own cultures. Though this would mean a true dialogical involvement in the local struggles for liberation and self-determination, many churches have not dared to enter into this responsibility. Too many churches are still imprisoned by forms and structures inherited from other countries and are thus not free to establish such signs of the kingdom of God as make use of their own cultural contexts.

The Bible as the canon of the churches' proclamation must be read and acted upon by the people in the light of their local struggles. The churches must live with the tensions between the Gospel and their local cultures. There is the risk of syncretism for all churches in relation to their context, but that must not prevent the churches from struggling with the necessity of relating the local cultures to the kingdom of God.

The prophetic stance of Third World churches

12. The Third World churches and nations often have to answer questions about their alignment, whether towards the West or the East. Such questions are misguided. What must be understood and respected is that the primary option in those countries as they try to witness to the Gospel, is for the poor and the oppressed and not for the political ideology. The position taken by the Roman Catholic Church in Puebla, Mexico, of "preferential option for the poor" is a clear example of this stance.

In Nicaragua the involvement of Christians in the revolution and national reconstruction is motivating the Marxists to reformulate the concept of and relationship to Christians and their faith.

If a church or members of a church should choose to use Marxist or any other ideological instruments to analyze the social, economic and political situation in which they find themselves, it will be necessary to guard against the risk of being subtly instrumentalized by such ideologies so as not to fall into the same trap as many churches have done in relation to the ideology implied by capitalism, and thus lose their fidelity to the Gospel and their credibility.

The World Council of Churches has expressed in various ways its solidarity with the struggles of liberation and has thus become a sign of the kingdom of God to many people. That sign has sustained them in their struggle and because of this the churches did not lose credibility in the minds of those involved in the struggles. This should challenge many churches to a more overt support.

B. *The kingdom of God and the struggles for human rights*

13. In the prayer our Lord gave to his church we are encouraged to pray in solidarity with all peoples for the coming of God's kingly rule and that God's will be done on earth as it is in heaven. In the light of this we realize that the structures of our societies—be it the religious, the political or the economic—have become hindrances to, or have actively repressed or even prevented the development of women and men into the fulness of life, thereby denying people their God-given right to dignity and growth.

The worldwide church is itself a sign of the kingdom of God because it is the Body of Christ in the world. It is called to be an instrument of the

kingdom of God by continuing Christ's mission to the world in a struggle for
the growth of all human beings into the fulness of life. This means proclaiming God's judgement upon any authority, power or force, which would openly or by subtle means deny people their full human rights.

Areas within which human rights are violated

a) *Unjust economic structures*

14. The kingdom of God brings in shalom—peace with justice. Any socio-
economic system that denies the citizens of a society their basic needs is unjust and in opposition to the kingdom of God. The churches have to exercise
the prophetic gift of assessing the effectiveness of the various socio-economic
systems in the world and speak in favour of exploratory models of a new international economic order in the light of the thrust of the Gospel. The churches are called upon to take sides with Third World peoples who suffer from
repressive systems in order to maintain the standard of living of affluent
countries, and with those who are forced into foreign economic patterns.

b) *Voiceless peoples*

15. The churches have a responsibility to analyze in depth various types of
inhumanity and injustice and perceive that some peoples' plights are more
desperate than others. This means responding not only to the loudest and
most noticeable cries for help but to seek out the overwhelmingly oppressed
and silenced to become their advocates and nurturers.

Often the most repressive political and economic systems are not even
perceived by people who live under them because they are not exposed to
other value systems and options for lifestyles. If they become aware, they are
not allowed to express their oppression and their plight because there is no
free exchange with people outside the system. In some repressive societies the
citizens are prevented from exposing and sharing their pain by threats and
reprisals directed against not only spokespersons but also against people who
can be identified with such spokespersons.

c) *Escalating militarism and doctrines of national security*

16. The arms race and the escalation in nuclear capability, the failure of
peace talks and the strong militarism of many national governments threaten
world peace and infringe upon human rights (as is clearly shown in the WCC
Executive Committee document "Threats to Peace", February 1980). This
situation calls the churches to urge all those involved to look upon war
preparations and the infringement of human rights in the name of national
security as countersigns to the kingdom of God. It is the task of the churches

to plead with all governments to ensure, in the name of human dignity, freedom of dissent on conscientious grounds.

We call for a cessation worldwide of the research, testing and production of nuclear weapons. Unilateral first steps should be encouraged by the churches. We also urge the early destruction of nuclear weapons now in existence. We further encourage our churches to support all efforts designed to place an immediate moratorium on the development, use and export of nuclear power until such time as there may exist clear and enforceable international guarantees against the dangerous uses of nuclear power and its wastes. Also urgent is the struggle against the export of and traffic in arms which often foster regional wars.

d) *Gross infringement of the sovereign rights of other nations*

17. During recent years many countries have used their military capability to intervene in the internal affairs of other nations. It has deprived nations of their right to determine their own future and inflicted further suffering on the people. The result is a new critical escalation of world tensions.

As Christian individuals and as churches responsibly working within our societies, we are called to advocate that our governments respect and uphold the freedom of peoples and nations, and avoid the use of military or economic intervention to gain sovereignty over other nations.

e) *Situations where human rights are violated on the false pretensions of ensuring human rights*

18. In many situations the churches as well as the people in general are faced with the false pretensions of ensuring human rights. Christian groups working for human rights, democracy and freedom, have been imprisoned together with some of those they work among on a variety of charges that do not make sense.

A "state of emergency" makes violence and terror the main pillars of the government of many military juntas. Popular movements are wiped out and dissidence silenced. Revelations of mass imprisonments, discoveries of clandestine cemeteries and the fact that certain forms of enforced economic models lead to unemployment, poverty and malnutrition show that the introduction of a "state of emergency" is not meant to protect the poor and the weak.

Similarly, indigenous political opinion has for long been ruthlessly suppressed unless it could be used for furthering the established ideology of separate development. There are countries where the churches together with all other citizens are faced with the fact that the government claims to be pro-Christian and democratic and yet upholds a system by which people are imprisoned or even murdered because they try to organize themselves to solve their common problem. The recent martyrdom of Archbishop Romero and many others symbolizes the role of a suffering servant that some churches may have to take on in this struggle.

Many Freedom of Religion Acts have been passed within our generation on the pretext that such an act will guarantee a religiously plural society, whilst in reality it has been proved to be a major oppressive force for the churches as well as for other religious communities. Sometimes the religious and political freedom is being violated on the pretext that a liberating political system has to be upheld for the good of the people.

Evangelism and mission in the struggle for human rights

19. When the churches and individual members of the churches get involved in the struggles for human rights they do so because they have seen in Jesus Christ as the Lord of the kingdom of God a radical challenge of all attempts at depriving women and men of their human rights. Churches and Christians are called to participate in such struggles as those who witness in their obedience to the unique character of the Gospel's demand for love towards the enemy, forgiveness and reconciliation. Evangelism is part of the local mission of the church in the social, economic and political life of human societies. Thus such participation in struggles for human rights is in itself a central element in the total mission of the church to proclaim by word and act the crucified and risen Christ.

In the struggles for the values of the kingdom, the churches must confront the evil aspects of the transnational companies which are, perhaps, the most potent agencies today for the counter-kingdom of Mammon.

The churches, representing the Body of Christ in their contexts, must also structure themselves in a way that allows all to be partners with God and have a voice in decision-making processes.

The churches must speak out prophetically on questions of human rights but also be prepared to be a people under the cross in their milieu, bearing silent and suffering witness to the hope which is in them.

In the churches it is not individuals who are struggling but Christ working through them and it is through the small events of our daily lives that the wider changes in society may come about in the direction of the kingdom of God.

The churches have to point out these small events in the struggles for human rights as signs of the kingdom and offer them as a hope for the world.

C. *The kingdom of God in contexts of strong revival of institutional religions*

The multifaceted picture of religious struggles

20. In the many human struggles today not least important is the struggle we face in the revival of religions, whether Hinduism, Buddhism, Islam or others. The question of religion touches the deepest points of human self-awareness as well as all the realities of daily life in the struggles of human beings for fulfilment. As general features of the present revival of religion we notice the urge for a reassertion of traditional values, the search for self-identity, the efforts to find a way out of the complexities of our modern time and not seldom also a new quest for religious experience and a missionary zeal for sharing one's convictions. The character of the struggles in specific situations varies greatly. This is true not only of the different religious communities but also inside one particular religion where there are not only differences between geographical areas, but also within one particular geographical area.

The positive and negative elements of religions and religious revivals

21. The question whether God is at work in the revival of religions cannot be answered by a simple "yes" or "no" response. In the various religions and in their revival, there are positive and negative elements and even this ambiguity takes on a different character from situation to situation. Wherever a religion or its revival enhances human dignity, human rights and social justice for all people, and brings in liberation and peace for everybody, there God may be seen to be at work.

Wherever people seek God and even touch and find God, there God is certainly not far from any one of them (Acts 17). The churches should not forget, however, that when these criteria are applied to the history and the present life of the Christian churches themselves, similar ambiguities come to the surface.

A humble and open attitude to people of other faiths

22. The attitude of the churches to the ongoing revivals or reassertions of institutional religions will have to vary according to the specific situation. In some countries the situation of the churches has become extremely difficult, particularly where the revival has led to erosion of civil liberties including, in some cases, the freedom of religion.

The prayer of the worldwide church must be that the Christians in those situations may find strength in the Holy Spirit to witness for the kingdom of God in humility and endurance, that oppression can be met with love and that God may use their sufferings to bring about a renewal of their own Christian faith.

We express our solidarity with them as with all oppressed people.

In all situations of religious conflicts the churches are called upon to help their individual members to re-examine their own basic loyalties and to understand better their neighbours of other faiths. On all accounts, the churches must try to find meeting-points in their contexts for dialogue and co-operation with people of other faiths. The above-mentioned criteria as well as the common cultural heritage and a commitment to national unity and development could be the starting points for a mutual witness in dialogue. This presupposes a mind of openness, respect and truthfulness in the churches and among their members towards neighbours of other faiths but also courage to give an account of the hope we have in Jesus Christ as our Lord.

23. As has been pointed out in the Guidelines on Dialogue, received by the Central Committee of the WCC, Jamaica 1979, a dialogical approach to neighbours of other faiths and convictions is not in contradiction with mission. Our mission to witness to Jesus Christ can never be given up. The proclamation of the Gospel to the whole world remains an urgent obligation for all Christians and it should be carried out in the spirit of our Lord, not in a crusading and aggressive spirit.

"Let us behave wisely towards those outside our number; let us use the opportunity to the full. Let our conversation be always full of grace and never insipid; let us study how best to talk with each person we meet" (Col. 4:5, 6).

D. *The kingdom of God in the context of countries with
   centrally planned economies*

24. The frequent inconsistency of the churches, the contradictions in their life, their age-old estrangement from the poor, their entente with power—all these factors have undermined the credibility of Christian faith among many of those who are committed to work for a new world.

This makes it urgent for the churches to equip their members to participate in building a better community where women and men live together in equality, justice and the sharing of God's gifts.

**The message of the kingdom in the context of countries with
a centrally planned economy**

25. The signs of the kingdom of God need to be discerned and proclaimed within every society. The prophetic teaching of the Old Testament underscores the conviction that justice, faith and the longing for the kingdom of God are intertwined and condition one another. The eschatological visions

of the New Testament and the life and teaching of Jesus himself show that the kingdom of God is not unrelated to the building of a society which seeks equal opportunities for all. In countries with centrally planned economies the preaching of and witnessing to the kingdom should help people to rediscover Jesus as the liberator of human beings from all forces which oppress, alienate and threaten them, either in the old or the new structures.

The participation in building up and ameliorating societies with centrally planned economies

26. At the level of practice, faith in and witness to the kingdom of God are not exhausted by participating in the building up and ameliorating of societies with centrally planned economies. Certain lines of Christian action arise not so much from need for political strategies but from the wish to be obedient to the will of God. A truly Christian style of life has to be redefined today, surpassing any identification of Christian faith with any ideological search for moral standards. The primacy of compassion, reconciliation, love of enemy, forgiveness and eschatological vision of history—all these are aspects of Christian faith which are beyond a merely passive participation in building up a new and better society.

A struggle within the struggle

27. To witness to the kingdom of God in the struggles to build a new society is to be involved in a struggle within the struggles, "for we are not contending against flesh and blood". The churches cannot overlook the fact that if the message of the kingdom of God creates faith it also provokes opposition, and they may have to face real problems. They have to be aware of the fact, however, that God, through the coming of some new forms of society, has opened a new page of God's history for humanity. In the presence of some of these new forms of society, God calls the churches to a new obedience, new praise, new prayer and renewal of their own forms of service to their fellow human beings.

28. The experience of actually living both in societies with free or centrally planned economies, has opened a wide field of possibilities for many Christians as individuals and for the churches, e.g. to speak against the assertion of military might in international relations, to support a comprehensive reordering of economic priorities, to undergird the morality of social structure and inter-personal relations, to challenge the values and consumerism and self-indulgence that could develop in any society. In their own faith in Jesus Christ and in their witnessing to the coming kingdom of God they find a comprehensive and liberating means of interpreting the ongoing struggle in its wholeness and totality.

E. *The kingdom of God in the struggles of countries dominated*
   by consumerism and the growth of big cities

The churches as part of consumer societies

29. Capitalistic-oriented society creates constant challenges to the churches in their witness to the kingdom of God. It sets forth false goals for life, exploiting the greed of the people. Christians living in such societies are tempted to acquire more and more wealth and to over-consume. People seldom realize the manipulative forces and powers behind the advertising business.

In such societies there are many, and in some the majority, who are free from the struggle for survival.

They enjoy easy access to all good things as well as to luxuries. These people belong to the inner circle of the system. Others are exploited and deprived of basic needs and resources and thus belong to the outer circle of the system.

Those who are free from material need often find themselves in new forms of enslavement. Quantity of things becomes more important than quality of life and personal gratification replaces concern for others. The search for legitimate security is misused to provoke fear and overproduction of arms to defend the control of the world's resources.

The intensive concentration of economic power attracts people to industrialized centers where many traditional patterns of family and community break down. As the growth of big cities does not provide equal benefits for all, gaps develop between rich and poor.

The Gospel as an invitation to change lifestyles

30. The churches as institutions usually reflect the values of the consumer society to which they belong. The kingdom of God in this situation becomes a challenge to the credibility of the churches. The crucified and risen Christ is a judge of shallow lifestyles and invites the churches to repentance and new life. In many situations today, renewed lifestyles will be the most authentic and unambiguous way to proclaim and live out the Gospel. This will involve forming and supporting groups within the Church which are experimenting with new forms of Christian community and family relationships. It further involves participation in the changing of those structures which cause imbalances in the world today. As those committed to the kingdom of God have become a minority within the secular affluent societies, this task may seem too difficult. Nevertheless, there is a call to those who wait for the kingdom of God to be the leaven in the lump, the salt of the earth and a sign of the kingdom to come.

The witness to the kingdom of God in action for change

31. When Christians convert or change the patterns and structures of life in consumer societies, their witness to the kingdom of God can be taken seriously. This is true also of missionaries who are sent out from consumer societies to developing countries.

The churches are called to conscientize their members about the inter-relationships of the whole world, about the injustice, exploitation and dehumanization caused by the greed for profit and consumption, and provide information and analyses of the effects of the selfishness of the consumer society on its own, but also and even worse, on other societies. A witness in action will mean involvement in the struggles of those in the outer circle: racial, ethnic and religious minorities, women, the handicapped, those asking for political asylum, etc.

The churches will have to promote action and reflection among their members to maximize the use of various gifts for involvement in the affairs of society, including a more accountable control over power concentrations which affect the life of people, such as the transnational corporations.

Special attention should be given to the defence of free and honest information through the mass media which in many countries are increasingly dominated by people who have an interest in distorting the news to con solidate their own power. Christians should be at the forefront of attempts at creating a new economic order and involved in national and international programmes for a more just, sustainable and participatory society. In this context the whole question of ecology is relevant.

The churches should encourage co-operation with groups outside the churches who show signs of the kingdom of God at work on behalf of those who are marginalized by the system of the consumer society.

The churches themselves should take courage to witness to the fact that a general decline in the economy of the consumer societies need not only be a negative thing but can open up new ways of life which better conform to the vision of the kingdom of God.

III. Conclusions

32. The work in Section II on the kingdom of God and human struggles reiterates what the last CWME Conference in Bangkok said, and presses upon ourselves and our churches an even more urgent need to become involved fully in the ongoing human struggles, and become even more aware of the fact that the Gospel about the coming of the kingdom of God is related to the struggles of this world.

We also felt a need to express repentance about our inability to be more specific in particular cases. This reflects both the painful situation many people continue to find themselves in and the sensitivity we feel towards those where specific mention might be dangerous.

The churches have a prophetic task to discern, in these struggles and in the ambiguities which they represent, where the forces of the kingdom are at work and where countersigns of the kingdom are being established. The church must awaken to exercise anew its prophetic role and itself ask for the gift of the Holy Spirit to establish effective signals of the kingdom of God.

There is a need for the churches to change their own attitudes and styles of life and let themselves be renewed by the Gospel which is entrusted to them that they may serve humankind with a true interpretation of what is going on in the many struggles, pointing to Jesus Christ as the one in whom God sums up all things.

The churches have a message that gives meaning to the struggles and a message about the possibility of reconciliation in the midst of struggles. They must spell out that message clearly because there are so many who are at a loss and who suffer evil in the many human struggles which are going on in the places where they live.

The Church Witnesses to the Kingdom

1. This title is a frightening claim, but a wonderful reality. It is frightening because it causes everyone of us to examine our personal experience of the empirical church, and to confess how often our church life has hidden rather than revealed the sovereignty of God the Father whom Jesus Christ made known. Yet there is reality here. The whole church of God, in every place and time, is a sacrament of the kingdom which came in the person of Jesus Christ and will come in its fulness when he returns in glory

2. The life and witness of our present churches is very diverse, and it is not our calling to be judges of their value to God. We can only look at some aspects of that life and witness to see how the church can more effectively carry the marks of Christ himself and be a sign of the kingdom.

The proclamation of the word of God is one such witness, distinct and indispensable. The story of God in Christ is the heart of all evangelism, and this story has to be told, for the life of the present church never fully reveals the love and holiness and power of God in Christ. The telling of the story is an inescapable mandate for the whole church; word accompanies deed as the kingdom throws its light ahead of its arrival and men and women seek to live in that light.

The church is called to be a community, a living, sharing fellowship. This sign of the kingdom is evident where our churches are truly open to the poor, the despised, the handicapped, for whom our modern societies have little care. Then a church becomes a witness to the Lord who rejoiced in the company of outcasts.

There is a healing ministry which many of us have too readily neglected and which the Spirit is teaching us anew. It is intimately connected with evangelism, as the commissioning of the disciples by Jesus makes plain (Luke 9:1-6). It has to do with the whole person, body, mind and spirit, and it must be related to the healing gift of modern medical science and the traditional skills found in many parts of the world.

As the whole church is set in a world of cultures and nations, we have to witness to the kingdom by reflecting both the universality of the Gospel and its local expression. As Christians work together to serve the needs of struggling people, so they reveal the unifying power of Christ. As they honour the inheritance of each person (culture, language and ideals) so they witness to the personal care of God.

At the centre of the church's life is the Eucharist, the public declaration of thanksgiving for God's gift in Christ, and the participation of the disciples in the very life of Christ. It is a foretaste of the kingdom which proclaims the Lord's death until he comes. We celebrate the Eucharist during the "in-between", recalling God's act in history (anamnesis), experiencing the presence of the risen Lord, and anticipating the great feast at the end when God is all in all.

3. In all these aspects of the life of the church on earth we are aware of our weakness, our divisions, our lack of wholehearted commitment and our narrow view of what the church is. We have no proprietary rights on the kingdom, no claim for reserved seats at the great banquet. Therefore we seek the mercy and grace of God that we might be open to all those who are in the kingdom, whether or not they are part of the institutional churches. So we pray "your kingdom come", believing that God alone will enable the church as it is on earth to reflect the light and love of his ruling over the whole created universe.

I. Proclamation of the Word of God

4. The proclamation of the Good News is the announcement that the kingdom of God is at hand, a challenge to repent and an invitation to believe. So Jesus, in proclaiming that the kingdom of God is close at hand, calls for repentance and faith in the Gospel (Mark 1:15). The time has come when the ancient hope as expressed by the prophet Isaiah for that kingdom will be fulfilled. Jesus is sent to proclaim Good News to the poor, release to the captives and sight to the blind, to set at liberty those who are oppressed, to proclaim the acceptable year of the Lord (Luke 4:18-19), as Isaiah had seen in his vision. By Jesus, and in his name, the powers of that kingdom bring liberation and wholeness, dignity and life both to those who hunger after justice and to those who struggle with consumerism, greed, selfishness and death.

The kingdom of God is made plain as the Holy Spirit reveals Jesus Christ to us. The Word has become flesh in him, and his followers proclaim in ever new ways and words the glories of their Saviour. Paul says it with singular fulness and intensity: therefore if anyone is in Christ—new creation! The old has passed away; behold, the new has come. All this is from God who, through Christ, has reconciled us to himself and given us the ministry of reconciliation. It is the kingdom that we proclaim until it comes, by telling the story of Jesus Christ, teacher and healer, crucified and risen, truly human and truly divine, Saviour and Lord.

5. There are false proclamations and false gospels, which use the language of the Bible to draw people not toward God as revealed in Jesus but a god made by human imagination. One part of the church's teaching is to help people discern for themselves this distinction.

6. Proclamation is the responsibility of the whole church and of every member, although the Spirit endows some members with special gifts to be evangelists, and a great diversity of witness is found. Both the church and those within it who are gifted as evangelists are themselves part of the message they proclaim. The credibility of the proclamation of the Word of God rests upon the authenticity of the total witness of the church.

Authentic proclamation will be the spontaneous offering of a church (a) which is a truly worshipping community, (b) which is able to welcome outsiders, (c) whose members offer their service in both church and society, and (d) which is ready to move like a pilgrim. Such a church will not claim the privileges of a select group, but rather will affirm the God-given rights of all. It is the Lord who chooses his witnesses, however, particularly those who proclaim the Good News from inside a situation—the poor, the suffering and the oppressed—and strengthens them through the Holy Spirit with the power of the incarnated Word.

7. The proclamation of the Good News is a continual necessity and all people, believers and unbelievers, are challenged to hear and respond since conversion is never finished. We acknowledge and gladly accept our special obligation to those who have never heard the Good News of the kingdom. New frontiers are continually being discovered. Jesus our Lord is always ahead of us and draws us to follow him, often in unexpected ways. The Christian community is a community on the way, making its proclamation, both to itself and to those beyond its fellowship, even as it shows forth its other marks "on the way". On this pilgrimage, proclamation is always linked to a specific situation and a specific moment in history. It is God's Good News contrasted with the bad news of that specific situation. We therefore affirm present efforts within the church to contextualize the Gospel in every culture.

8. One area of concern is the widespread oppression of women in both church and society, and we look with gratitude and expectation to the work of those women who are seeking to proclaim a Gospel of liberation for both women and men.

9. Proclamation demands communication in deed and word, in teaching, learning and serving. The theory of communication as it applies to individuals and to groups, to listening and to speaking is a considerable area of

study and we value the work of those with technical and theological understanding.

We have considered the proclamation of the Gospel through the mass media, and are grateful to have been challenged not only to use the media for the proclamation of the Word, but also to relate the proclamation to the means of mass communication themselves, confronting the powers in the name of Jesus Christ. This will be a part of a theological understanding of communication.

10. Preaching expects conversion. Conversion resulting from the action of the Holy Spirit may be individual, spiritual or emotional—and these three elements are of vital importance—but much more is entailed. It involves a turning *from* and a turning *to*. It always implies a transfer of loyalty and means becoming a citizen of God's kingdom through faith in Jesus Christ. Conversion involves leaving our old security behind (Matt. 16:24) and putting ourselves at risk in a life of faith. This leads to a degree of earthly homelessness (Matt. 8:20), for even the church is only an emergency residence (paroikia).

Conversion implies a new relationship both with God and with others and involves becoming part of a community of believers. It is individual and societal, vertical and horizontal, faith and works (James 2:19-20). It has to do with those things which may not be bad in themselves, but which stand in the way of our relationship with God and our fellows (Gen. 22; Phil. 3:2-8; Luke 18:22; Luke 3:13). It is an ongoing process.

No one can know the kingdom of God present in Jesus and accept that authority except through the Spirit. This is so far-reaching and decisive an experience that Jesus referred to it as "being born all over again" (John 3:3-8) and Paul as "putting on the new self which is created in God's likeness" (Eph. 4:24).

II. In search of a living community at the local level, or living the future now

11. The church should be searching for an authentic community in Christ at the local level. This will encompass but be larger than the local church community because the kingdom is wider than the church. The kingdom is seen as an inclusive and open reality, stretching to include people irrespective of their sex, race, age and colour, and it is found in caring and fulfiling relationships and environments where people are reconciled and liberated to become what God wants them to be. It is not self-preserving but self-denying. The kingdom is found in the willingness to accept suffering and sacrifices for

others. Also in the willingness to reflect on and respond to needs and ideas beyond our own community, thus entering into dialogue and service. In the kingdom there is love, openness and respect for others. The concerns, convictions, aspirations and needs of individuals and groups are received with understanding. The kingdom encourages and stimulates the development of the unique identity of individuals and groups within the total human community.

12. As Christians, we recognize the discrepancy between the reality of the kingdom of God and the actual condition of our empirical local congregations. Some of us have therefore sought different ways for bringing the fellowship of the church towards a clearer likeness of the fellowship of the kingdom that Christ proclaimed. The institutional church is not to be rejected as it is one of the forms in which renewal can occur. Under the influence of liturgical and sacramental renewal, charismatic movements and parish weekend retreats, local congregations are attempting to realize the fulness of Christian fellowship. Home churches and other small prayer and study groups are providing greater opportunities for more honest and caring personal relationships than can be achieved in larger groups. Such small groups very often become ecumenical.

A particularly vital form of congregational life is known as Base Christian Communities. These communities, arising among the poor and disenfranchised and committed to the struggle for their liberation, express common concerns for identity and a new dignity. They are a gift of God; offering renewal to the church and calling it to a new presence among the poor and disenfranchised.

There are other experiments that arise as alternatives to parish life and that focus on particular aspects of the demands of the kingdom, e.g. seeking a simpler lifestyle, a concern for conservation, or as a political protest. Monastic communities, after a traumatic period of reassessment, are emerging with new confidence in their vocation in the modern world.

Arising from needs within the Christian community, study and research centres, youth movements and various women's organizations attempt to involve their members in the life of the community by focusing on their concerns and challenging the church to recognize them.

Clergy must learn to see themselves not only as the leaders of worship in the congregations but as enablers and coordinators of the various small groups in a district, linking them with each other and with the rest of the church in a united witness.

13. We discover that we must ask ourselves when shall we live in the kingdom, and how do we live the kingdom now. On this we make three observations. First, we are partially living the kingdom. Second, there are

severe limitations in our life. Third, we have hopes for our life that have not yet been realized.

The existence of the Church as it is true to its witness is a positive reality. The Church is the Body of Christ, and the witnessing life of the faithful speaks of the reality of the suffering and risen Lord. The whole life of the Church is oriented towards this witness in its total sacramental life—in prayer, proclamation, service and liturgy. This witness takes on different emphases and importance depending on the context in which the Christian community lives. In living this foretaste of the kingdom life, the Church is compelled to confront the values, structures, ideologies and practices of the society of which it is a part.

14. The local community usually includes children. Jesus teaches us how important they are as signs of his love to us. So we expect our churches not only to continue their work of cherishing and teaching, but also to search for the right ways in which children may participate in eucharistic worship and prayer.

15. The Church often hinders its own witness by its actions as well as its words. It is sometimes an exclusive body. It excludes people because of race, sex, class, those who have handicaps and, through its emphasis on verbal expression, those who are receptive mainly through images. It excludes women through its use of sexist language, and by refusing them full participation, especially in leadership. Class exclusion is very evident in the life of white middle-class western churches and those with that style in other countries. People of different classes feel unable to participate and be heard in this church. Racial exclusion may be direct or indirect; in the latter case it often arises in the same manner as class and cultural exclusion. In a similar manner the verbal nature of the Church excludes a great number of persons who find other forms of expression more helpful. These are only a few of the many forms of exclusion that the Church practices, consciously or unconsciously.

16. Because of the victory of Christ, we have hope. We acknowledge our responsibility for the various exclusions practised consciously or unconsciously. The Church must become a body that is truly open to people. This will occur when the structures and language that exclude persons from its life are removed.

An emphasis on human relationship within the community, which is healing and caring, will speak of the kingdom to which it is a witness. As local communities have courage to examine and challenge themselves as well as the societies in which they live, they begin to realize their witness. Here we see the hopes and aspirations of the people in the surrounding community being taken up in the life of the witness to the kingdom. The Church at the local level also shows witness to the kingdom when its membership reflects the membership of the community of which it is a part.

The Good News, the Gospel of Jesus Christ, remains the witness for which we exist. It is also the measuring rod by which we discover how close we are to the will of God in our attempts to give life to the Gospel in local community.

III. The Healing Community

17. Our Lord healed the sick as a sign that the kingdom of God had come near, and commanded his disciples to do the same (Luke 9:1-6). It is a healing of the whole person—forgiveness for the guilt-laden, health for the diseased, hope for the despairing, restored relations for the alienated—which is the sign of the kingdom's arrival.

Ill-health has many roots: oppressive political and economic systems that abuse human power and produce insecurity, anxiety, fear and despair; war and the displacement of refugees, natural disasters; hunger and malnutrition; marital and family problems; unhelpful attitudes towards the body and sexuality; alienation between the sexes, generations, races, classes and cultures; unemployment; competitiveness; the division of humanity into rich and poor. Basic to many of these factors is personal estrangement from God.

18. The churches in this response must commit themselves in fellowship with those who struggle to rid the world of these root causes. In their healing work they need to give priority to the poor, the aged, the refugees and the chronically ill who are particularly disadvantaged in health care. It is not only that poor countries lack basic medical services. It is also that the medical professions' concentration on spectacular achievement, expensive specialist treatment, and great hospitals diverts attention from basic health care for all.

The churches should therefore:

a) encourage and support community health and preventive medicine, small hospitals in the neediest places and medical care for the poorest people;

b) seek to engage doctors, nurses, patients and patients' families in study to discover how the dignity of each person may be respected, in view of the many ethical questions arising in modern medicine;

c) establish care systems in the style of the hospice care movement, to balance the care systems to which we have become accustomed;

d) encourage Christians to see service to the people as an essential and joyful part of Christian witness in society;

e) affirm death as a part of normal human experience in which the dignity of the person is respected and the hope of resurrection celebrated by the believing community.

19. The local congregation is to be a healing community. The Holy Spirit uses the loving service and open welcome extended by the congregation for healing. By listening to one another and bearing one another's burdens, the despairing receive hope and the alienated are restored. Those whose wills have been crushed receive new courage in the caring group. Worship and sacramental life is a powerful force for healing the sick—especially the prayers of intercession, the proclamation of forgiveness (absolution), the laying on of hands and anointing with oil (James 5:14) and participation in the Eucharist.

20. Today a variety of healing methods is practised. The inappropriateness or unavailability of western health care has revived interest in oriental medicine and other traditional healing methods. There are also two specifically Christian healing developments. The first is the holistic approach—a blend of psychotherapy, medicine, counselling, physiotherapy, the Word, prayer and support groups. We commend this form of holistic care as consistent with Jesus' concern for the whole person. The second is the renewed interest in charismatic gifts of healing through which many people throughout the world have been healed of various physical and psychosomatic illness and had their spiritual life quickened. In some cases, charismatic practices play a major part in holistic centres. Since scepticism or uncertainty exists among some Christians about certain healing practices, we encourage Christians to be more open in dialogue with each other on the subject, so as to prevent needless divisions, but we also recommend that serious discussion take place about what constitutes authentic healing. The WCC is asked to provide help in this respect.

IV. Common Witness to God's Kingdom

Common witness and cultural identity

21. In its mission in any culture, the Church is called to witness to the Incarnated Christ, in family life, in common celebrations, in art and in its struggles.

We affirm the need and the possibility for common witness to populations and groups not sufficiently acquainted with the Gospel, both in cultural groupings where the Gospel has never been proclaimed and in societies where many people no longer believe in the Gospel. We must co-operate in realizing where such populations and groupings exist and how they can be reached. What preparations and initiatives to proclaim the kingdom to them can be undertaken together? We must explore how to coordinate the efforts to witness to these various cultural groupings and how to avoid competition and proselytizing. We encourage all those who are working to enable the Gospel to take genuine root within different cultures.

22. We affirm the need and the possibility for common witness to people of other religions and ideologies, especially in societies where these religions and ideologies constitute a majority or have the power of the state at their disposition. Within this framework, we reflect on the role of martyrdom and the special meaning of common witness in situations of active persecution, whether of one church or of all Christian churches. Even churches that are not in full unity must struggle together to join efforts in securing more freedom of witness for all. No religious community, including Christian churches, must ask for privileges which it is not ready to grant to others. Common witness may be a crucial antidote for the attempt to set various Christian communities and denominations against one another in order to isolate them and prevent them from constituting a presence in public life. Dialogue with people of living faiths can show us how they and we may serve the common needs of humanity. We may also discover that God has fresh inspiration for us in the experience of other religions.

23. We affirm that common witness is especially relevant in pluralistic societies. The churches can best contribute by joint efforts to promote the expression of Christian values in public affairs and in lifestyles. In societies where Christian belief or one church is more closely associated with national identity, common witness provides an opportunity to strengthen the critical function of the Christian faith toward the transformation of the culture. Common witness implies respect for varying cultural heritages and the avoidance of even the more subtle and hidden forms of cultural invasion. The churches use the language of a culture to create genuine and indigenous expressions of faith. The danger lies in an absolute identification with a culture, thus leading to a kingdom of human culture rather than the kingdom of God.

24. This common witness of the Church to the world we celebrate by dancing, singing and eating our food with one another. In celebrating, we witness to the power of the Gospel to set us free. We can only celebrate in honesty if the churches realize the damage done to their common witness by the scandal of their comfortable life in division—we believe that unless the pilgrimage route leads the churches to visible unity, in the one God we preach and worship, the one Christ crucified for us all, the one Holy Spirit who creates us anew, and the one kingdom, the mission entrusted to us in this world will always be rightly questioned.

Common witness in the socio-political context

25. a) Common witness takes place within the context of particular social and political situations, on both global and local levels. The credibility of the churches in large measure depends on the integrity of their moral choices and political goals in society.

b) It is not for the Church to assume the powers of the state; yet the churches corporately and through their members should be involved in common witness and action in the political realm even while recognizing the ambiguities and the diverse views and solutions that may be proposed.

c) Certain social and political situations and options prevent Christians from witnessing together. This may be due to matters of clear and basic principle: in such cases the duty of witnessing leads to a break. If a church member or a church community adopts or condones an ideology of contempt for people in theory or in practice, their stand is an action of contempt for God's love and consequently for the unity of his church, and must publicly be condemned by other Christians. In such cases solidarity can only be expressed by prayer for repentance, by bearing in mind that the oppressors and enemies are, nevertheless, fellow human beings and that there is an element of tragedy, shame and pain in the break in communication and in the sometimes unavoidable recourse to violence.

Common witness and confessional diversity

26. a) We all share in a common basic faith commitment, the core and fount of common witness to the kingdom.

b) Common witness is obscured, hampered or prevented, for example, where:

(i)   interchurch aid in human, financial and other forms leads to cultural insensitivity, church dependency and inappropriate lifestyle, which deform the Gospel, deny a culture and bribe a people;

(ii)   interchurch aid fosters church divisions, when partner churches, agencies and groups work separately and even competitively in mission and development; and

(iii)   interchurch aid disregards existing local churches, their identity and mission within their own contexts.

c) Efforts can be made, are being made and should be made to overcome disruptive efforts on common witness. Such efforts are:

(i)   putting together shared resources to be allocated locally in an ecumenical style;

(ii)   recognizing national and local councils of churches as places and opportunities to share the strength as well as the weaknesses of all members, not seeking to retain the best assets for each church's purposes;

(iii) promoting corporate Bible translation and distribution;

(iv)   developing theological training of clergy and laity ecumenically, whenever, wherever and to whatever extent possible;

(v)   strengthening co-operation in pastoral and diaconal ministries, as a means of practical mutual recognition of common ministry and witness, despite the remaining obstacle in the mutual recognition of ordination and as an appropriate approach to overcoming this obstacle;

(vi)   fostering common pastoral care for mixed marriages, co-operation in the use of mass media, the press and publication, common initiatives in the realm of spiritual life;

(vii) forming life style of congregation and community in accordance with the local context and in reference to the least and the last in society; and

(viii) respecting the membership and the worship of other churches, and discouraging a competitive attitude towards one another or proselytizing among other churches.

27. To fulfil common witness in each and all places, three levels are particularly sensitive and are to be focused on:

a) the local and national level, where the churches should seek and foster unity in and for common witness;

b) the international level, where the relations between churches should be more thoroughly tested towards a fruitful responsible sharing of resources which enhance, not hamper, common witness. We commend the great possibilities of ecumenical team visits;

c) the interconfessional level where promising ecumenical dialogue is taking place.

We recognize the emergence of new lines of division which offer new fields for bridge-building and which open new areas where we must develop common witness.

V. The Eucharist as a witness to the Kingdom of God and an experience of God's reign

Word and sacrament

28. As we speak of worship and of our understanding of what is central to it, we are aware of different emphases, but believe there is a growing

ecumenical consensus. We value the Faith and Order documents on baptism, Eucharist and ministry which help us to see our increasing unity. We would seek to value the spoken word as having a sacramental quality, for in preaching we ask the Spirit to take our crude words and thoughts and make them effective and loving to touch the hearts of our hearers. We would seek to receive the Eucharist as God's word which speaks freshly each day of sacrifice and victory. We believe that as our churches hold together these two aspects of Christian sharing, we may avoid both the excessive intellectualism of some preaching traditions and the excessive ritualism of some who have focused entirely on the Eucharist.

Unity with Christ in his mission

29. "The sharing of the broken bread and the poured-out wine was the symbol Jesus gave to the disciples to show that they were still included in his own vocation to be the Son of Man" (John V. Taylor). They were eager to share the rights of their hoped-for kingdom. But they could not accept the way of suffering which Jesus knew to be his baptism and his cup. So Jesus went to the cross alone. Yet on the very night of his betrayal, when agony and distress were powerful, he offered this food that the disciples might know their unity with him. We are now in a world where agony multiplies, and where there are no easy roads to peace.

On this betrayal night Jesus still invites us to share bread and wine that we may be one with him in sacrificial love. "The koinonia of the church is nothing less than the most literal partaking in the sufferings and the resurrection of Christ, to make up the balance of what has to be endured in order to open the kingdom for others to enter in" (John V. Taylor). To be incorporated into Christ through the work of the Holy Spirit is the greatest blessing of the kingdom, and the only abiding ground of our missionary activity in the world (II Cor. 1:7; I Peter 4:13; Col. 1:24; Gal. 3:27-28).

Unity with the people of God in the fulfilment of Christ's mission

30. a) Communion with God in Christ and community with God's people are two aspects of the one sacrament. Yet often the worshipper who participates in the Eucharist does so as a lonely individual, although surrounded by other people. The congregation is not automatically a community. It may be a collection of isolated persons, each intent on an interior life and a personal word from the Lord. This is particularly a danger in large congregations. It leads to weakness in our witness, for we may have no sense of corporate action in the world but only of private action. We therefore hope

that the churches will regularly examine the nature of their community life.

b) We have noticed that there is very often a distinction or even a division between Christians who are socially active in Christ's name and those who offer themselves in prayer, study and liturgy. Both gracious offerings are enfeebled and distorted by such a separation. Social action may become impatient activism supported only by vague ideals. Worship may become a private indulgence with no active concern for others. We believe that both aspects of discipleship are to be held together in Christian life. Gathering *and* dispersing, receiving *and* giving, praise *and* work, prayer *and* struggle—this is the true rhythm of Christian engagement in the world.

c) We live in a world of divisions, and we have become too easily accustomed to divisions within the church. The fact that the table of the Lord has been divided remains a great scandal. There are many historical sources of this disunity. Yet today it still remains a process of the greatest difficulty to bring all Christians into one fellowship at one table to eat the one bread and drink the one cup. This is a weakness for our missionary witness and its root must surely lie in our disobedience. If Christ invites his people to his feast, how can we fail to celebrate in full communion with all those who love him and are his forever? We plead with our churches to continue the search for that unity which will reveal the Lordship of Christ.

The Eucharist — Pilgrim Bread

31. a) There are times and places where the very act of coming together to celebrate the Eucharist can be a public witness. In certain states Christians may be discouraged from attending such worship or penalized for it. We hear of those who come together at great risk, and whose courage reveals to those around them how precious is this sacrament. In other situations the Eucharist may be an open-air witness so planned that many may see it. Such a joyful celebration as this may offer fresh hope in cynical, secular societies. There is, at the Lord's table, a vision of God which draws the human heart to the Lord.

b) Yet the experience of the Eucharist is primarily within the fellowship of the church. It gives life to Christians so that they may be formed in the image of Christ and so become effective witnesses to him. The Easter celebration (for example, in Orthodox churches), when candlelight is spread from the celebrant to all, and through all to every home, makes this very vivid.

c) In order that this process of growth may be encouraged, we seek through the liturgy to help the Eucharist speak to our condition. Each Christian minister and congregation has to seek this understanding, and we can only give some indications:

Where a people is being harshly oppressed, the Eucharist speaks of the exodus or deliverance from bondage.

Where Christians are rejected or imprisoned for their faith, the bread and wine become the life of the Lord who was rejected by men but has become "the chief stone of the corner".

Where the church sees a diminishing membership and its budgets are depressing, the Eucharist declares that there are no limits to God's giving and no end to hope in him.

Where discrimination by race, sex or class is a danger for the community, the Eucharist enables people of all sorts to partake of the one food and to be made one people.

Where people are affluent and at ease with life, the Eucharist says, "As Christ shares his life, share what you have with the hungry".

Where a congregation is isolated by politics or war or geography, the Eucharist unites us with all God's people in all places and all ages.

Where a sister or brother is near death, the Eucharist becomes a doorway into the kingdom of our loving Father.

In such ways God feeds his people as they celebrate the mystery of the Eucharist so that they may confess in word and deed that Jesus Christ is Lord, to the glory of God the Father.

Conclusion

32. Having examined these ways of the Church's witness to the kingdom, we are compelled to ask, what does this mean for the congregation where I shall worship next Sunday, bearing in mind the global context of our local Christian obedience.

Each of us has to make a personal interpretation in his or her own context. But as a summary we see each of the five chapters presenting a pressing challenge to every congregation.

a) Do we know Jesus Christ in such a way that we can speak convincingly of him?

b) Is our congregation reaching out and truly welcoming all those in need, and all those who seek?

c) Are we expressing the Spirit's ministry of healing for those with broken hearts, disturbed minds and sick bodies?

d) Are we sharing with all Christians the deep concern in our neighbourhood and nation for better ways of living?

e) As we receive the Eucharist, God's all for us, are we giving our all to him and his needy children?

No congregation can ever give entirely adequate answers to these questions. They are always a spur to self-examination, to repentance and to growth. All Christians live in hope, expecting the powers of the Spirit to transform life, and trusting in God's mercy when the Lord comes in judgement and kingly rule.

Christ—Crucified and Risen—Challenges Human Power

I. We stand accused

1. We gathered at Melbourne in obedience to the crucified, risen and ascended Christ, and to examine our calling to be witnesses to him in all the world. It has once again been sharply brought home to us that the colonial expansion of the West is perceived by many "Third World" people as a barbarian invasion. Not all the wounds have healed.

The end of the colonial era has not, however, got rid of the fact of domination. One power has been removed and seven others have come in. Large parts of the developing world have become an arena and victims of a struggle between the super-powers, directly or through intermediaries. Some countries have suffered military occupation, political repression and ideological aggression. Others experience an onslaught from transnational companies who, with local elites, have established new centres of power that now encircle the globe. Patterns of technological and bureaucratic development produce benefits that accrue to everybody except the poor.

Since the CWME Bangkok Conference in 1973, conditions have deteriorated sharply.

The Asian experience was described in 1977 in the following terms:

The dominant reality of Asian suffering is that people are wasted: wasted by hunger, torture, deprivation of rights.

Wasted by economic exploitation, racial and ethnic discrimination, sexual suppression.

Wasted by loneliness, non-relation, non-community.

(Report of the Sixth Assembly of the Christian Conference of Asia, June 1977.)

2. We in Melbourne have had to face the fact that the churches' complicity with the colonial powers, so frequently condemned in the past, has been carried over and continues to the present day. In the consumer societies now flourishing in the rich centres in many lands, good Christian people and others are now, with "cruel innocence", eating up the whole world. A vast fertility cult expects a wild, egotistical, statistical increase, demanding human sacrifice as the price of building and sustaining our industrial cities, in rich

and poor countries alike, for the economic benefit of a minority of individuals. The cries of the hungry are lost amongst the pleasures of the rich.

As representatives of the churches of all parts of the world, we stand accused by our own consciences in the presence of the crucified Christ, at our acquiescence in such suffering and our involvement in this shameful and continuing injustice. We accept this indictment not only as representatives of rich churches but also of poor. Just as the rich churches are being asked to share the pain of the oppressed, so the oppressed Christians stand alongside the accused and share that pain. For we remain brothers and sisters in Christ. This is an expression not only of the unity of the church and the solidarity of the people of God, but also of the pain of realization that we are all part of the oppressive world.

We intend that our repentance should lead, by the grace of our forgiving Lord, to amendment, and our intentions are set out in this report. Only as we stand together in this solidarity can we be liberated from being locked into the structures of power in our societies. How are we to understand these powers in the light of our prayer "Your kingdom come"?

II. The realities of power

3. The world as created by God is essentially good. The proclamation of God's reign is the announcement of a new order which challenges those powers and structures that have become demonic in a world corrupted by sin against God. The Old Testament traces the long story of the need to ensure that human power is subject to law and to constant scrutiny in the interest of right dealing. Jesus of Nazareth rejected coercive power as a way of changing the world. Rather, as signs of God's inbreaking reign, he had power to forgive sins, healing power and an authority over demonic, dehumanized powers. He taught and embodied a thorough-going love and a transcendent judgement which presented a radical challenge to the powers in his society. The religious, political and military powers contrived with the power of the Jerusalem crowd to put him to death by crucifixion. The eye of faith discerns in that cross the embodiment of a God who out-suffers, out-loves and out-lives the worst that powers do. In the decisive events which followed the crucifixion, something radically new happened which seems best described as a new creation. An altogether new quality of power appeared to be let loose among humankind. Those who responded, found that they shared in this power. The inexorable bondage of cause and effect appeared to be broken, and they experienced a liberation which enabled them to face their

persecutors without fear and to claim that the powers had been overthrown, disarmed, in a decisive way, even though the powers were somehow permitted to function in the meanwhile until the final consummation of history.

The early Christians used many analogies to describe what they had experienced and what they believed had happened. The most striking picture is that of a sacrificed lamb, slaughtered but yet living, sharing the throne, which symbolized the heart of all power and sovereignty, with the living God himself. The principle of self-sacrificing love is thus enthroned at the centre of the reality of the universe.

With this as our faith, what is our response to the shameful realities of our world? How must we confront the powers?

III. Our response

A. In relation to powers

4. The crucified Christ speaks directly to the central issues confronting humankind both in personal and political life. An example may help to explain this assertion. Our generation is earnestly searching for the answer to the question: what does it mean to be human today? How can we affirm our humanity and put an end to all that demeans and degrades humankind? My identity is my tribalism. I exist as part of my group. But my tribalism is not only the means by which I necessarily express my being, it is also the way—in the form of racism—in which I attempt to humiliate, to destroy your identity, your being. Only if I can, as it were, die to my tribalism ("letting it be taken up on to the cross"), can I affirm my tribal identity ("in Christ") without demeaning you. In this way, the demonic power of racism can be broken both in individuals and in groups, as the crucified Christ confronts the powers.

5. But, of course, not everyone is willing to die to his identity in this way. Racism and other powers such as militarism, aggressive nationalism and super-power ambitions continue to exert a demonic influence with an immense power of evil. How are we to confront them?

So long as the churches use various kinds of power, they should avoid imitating the patterns of the powers they seek to challenge, or else they will become indistinguishable from them. In the light of the reign of God, the fundamental criterion for their use of power must be the good of the poor and their liberation from oppression. With this criterion, the churches may use their institutional power in any way possible, including through the systems of law or in spite of them. The churches will then run the risk of putting their institutional life on the line. In doing this they are in constant danger of being used by the powers. This danger is not avoided by the churches avoiding involvement in the struggle. To stand aside is to be aligned with the oppressor.

Challenging the Powers

6. There are many different situations in which the churches are called to challenge the powers. In some situations the powers are clearly oppressive; other situations are "mixed", that is to say that at some points the powers are seen to be acting in ways which affirm the humanity of the people; sometimes by the grace of God they positively embody higher levels of justice because of their responsiveness to the needs and rights of all citizens. The criterion for determining the relation to the powers is the extent to which God's creative, liberating and serving power is evidenced in their actions, and the extent to which equality is established. We have aharil from churches that have found that siding with downtrodden or marginalized people and being sensitive to their needs means sharing in their suffering.

7. When the churches challenge the powers in the name of people who are being dehumanized, the credibility of the churches with the oppressed is put to the test. They lose their credibility if they are not consistent in their concern for the people in greatest need. In such situations the churches act as agents of renewal and they must be prepared to be minorities, but they can be creative minorities if they pick up issues which are vital for the community and thus motivate others to join in the struggle for the full humanity of all the people.

Another possibility for the churches to act as agents for transformation lies in their potential to influence attitudes and values and to raise consciousness. This demands in the individual churches envisioning alternatives in such matters as the handling of violence, the sharing of economic resources, the use of natural resources, the application of appropriate technologies and the different kinds of political organization at local, national and international levels. In particular we believe that a radical change is needed in the lifestyles of those who are not poor.

We have become aware that the powers of the world make themselves felt also in the life of the church. The tensions that are present in the community are also present in the church, and the churches must struggle with these tensions in their own lives as well as outside. This struggle can be spiritually exhausting and we have heard of Christians becoming "burnt out". We acknowledge our need to engage more faithfully in profound wrestling in prayer as essential to our commitment. It becomes therefore a missionary obligation for the churches to develop a dynamic spirituality including renewed resources for education and a supportive community.

We do not, of course, suggest that the church has any monopoly when powers are challenged. God has many ways of working out his purposes of mercy and judgement far beyond the borders of the visible church. His instruments often include the courageous witness of those who do not name his name, the actions of individuals and groups of other faiths and in secular bodies, with whom we can join in common action.

Experiencing the power of the Crucified Christ

8. By his resurrection the crucified Christ has changed the context of human life. We have shared many ways in which Christians have experienced and are experiencing this power of the crucified Christ, foremost in the sacraments of baptism, the Eucharist and the liturgical life of the church. The faithfulness of disciples in "small things" is honoured; but this does not exempt us from responding to the wider vision. The marks of the crucified Christ will determine the style of social action of the church and its members; these are unlikely to reflect "short-cut" methods; these marks are powerfully present in the suffering, imprisonment and martyrdom of Christians today. Those who are persecuted for their faith share too in this experience of their crucified Lord.

9. We rejoice that in certain revolutionary situations of our time the power of forgiveness is seeking to replace the power of vengeance. In other situations the experience of losing status has been the source of spiritual strength. Elsewhere, the churches, trusting in the power of Christ, have enabled ethnic minorities to recover their identity and to stand up against unjust government powers.

None of these situations has been permanently transformed; it therefore remains for all of us to persevere in the challenge of the powers. We cannot, however, overlook the fact that many Christians lack the experience of the power of the crucified Christ. Too easily we are overcome by grief, pain or fear, or a sense of outward oppression. This reminds us that we are never free from the need for renewal and the need to rediscover the strength that comes from challenging the powers.

Suffering and violence

10. We believe that the crucified Christ shares in the agony of the suffering of the world and that the risen Christ can bring about an inward transformation of suffering, so that it takes on a power, derived from the power of the cross. A new solidarity is generated among those who suffer together, and new resources are discovered.

As we think also of those Christians who are suffering because of their Christian faith under different political regimes, we strongly urge that human rights and religious freedom be respected in their case. We recognize with repentance that in the past and still today in other ways, we Christians have not respected religious liberty as an inalienable right of human beings.

11. The challenge of the powers and the suffering which results from it reveals the all-pervasive presence of violence. Violence is a fact of life whatever our situation may be. But it is a fact and not fate, and Christians must therefore resolutely resist the power of violence.

We are aware that Christians today choose different ways to resist violence. We wish to affirm the practice of non-violence as an inalienable part of the Christian obedience, and we call on the churches to provide support for all those who commit themselves to the life of non-violence. In certain cases redemptive and vicarious suffering such as that of our Lord may have to be chosen by his followers to counteract violence by suffering love—the way of the cross. Nevertheless there are situations in which Christians find their communities involved in violence and, in these circumstances, without identifying totally with any political movement, the churches should act out in concrete forms their solidarity with those Christians and others who become involved in counter-violence in order to free themselves from the unbearable violence of the oppressors. It is necessary for all to take into account that the global threat caused by increased militarism may in the years ahead give added importance to the option of non-violence.

The difference just described which separates Christians regarding the morality of violence is not a complementary harmony but an unresolved ecumenical debate, which this conference has not studied directly. The urgency of this debate is increased by political developments of recent years. We urge the WCC to give priority to direct study of this problem.

B. In relation to church structures

12. Our response to dehumanization and oppression cannot be, as it were, from an innocent church to a guilty world, for we know to our shame that power exercised within the church (in the empirical reality of its earthly form) can be abused. Judgement must begin at the household of God.

13. We have to discern how we may judge whether power is for or against God. What are the criteria by which we make that judgement?

a) Fundamentally we have to ask how the power is used. Is it used for self-aggrandisement and self-preservation of the community, institution or leader, or is it essentially selfless?

When we look at a community, for instance, do we see it as being primarily concerned with the needs of those who are poor and have no power—they may be inside or outside the community—or is it preoccupied with its own rights, privileges and future? We have to ask whether it belongs in sympathy and identification with the oppressed or whether it finds its home with the oppressors.

b) Turning to leadership, we must pose two questions. The first concerns motive, and asks whether the power is exercised as an expression of selfless love, which serves to release and encourage the gifts contained within the community on whose behalf the power is exercised for the fulfilment of its true purpose, or whether the leadership draws on these gifts for its own purpose. A church within which power is exercised in humility and love stands as a sign of the kingdom to the world.

c) But motive alone is an inadequate test. Those who use power are prone to self-deception about motives and the effectiveness of their methods. Churches and their leaders must seek the perceptions of the community on whether their power is helping to free the poor and oppressed. The exercise of leadership has an edifying purpose: it is to build up the body so that every member may attain to the fulness of the maturity of the stature of Christ, in order that they may realize their full humanity. This, it must be noted, does not imply the development of a new breed of successful super-persons with brilliant brains and exquisite physique. Full humanity has to be seen in the likeness of the self-giving love of the crucified Christ.

d) This leads us to a further criterion. Power which reflects the power of the Christ is a power that is exercised within the community of sharing, built on communion with the Triune God. It is a power that is shared, as life within the Trinity is shared.

The question we ask here is whether all persons, as children of God, participate in the agencies of power, or whether there are groups that are excluded, for example on the basis of sex, age, handicaps, economic circumstances, social marginalization. In asking that question it should be noted that we have to think not only of sharing in decisions, but of the exercise in common of all the gifts given within a community such as, for example, healing, teaching, organizing, caring.

Any use of power that suppresses the loving exercise of gifts is an abuse that ultimately leads to the dehumanizing of persons. The clericalization of the church and the resultant withdrawal of power from the laity is a blatant expression of the abuse of power. This problem is heightened by the fact that when church structures place power in the hands of a few or even one person, a pyramidical system is created with the inherent danger of the monopolization of that power.

The Spirit's empowerment is bestowed upon the whole people of God. Therefore structures and policies should provide equality of opportunity for women and men to exercise their gifts throughout the life and leadership of the new community in Christ. In this way the ecclesial community will be a witness of a new society in which power is shared and gifts recognized as complementary.

e) In this regard, we especially deplore the lack of power exercised by women in so many churches. The Bible teaches that women are created equally in God's image and are baptised equally into the one church of Christ in whom there is neither male or female.

f) To indicate one other criterion, the question has to be raised about the exercise of power through the dissemination of knowledge. An institution or leader exercises control over interpretation, release, and retention of knowledge. Consciously or unconsciously, the truth may be subtly distorted. Highly technical language not only excludes many from taking part in discussion of faith, but can also become an idol to be worshipped. We must ask whether what is being propagated or taught is open to the truth that is Christ, or is it instead closed idolatrously within itself as ideologies are closed.

As we have already noted, patterns of theology, too, can be evolved which are used as instruments of power and oppression, not least because such formulations cannot be used by oppressed people to express their understanding of God in Christ. The fact that different theological formulations are now being developed with accents on God's action in the liberation of the oppressed, of women, of black peoples—asks new and demanding questions of traditional theological expressions.

Money

14. The use of financial power has to be judged by these criteria. Where money comes from and how it is used within the church is an important aspect of the church's use of power. The source of money affects the ways in which it can be used. Some churches receive money from church taxes and/or from their governments. This may place limitations on its use and on the freedom of the church itself. The church can be used as a tool for political power. Voluntary contributions from some organizations and individual sources can also have a similar effect.

By what right do we assume that churches should accumulate funds to be invested? This question, we feel, requires a great deal more consideration than we have been able to give it. Even where this is accepted, the investment policy of the churches can reflect where they stand in relation to the oppressed. Where money for the work of the churches is received from rich churches or organizations, a feeling of dependency can be created and the relationship between donor and recipient affected. Money must be considered as a tool of common sharing. The economically poor have a right to play an equal part in the common sharing of the resources of earth. Church money should be used to support the struggle of the poor to end the unjust society.

Community in Christ and church structures

15. In the New Testament the church is affirmed to be the Body of Christ, a community of believers which assumes institutional form within history. In the exercise of power to fulfil its mission, the church in its members has sometimes engaged in the subtle or obvious abuse of the authority granted to it by God. It may refuse to accept new forms of communal life and mission, especially if they directly challenge such abuses.

In these cases, the community-in-mission, for example, a "communidad de base", becomes a victim of unyielding forms or structures rather than being served by them.

Such "communidades de base", which have in the last twenty years developed in very large numbers, particularly in Latin America, alongside the institutional churches, present the ecclesiastical institution with a challenge, particularly in relation to the structures of power within the church as they now operate. Power structures in the church are often regarded as unchangeable because they are thought to be sacred. Instead of presenting an image of a serving, sharing community, the ecclesial institution can thus reflect the structures of domination and exploitation present in society. It may then take these and reinforce them by a process of sacralization. Where this occurs it has led to a distortion between the practice of the church and its real message as Good News to the oppressed. Nevertheless each new form can be tempted itself to become in some ways a new structure of oppression if it is not constantly open to the changing needs of its members.

16. Without attempting to build a new model, we can underline some of the key features which shape these "communidades de base" and which confront the structures of the institutional church as it looks forward to its continuing task of mission and evangelism:

— the mission of the community in Christ is to prepare itself and all people for the coming reign of God by the proclamation of the Good News;
— the structures at the service of this community must be dynamic, flowing and flexible, allowing for the creativity of all members of the community and the emergence of all kinds of ministry;
— the ongoing process of formation has to be based on the daily living experience of the people for the full realization of their humanity;

— this necessarily requires that the church be politically and socially aware of the struggles of the oppressed and involved in them;
— consequently the Word of God must be read from the point of view of the oppressed.

Repentance and Restructuring in Mission

17. In the light of this we must affirm that the crucified Christ not only challenges the structures of society, but also the institutional churches' structures. An effective response to this challenge is crucial to the fulfilment of the mission entrusted to the church by the risen Christ. It calls for repentance and restructuring:

Churches are tempted to be self-centred and self-preserving, but are called to be serving and sharing. Churches are tempted to be self-perpetuating, but are called to be totally committed to the promises and demands of the kingdom of God. Churches which are tempted to continue as clerical and male-dominated are called to be living communities in which all members can exercise their gifts and share the responsibilities. Churches which tend to be decaying or moribund from stifling structures are called to be living communities in which all members can exercise their gifts and share the responsibilities. Churches are tempted to be exclusivist and privileged but are called to be servants of a Lord who is the crucified Christ who claimed no privilege for himself but suffered for all. Churches tend to reflect and reinforce the dominating, exploiting structures of society but are called to be bodies which are critical of the status quo. Churches are tempted to a partial obedience but are called to a total commitment to the Christ who, before he was raised, had first to be crucified.

18. It would seem to many of us that biblically, theologically and pastorally there is no reason why women should be excluded from any position in the churches. Those who affirm this feel bound to urge upon those churches which exclude the full participation of women in top leadership that ways be sought in which women can be increasingly involved in positions of full responsibility. We have to acknowledge, however, that sharp differences of opinion have been expressed on both sides of this issue, and that no consensus can be reached in our section. We urge that the mission of the church demands a sustained exploration of this unresolved ecumenical debate. A further issue concerns the pyramidical pattern of the structure of some churches. The teaching and example of Jesus on power and leadership is that these functions must be exercised in service. The churches are called to bear witness to this. Traditionally this has been seen as affecting the style with which power is exercised. Many of us feel bound to ask whether it should not also determine the structure of authority. We report that we were unable to

reach unanimity on this sensitive issue which raises difficult questions for all churches. But as the section was asked to examine church structures in the light of the crucified Christ, we cannot lightly pass over this question.

C. In relation to evangelism

19. Jesus charged his disciples with the mandate to announce his Gospel to the ends of the earth till his return at the end of time. "Go and make disciples of all nations teaching them to observe what I have commanded." It is important that the content and mode of evangelism be reviewed in our day in the light of the advance of biblical knowledge, of our own mistakes of the past, and the emergence of new forces and problems in the present. Jesus is the core of the Gospel. "Love one another as I have loved you" is the message of his life and "repent and believe the Good News" was his teaching. This demands a radical change of attitude on the part of all who respond.

Genuine evangelism therefore is the proclamation of Jesus as Saviour and Lord who gave his life for others and who wants us to do likewise, setting us free by declaring God's forgiveness. Evangelism is true and credible only when it is both word and deed; proclamation and witness. To say this is not to suggest that evangelism derives its power from the good deeds of Christians; our failures in obedience, however, can act as stumbling blocks.

In a world of large-scale robbery and genocide, Christian evangelism can be honest and authentic only if it stands clearly against these injustices which are diametrically opposed to the kingdom of God and looks for response in an act of faith which issues in commitment. Christian life cannot be generated, or communicated, by a compromising silence and inaction concerning the continuing exploitation of the majority of the human race by a privileged few. "You cannot love the God whom you do not see, if you do not love the neighbour whom you see" (I John 4:20). The neighbour today also is fallen among robbers as in the Gospel parable. Woe unto the evangelizer who proclaims the word but passes by this neighbour like the priest and the levite in Jesus' parable.

The unity and integrity of social action and evangelism has been suggested to us by the proposition that to issue a political challenge to the oppressor in the name of Christ may be the only authentic way of putting to him what it means to make Jesus Christ the commanding reality in his life. We thus affirm and seek to obey the mandate to bear witness among all nations to Jesus and him crucified. We reject as heretical any proclamation of a discarnate Christ, a caricatured Jesus, who is presented as not being intimately concerned with human life and relationships. Our evangelism must be set in the context of structures for global mission.

D. In the context of mission

20. In the course of our meetings, we have been led to study the significance of the crucifixion of Jesus outside the city wall. We see this as a sign, consistent with much else in his life, that he who is the centre is constantly in movement from the centre towards the periphery, towards those who are marginalized, victims of the demonic powers, political, economic, social, cultural and even—or especially—religious. If we take this model seriously, we find that we must be with Jesus at the periphery, on the margins of society, for his priorities were clear.

Mission and evangelism must be seen in the context of the crucified Christ's words to his own people: Luke 4:18-19:

The Spirit of the Lord is upon me because he has anointed me to preach good news to the poor, he has sent me to proclaim release to the captives, and recovering of sight to the blind, to set at liberty those who are oppressed, to proclaim the acceptable year of the Lord.

This mission and evangelism are concerned with the poor, blind, captive and oppressed and their condition which is brought on by unjust economic, political and religious structures. For many years, the churches have taken these needs seriously in their charitable work. Such charity is increasingly seen as one-sided if it implies a failure to tackle causes and structures.

21. Our study and prayer together on the theme "Christ—crucified and risen—challenges human power" has led us to see special significance in the role of the poor, the powerless and the oppressed. Might it not be that they have the clearest vision, the closest fellowship with the crucified Christ who suffers in them and with them? Might it not be that the poor and powerless have the most significant word for the rich and powerful: that Jesus must be sought on the periphery, and followed "outside the city"? That following him involves a commitment to the poor? Who but the church of the poor can preach with integrity to the poor of the world?

In these ways we see the "poor" churches of the world as the bearers of mission: world mission and evangelism may now be primarily in their hands. Perhaps they alone can waken the world to an awareness of the urgent call of Christ to costly and radical response. We commend these thoughts to the consideration of all who care about mission.

22. A second context of mission today is dominated by interconnected powers which form a vicious cycle.

a) The power which shapes beliefs, attitudes, culture, theology, ideas and values.

b) The organizational power, types and patterns of ministry; nature of leadership; bureaucracy; discipline; etc.

c) The remunerative power: salaries and subsidies; resources for maintenance of institutions; scholarships and similar opportunities; investments; grants of various kinds; budget allocations.

d) The punitive power—law and order: withholding or withdrawing of recognition; withdrawing of support; breaking of relationships and cutting off of finances.

These four powers and their interaction reflect the pattern of a vicious cycle, both within our societies and our churches. In this reality the church imitates the patterns of world power rather than the redeeming power of the crucified Christ.

This cycle needs to be broken if a new starting point of relationship in mission is to be established. The points at which it can and must be broken will depend upon each situation and context. Not only in the "dependent" parts of the world, but also the churches in the "dominant" parts of the world.

Once the cycle is broken a process of change is initiated which challenges all powers—this is true dying and rising in Christ.

Mission at the peripheries

23. The concept of mission being from "sending" to "receiving" countries has long been replaced by a mutuality in shared mission involving a two-way flow between the churches in the industrialized countries and the so-called Third World. We would like to point to the following:

The Christian community of the People's Republic of China reminds us of the power of the crucified Christ to sustain faith and witness apart from the structures of power on which it had long been dependent. The Christian community has long shown the correlation between self-reliance and commitment to the national struggle of the people to achieve justice. As relations increase with other churches, it will be an advantage to all to learn from the experience of the church in China in wrestling with the issues of cultural identity and authentic faith.

24. We perceive a change in the direction of mission, arising from our understanding of the Christ who is the centre and who is always in movement towards the periphery. While not in any way denying the continuing significance and necessity of a mutuality between the churches in the northern and southern hemispheres, we believe that we can discern a development whereby mission in the eighties may increasingly take place within these zones. We feel there will be increasing traffic between the churches of Asia, Africa and Latin America among whose numbers both rich and poor are counted. This development, we expect, will take the form of ever stronger initiatives from the churches of the poor and oppressed at the peripheries. Similarly among the industrialized countries, a new reciprocity, particularly

one stemming from the marginalized groups, may lead to sharing at the peripheries of the richer societies. While resources may still flow from financially richer to poorer churches, and while it is not our intention to encourage isolationism, we feel that a benefit of this new reality could well be the loosening of the bond of domination and dependence that still so scandalously characterizes the relationship between many churches of the northern and southern hemispheres respectively. We must in any case work for a new world order, joining in a common confrontation with powers at the centre.

In this way we have recognized that the churches in each of the three "worlds" bear primary responsibility for mission and evangelism in their own countries and regions, that it is they who are called to assume a critical stance in the name of the crucified Christ in relation to their own structures and governments, and that it is they who exercise control over their own interest as well as over all the means used in the fulfilment of their missionary and evangelistic task.

25. Only thus can we be in solidarity with churches in other regions than our own, in the exercise of mission and the pursuit of justice legitimized as service of the crucified Christ, who challenges all human power. To build inter-church relations without challenging our own power structures, which dehumanize and betray the kingdom, is to build on sand.

We feel a sense of frustration, for much of this was clearly stated during the Salvation Today conference in Bangkok in 1973. But we confess that we have continued in our sin. We need to be converted both as individuals and church communities toward an action that reflects the crucified Christ in the way we use our power in mutual relationships among our institutions, church and secular, and especially in our relationships with the poor, alienated and oppressed.

We challenge our member churches to review their reflection and action in the light of the crucified Christ and his kingdom, facing the international economic system in our world today.

26. In light of the above reflections *we recommend* the following:

a) Churches should engage in a constant dialogue among themselves and with others in order to understand and identify with those who are socio-economically alienated on grounds of race, ethnicity, sex, culture and religion.

b) Western churches have billions invested in transnational corporations and commercial banks. These investments must be turned into a resource for the mission of Christ's Church which is to stand alongside the poor and the powerless. This may mean disinvestment from such transnational corporations and banks. We commend in particular the decision of the Central Committee of the World Council of Churches in

Kingston, Jamaica (1979), to reaffirm the Ecumenical Development Co-operative Society (EDCS) to make money available in soft loans to the poorest of the poor and their development projects. We recommend that the CWME urge its national members to support this new ecumenical channel for alternative investment.

c) We further urge the encouragement and support of church organizations which are attempting to call transnational corporations and banks to a corporate responsibility by avoiding investing in countries which brutally oppress their people.

d) We also urge that the Church support international bodies working for a new international economic order: United Nations, UNCTAD, etc., and the challenge to participate in a global tax.

e) That the development programmes and sub-units of the World Council of Churches—CICARWS, CCPD, UIM-URM, ECLOF, Ecumenical Sharing of Resources, etc., be interpreted and supported on all levels of the member churches of the WCC.

f) That CWME and national or regional councils of churches be called upon to take the initiative in challenging churches to implement better structures of co-operation in mission, helping them to come together for the study of new possibilities for sharing in decision-making, better approaches to mutual support, ecumenical exchange of personnel, and united witness in the light of this report. In particular they should give new consideration to the reasons that led to the proposal for a moratorium. Such reasons have lost nothing of their urgency since the Bangkok conference in 1973.

g) That churches and organizations that receive economic assistance adapt their orientations and lifestyles to the poor whom they serve.

IV. "Do this..."

27. Central to the worshipping life of the community of the followers of the crucified Lord is the Eucharist. In our own ways we remember the Lord's death until he comes. Here at this banquet the mystery of the kingdom takes tangible form. In that act we are brought face to face with the servant nature of the community of the crucified—its need to be broken bread and poured-out wine. We are joined in faith with the multiplicity of Christian experience around the world, and rejoice in those saints of confessing churches whose witness is a sign of the kingdom today.

Jesus' command "do this..." impels us to be faithful to the truth we have already been given. We do not need more words, but the will and the courage to act. We know that such action will lead us to conflict with the powers of this world along the way of the crucified.

28. In the midst of our conference we are aware that we live in a period when international tensions have once more become dangerously intensified, and when the fate of the world is again subjected to great-power rivalry. As we go from this conference we shall not rest silent in the face of the danger of a new world conflict. We shall not accept that the future of humanity should be determined by some of the "great", whatever may be their sense of responsibility. They are prisoners of the demonic game of competing for power. Controlled as they are by the uncertainty of maintaining themselves in power as precarious leaders, they are all the more prisoners of the incensed desire of the wealthy nations to maintain the national privileges of the rich and the powerful and to do this at any price, even the price of a possible nuclear apocalypse. As we go from here in the name of him who renounced everything for the love of all, we appeal to Christians throughout the world to open their eyes to the deadly consequences of the competition for wealth, and to raise a powerful voice for the defence of peace, remembering that peace can only be assured through a just distribution of the world's resources. National egotism is a sin whose wages can only be death, perhaps the death of the whole world. Our faith in the reign of Christ must always exclude the resigned acceptance of fatalism. Therefore we must reject and resist the counsel of despair which accepts the inevitability of war.

Christ is risen!

Come Lord Jesus.

REFLECTION AFTER MELBOURNE

Theological discussions on the topics of the Melbourne conference will never do justice to the spiritual event; that was the privilege of the participants and of many people in the local churches of Melbourne. We remember the warm hospitality provided by the host churches, which included meeting participants at the airport and generously opening their homes to them before the conference started. Worshipping together in St. Patrick's cathedral and participating in the mass rally provided some of the most precious moments of the conference.

The Bible study during the conference provided an opportunity for people to share their hopes and anxieties and to encounter those of others, under the authority of Scripture. Participants coming from the most diverse theological schools and confessional families brought with them, of course, their hermeneutical *a priori*. But the Word of God was able to capture our pre-judgements and open our hearts to the message of the King and to the testimony of our brothers and sisters. How can we forget the passion with which the Korean delegates looked for news of the events taking place in their country, or the joy of the Zimbabwean delegation sharing with the churches of the world the reality of newly acquired freedom, or the anguished pain and hope of delegates from Central America? In those moments of sharing and studying, the World Council as a family of churches that confess Jesus Christ according to the Scriptures became a reality for the participants.

We did not lack frustrations. There were too many speeches during the first few days. Each of us had to overcome the limitation of his or her local situation. But in the worship around the prayer theme of Melbourne, "Your Kingdom Come", most of the frustrations, the anguish and the dreams of the participants found the right expression. To face the missionary challenges of today, the predicaments of humankind, we need to go deeply into the spiritual roots of our Christian life. **So we gathered, not to make a theological study on the kingdom theme, but to pray together, looking for vision and inspiration for our personal and communitary mission.**

A new creation

First, the topic of the kingdom invited us to take a look at the whole of creation and to recognize links between the hopes of all people and the promise of the kingdom of God in Jesus Christ. But the conference was not embracing a general theory of history, a metaphysical affirmation of the whole of reality. **The kingdom we pray for, the one we try to understand, was the kingdom fully manifested in the person of the servant king, Jesus Christ.**

It is the kingdom that has come in his person which commands our loyalties and sends us in his name into the world. We learned to pray "Your Kingdom Come" and *Maranantha*, "Come Lord Jesus". It is only through a personal encounter with the servant king that it is possible to discern the signs, the manifestations of his kingdom in the world. Jesus came as poor among the poor, walked among the sinners, died on the cross, powerless in human eyes. But in him, despised by all men, a new power was being manifested. So Section IV, 3 reads: **"In the decisive events which followed the crucifixion, something radically new happened which seems best described as a new creation: an altogether new quality of power appeared to be let loose among humankind. Those who responded found that they shared in this power.** The inexorable bondage of cause and effect appeared to be broken and they experienced a liberation which enabled them to face their persecutors without fear, and to claim that the powers had been overthrown, disarmed, in a decisive way, even though the powers were somehow permitted to function in the meanwhile until the final consumation of history. The early Christians used many analogies to describe what they had experienced and what they believed had happened. The most striking picture is the one of a sacrificed lamb, slaughtered but yet living, sharing the throne which symbolized the heart of all power and sovereignty with the living God Himself. The principle of self-sacrificing love is thus enthroned at the centre of the reality of the universe."

The kingdom of the crucified Christ. These words remind the churches to reconsider their missionary style, strategies, priorities. One of the important realizations of the delegates in Melbourne was that the Church everywhere is increasingly called to confront the powers of the world. How do we express the power of the Lamb in terms of the power of the Church confronting the powers of the world?

A few weeks after Melbourne, several pastors were taken to jail in Australia because they were showing their solidarity with aboriginal peoples defending one of their worshipping places against the voracity of the oil companies.

This same confrontation takes place in many countries of the Third World where churches face the tensions of the doctrine of national security or in the powerful countries of the world where the craziness of militarism invites the churches to counteract with the craziness of the cross, where non-violence becomes a rejection of the growing potentialities for mass murder.

In the King Jesus Christ we discern the power of the cross as a clear challenge to all missionary organizations to come under the discipline of the powerless Christ. We have also a personal challenge, an invitation to assume voluntary poverty, to follow Jesus the King who empties himself in order to be counted among the poor, to work among them for their salvation and liberation.

Some persons have pointed out that the concentration on the incarnational kenosis of Christ did not pay enough attention to the atonement dimension of his death on the cross and of his resurrection. **While several** **passages from the documents of Melbourne make reference to the once forever event of Jesus Christ, it is clear that much more effort should be made to relate the reality of the forgiveness of sins through the atoning death of Jesus Christ to our participation in the historical struggles of today.** By experience we know of the tremendous power that is generated by the assurance that God in Jesus Christ reconciled the world with himself, liberating us from all our pretensions and releasing us for historical actions in the ambiguities of daily history. This theological task remains before us.

Another symbol that made an impact in the Melbourne conference was **that of Jesus crucified** *outside* **the gates of Jerusalem; Jesus walking towards the periphery of life, looking for the marginals, the down-trodden and with them and through them working for the transformation of the whole of society.** The growing numbers of independent churches, pentecostal communities, basic ecclesial communities—all working fundamentally from the bottom of society—are contemporary indications of this Christ who is at the margin, working with those who have no social powers. To announce the kingdom of God is to call people to receive Jesus Christ as King and to join with him in his movement to serve, to love all those who even today are marginal to the life of our world.

Melbourne discerned "a change in the direction of mission, arising from our understanding of Christ who is the centre which is always in movement towards the periphery. While not in any way denying the continuing significance and necessity of a mutuality of the churches between the Northern and Southern hemispheres, we believe that we can discern a development of worldwide mission in the '80s which will increasingly take place within these zones. We feel that there will be increasing traffic between the churches of Asia, Africa and Latin America among whose numbers both rich and poor are counted. This development we expect will take the form of a strong initiative from the churches of the poor and oppressed at the peripheries" (Section IV, 24).

The missionary yardstick

The second concentration point of Melbourne is the affirmation of the poor as the missiological principle par excellence. The relation to the poor inside the Church, outside the Church, nearby and far away, is the criterion to judge the authenticity and credibility of the Church's missionary engagement. The Roman Catholic Bishop's Conference in Puebla, Mexico, spoke of the preferential option of God for the poor. That is discerned in the Gospel. **Jesus established a clear link between the coming of the kingdom and the proclamation of the Good News to the poor.** The missiological principle, the missionary yardstick, is the relation of the Church to the poor. It would be very difficult to find today a theological justification for the missionary outreach of the Church without this deep concern for the poor. **"The Church of Jesus Christ is called to preach Good News to the poor, even as its Lord has done in his ministry announcing the kingdom of God. The churches can not neglect this evangelistic task. Most of the world's people are poor, and they are waiting for a witness to the Gospel that will really be Good News...** The mission which is conscious of the kingdom will be concerned for liberation, not oppression; justice, not exploitation; fullness, not deprivation; freedom, not slavery; health, not disease; life, not death. No matter how the poor may be identified, this mission is for them" (Section I, 16). We were led at Melbourne to study the significance of the crucifixion of Jesus outside the city walls. We see this as a sign, consistent with everything else in his life, that he who is the centre is constantly in movement towards the periphery, to the margin of society, because his priorities were clear. We are invited to read the Bible anew, to see history from the perspective of the poor, with the eyes of the downtrodden. **Of course the Gospel is for all and not only for the poor. But God is a personal God who addresses himself to each one of us personally in each one of our own situations.** So Melbourne said (Section I, 4), "To the poor this challenge means the profound assurance that God is with them and for them. To the rich it means a profound repentance and renunciation. To all [both rich and poor] who yearn for justice and forgiveness, Jesus Christ offers discipleship, and the demand of service." This preferential option for the poor is not an elimination of the invitation to faith, to conversion, to discipleship. The poor are not only the recipients, the objects of God's love: they are also called to grow into faith, into community, into discipleship. The decision for Christ also belongs to them, because they are invited to be protagonists with God, to organize themselves to shape history, to become evangelists. And Melbourne saw quite clearly that the poor of the earth are those who will have the credibility to announce the Gospel of the poor Jesus Christ to the poor of the world today.

Several practical consequences follow immediately. The churches are called to repentance, because the credibility of the kingdom is at stake in the attitude of the Church towards the poor. Second, our concern for the poor should be a priority judgement in all our missionary strategies and in our missionary vocation. When we speak of the billions of "unreached" people who have not yet received the Gospel of Jesus Christ, we are talking of those against whom we Christians have sinned; those who have perhaps hardened their hearts because of the poverty of the testimony of nations that were confused with Christian nations. **If we take seriously the fact that the proclamation of the gospel of the kingdom is above all for the poor, we are faced with a clear calling to our world missionary commitment, and within that same commitment, an engagement towards justice, in order to announce the Gospel that really is Good News to the downtrodden of the earth.**

Third, to announce the Good News to the poor is to call them to become protagonists, to organize themselves to claim the promises of the kingdom. It is to call them to become evangelists. "Our study on 'Christ crucified and risen—challenges human power' has led us to see special significance in the role of the poor... Might it not be that they have the clearest vision, the closest fellowship with the crucified Christ who suffers in them as with them? Might it not be that the poor and powerless have the most significant word for the rich and powerful: that Jesus must be sought on the periphery, and followed 'outside the city'? That following him involves a commitment to the poor? **Who but the Church of the poor can preach with integrity to the poor of the world? In these ways we see the 'poor' churches of the world as the bearers of mission: world mission and evangelism may now be primarily in their hands"** (Section IV, 21). The priority of the poor also means that we need to join forces with them in their struggles for change of their destiny. And this brings us to the next concentration point of the conference.

The Church must dare to be present
The kingdom of God is related to the struggles taking place in history. Melbourne tried to see the relation of the kingdom to history, and the specific responsibility of Christians in this encounter between the kingdom and history. There is no easy optimism here. There is no affirmation at all that we are building the kingdom or that the kingdom could be confused with any social system. **No social system can be exempt from the prophetic challenge**

of the Church that proclaims the kingdom. "As the kingdom in its fullness is solely the gift of God himself, any human achievement in history can only be approximate and relative to the ultimate goal—the promised new heaven and new earth in which justice abides. Yet this kingdom is the inspiration and the constant challenge in all our struggles" (Section I, 4). The kingdom is the permanent inspiration to enter into the penultimate struggles of humankind. It is only possible to proclaim the name of Jesus Christ, to invite people to faith, to conversion and to participation in the fellowship of the church in terms of the clear spelling-out of the relation of this Good News in Jesus Christ to the work that is going on in daily life. The incarnation of God in Jesus Christ, his invasion of love, is fully manifested in relation to family life, children, disease, oppressors in society, in human structural life, and the pressures of love confronting the powers of the day.

Now, how should the churches and Christians enter into the historical struggles in the name of the kingdom of God?

Assuming with *Romans* 8 that "the world is groaning for fulfilment, that God is at work", the Church must dare to be present where there are risky decisions to be taken in the ambiguities of the world, knowing that we cannot escape these ambiguities by retiring from the world. "In their witness to the kingdom of God in words and deeds the churches must dare to be present at the bleeding points of humanity and thus near those who suffer evil, even taking the risk of being counted among the wicked. The royal reign of God appears on earth as the kingdom of the crucified Jesus, which places his disciples with him under the cross. Without losing sight of the ultimate hope of the kingdom of God or giving up their critical attitude, churches must dare to be present in the midst of human struggles for penultimate solutions and welcome all signs of a hopeful development" (Section II, 4). Churches must be there interceding for the problems of the world. The churches must be there with repentance and self-criticism, recognizing their own complicity with much of the tragedy of the world. The churches must be there to join forces with others, knowing that God's kingdom works with several means and instruments. The churches must be there to plant signs of the kingdom, especially the signs of reconciliation. **But fundamentally, the churches are called to witness in the midst of those struggles to the hope that is in Jesus Christ, to invite all to see what is going on in the search for justice, to what went on the cross and in the resurrection of Jesus Christ.** Evangelism is affirmed in Melbourne, not as a professional programme outside of one's participation in the struggles of the world, but precisely in the moment in which we are cooperating with others, praying for others, trying to plant signs of reconciliation, we are there to give reason to the hope that is within us. We are there to *"witness to the fact that there is a common hope for humankind* *and for the whole of creation in the life and death, the resurrection and the ascension of the Son of God, and that the coming of the kingdom of God is linked with the turning of human minds to Christ as the Lord of the kingdom"* (Section II, 5).

I emphasize this phrase because I think that we are overcoming the division between social ethics on the one hand, and the Gospel on the other. Here we understand the kingdom struggling to be manifested fully in daily history, the churches struggling to discern those signs of the kingdom, joining forces with others instead of wanting to hold on to the monopoly of that kingdom, but joining forces as Christians, as churches: this means illuminating or highlighting the hidden meaning of these human situations by pointing to the link between them and the history of Jesus of Nazareth.

The concern for the struggles of the world is not simply a concern for the social-ethical dimensions of the Gospel, but a clear invitation to announce the name of Jesus Christ in relation to the cutting issues of human concern. The discernment of the powers and the nature of their manifestation in history should become an invitation to exorcise them, to control them in the name and in the power of the crucified king.

For CWME and for many missionary agencies the main task is how to transform a vision of Melbourne into daily decisions. And that will keep us busy in the years to come.

Melbourne did not explore fully the relation of Christianity to other world faiths, but it invites us to discern signs of the kingdom in the struggles of history among people who identify themselves with different ideological or religious loyalty, thus giving us a new evangelistic motivation, a new missionary passion, free from imperialistic connotation. We go as Christians who come from the revelation of the Lord Jesus Christ, who know the story of the Bible, to join forces with others, to participate with them in common struggles and, in the midst of that belonging-together, in that incarnational style, to indicate the relations between those situations and the story of God in Jesus Christ. We are not making general affirmations about general revelation, about salvific value, or this or that article of religion. **Melbourne is saying that it is in the actual participation with people in the search for solutions to common human problems that we find natural opportunities to name the Name of Jesus Christ, to render witness to his saving and liberating powers.** Christians living in minority situations or cross-cultural missionaries following their vocations to enter into other religious or ideological milieus will find here not only encouragement for their mission, but also inspiration for this style of missionary approach which corresponds both to the Gospel and to the human situation. Only God knows what really happens when Christians are able to indicate the existing link between the manifestation of goodness and love among nations of the earth and the revelation of the supreme love and goodness of God in the cross of Jesus Christ; or to point to the tragic complicity between all those forces that dehumanize human beings, inside and outside religious and ideological systems, and the forces of inhumanity that put Jesus Christ to death on the cross.

The Good News of the Kingdom includes the announcement that God has not remained without witness anywhere, but as Christians we are called to point our finger like John the Baptist to the Lamb of God who takes away the sins of the world.

The fourth concentration point in Melbourne is the emphasis on the Church as a sacrament of the kingdom. Melbourne is criticized by some who say that it was not a missionary conference in the classical sense, i.e. an assemblage of people concerned mainly with foreign mission. In Melbourne, representatives of all aspects of the life of the churches were gathered, because *all those aspects* needed to be looked at, to be screened through the eyes of the missionary calling. It is no surprise, therefore, that Melbourne placed such a great emphasis on the reality of the Church as a sacrament of the kingdom, the very same Church whose sins we recognize and confess. Perhaps in a first reading of the reports, one has the same feeling I had in Melbourne, that they are too masochistic in pointing to the sins and failures of the churches. In any case, once the beautiful affirmation that the Church is the sacrament of the kingdom is made, it is good and necessary to remind ourselves of our reality: that we are rooted in this Church which has not yet reached the kingdom, but which does have the gift of the Holy Spirit to direct us to that path.

This sacramental reality of the Church, which moved us so much in Melbourne, is fully manifested in the celebration of the Eucharist. **The Eucharist is described as the pilgrim bread, missionary bread, food for a people on the march. At the centre of Church life is the Eucharist, the public declaration of thanksgiving for God's gift in Christ, and the participation of the disciples in the very life of Christ. It is a foretaste of the kingdom which proclaims the Lord's death until he comes. From that centre of the eucharistic life of the Church, the proclamation comes naturally, the unashamed announcing of the acts of God in Jesus Christ, the calling to build up a church community, a fellowship.**

The basic ecclesial communities, those grassroots churches or groups of churches that are emerging all over the world, multiply the participation of the poor in the body of Christ. They are referred to in every Section of Melbourne as paradigms of the Church of the poor, as models, that challenge the lives of our churches and invite us to reconsider all our structures to see if they are really at the service of the crucified Christ whose kingdom we announce. Churches of the poor, rooted in the Bible and the Eucharist, searching for the missionary obedience which is called for in their local situations.

Churches in Melbourne were also called to recognize the relationship between mission and unity. We can only celebrate in honesty if the Church realizes the damage done to common witness by the scandal of our divisons. **Unless the pilgrimage route leads the churches to visible unity in the one God, the one Christ, the one Holy Spirit going towards the one Kingdom, the mission entrusted to us in this world will always rightly be questioned.** So God feeds his people and they celebrate the mystery of the Eucharist in order that they may confess in word and deed that Jesus Christ is Lord to the glory of God the Father.

This community rooted in the grace of God, manifested in the liturgical celebration, is entrusted with a responsibility for the proclamation of the Gospel to the whole world.

"Authentic proclamation will be the spontaneous offering of a church which is a truly worshipping community, which is able to welcome outsiders, whose members offer their service in both church and society, and which is ready to move like a pilgrim. Such a church will not defend the privileges of a select group, but rather will affirm the God-given rights of all. It is the Lord, however, who chooses his witnesses, particularly those who proclaim the Good News from inside a situation—the poor, the suffering and the oppressed—and strengthens them through the Holy Spirit with the power of the incarnated Word" (Section III, 6).

Crossing all human frontiers

This proclamation entrusted to the Church should be fulfilled both nearby and by crossing all human frontiers. Jesus our Lord is always ahead of us and asks us to follow him in unexpected ways. God's programming of the pilgrim people will always be linked to a particular situation and to specific moments in history. It will be the joyful telling of the story of God in Jesus Christ and the illumination of all contemporary situations from that perspective. Melbourne challenges all the churches to consider themselves as the sent body of Jesus Christ in the world. The liturgical inspiration comes as challenge to activitist groups and the invitation to proclamation comes as challenge to churches centring in the liturgical celebration. These reciprocal corrections should provide inspiration for the announcement of the Gospel everywhere.

Within the life of the Church are diverse vocations. **We need to recognize among those a call to the evangelists, a call to go beyond their frontiers, to share the Gospel of Jesus Christ.** It is possible to find in Melbourne clear references to this vocation. In the recognition of the poor as the unreached billions, or in the affirmation that it belongs to the task of the Church to proclaim the Gospel of Jesus Christ to every creature, in every time. This issue, however, did not receive in Melbourne a specialized consideration. Even if there were professional missionaries in Melbourne, this conference on the mission of the Church was not a conference called to consider specifically the professional missionary vocation. Now that we have a theological perspective—the Gospel announced to the poor, and a vision of God's own missionary style—Jesus emptying himself, going through the cross to the margin of life, we need to engage ourselves in practical discussions with all those who receive today the calling to go to the regions beyond. Here again there is a clear challenge for the future work of CWME.

But this special vocation should not become an alibi to let the majority of the congregation remain totally indifferent to the evangelistic calling of the mission of the Church. The prayer "Your Kingdom Come" belongs to all, to each one of the members of the churches; we all are challenged to make of that prayer the motivation of our lives. We cannot pray for the kingdom to come without announcing to the world the knowledge of the King whose kingdom we hope for. We cannot pray for the coming of the kingdom without calling everybody, everywhere, to recognize this servant kingship of Jesus Christ and that belongs as a responsibility to every Christian community and to every aspect of our ministry—liturgical life, healing ministries, proclamation of the Word—all belong together as we try to announce the glories of him who has called us from darkness to his wonderful light.

Of course, and happily, Melbourne was not the end of the road or the only expression of the search for missionary obedience in the church of Jesus Christ today. Other meetings are taking place this year in Pattaya and Edinburgh which bring together sectors of the Christian church, people with a particular theological perspective or even with a particular understanding of their missionary obedience; their voices also belong within the ecumenical forum where we all contribute our experiences, our convictions, our questions, our challenges, and our praise.

Emilio Castro
Director, CWME

APPENDICES

Message to the churches

Dear Sisters and Brothers in Christ:

We, more than five hundred Christians from many of the world's nations, have gathered in Melbourne, Australia, May 12-24, 1980, in the World Council of Churches' Conference on World Mission and Evangelism. In the name of Jesus Christ we have come. Our attention focused on the prayer Jesus taught us: "Your Kingdom come". This prayer disturbs us and comforts us yet by it we are united.

We meet under the clouds of nuclear threat and annihilation. Our world is deeply wounded by the oppressions inflicted by the powerful upon the powerless. These oppressions are found in our economic, political, racial, sexual and religious life. Our world, so proud of human achievements, is full of people suffering from hunger, poverty and injustice. People are wasted.

> Have they no knowledge, all the evildoers
> who eat up my people as they eat bread?
> (Psalm 14:4)

The poor and the hungry cry to God. Our prayer "Your kingdom come" must be prayed in solidarity with the cry of millions who are living in poverty and injustice. Peoples suffer the pain of silent torment; their faces reveal their suffering. The church cannot live distant from these faces because she sees the face of Jesus in them (Matthew 25).

In such a world the announcement of the kingdom of God comes to all. It comes to the poor and in them generates the power to affirm their human dignity, liberation and hope. To the oppressor it comes as judgement, challenge and a call for repentance. To the insensitive it comes as a call to awareness of responsibility. The church itself has often failed its Lord by hindering the coming of his kingdom. We admit this sin and our need for repentance, forgiveness and cleansing.

The Triune God, revealed in the person and work of Jesus Christ, is the center of all peoples and all things. Our Saviour Jesus Christ was laid in a manger "because there was no place for him in the inn" (Luke 2:7). He is central to life yet moves toward those on the edge of life. He affirms his lordship by giving it up. He was crucified "outside the gate" (Hebrews 13:12). In this surrender of power he establishes his power to heal. The good news of the kingdom must be presented to the world by the church, the Body of Christ, the sacrament of the kingdom in every place and time. It is through the Holy Spirit that the kingdom is brought until its final consumation.

People who suffer injustice are on the periphery of national and community life. Multitudes are economically and politically oppressed. Often these are the people who have not heard of the Gospel of Jesus Christ. But Jesus Christ comes to them. He exercises his healing authority on the periphery. We, participants in this Conference on World Mission and Evangelism, are challenged by the suffering of the poor. We pray that they may hear the Gospel and that all of us may be worthy proclaimers of the Gospel by word and life. We stand under the judgement and the hope of Jesus Christ. The prayer "Your kingdom come" brings us closer to Jesus Christ in today's world. We invite you to join us in commitment to the Lord for the coming of whose kingdom we pray.

Your kingdom come, Oh Lord.

Constitutional change

The CWME Melbourne Conference has adopted the following change in its Constitution.

I. The Constitution read...
A. Conference on World Mission and Evangelism
    4. Membership
    a) The membership of the Conference shall consist of not more than 250 persons in the following ways:...

II. The adopted change reads...
    a) The membership of the Conference shall be established by the Central Committee of the World Council of Churches on the recommendation of the CWME Commission prior to each world conference. These persons shall be named in the following ways...

This change has been accepted by the WCC Central Committee, Geneva, August 1980.

The ascent of human nature

ANASTASIOS (YANNOULATOS)*

With the development of the sciences and technology within our age, many have spoken about the amazing capabilities of man. Indeed, sometimes, pompous statements have been expressed, such as "God is dead" and "We are gods." This sounds as a direct echo of the old voice of the Devil in Eden: "and you shall be as God, knowing good and evil" (Gen. 3:5).

But the Devil cannot produce a new idea. He cannot create. He can only pervert creation. Here he is seen twisting the truth, and turning it into a lie. Also then in Eden, he used as a starting point a basic truth, but he spoke it in a way that set humanity in a wrong direction: pushing humanity in the way of arrogance, of self-realisation. Man has followed the Devil's distortion in self-divination.

In the same way, the desire of man to elevate himself to the throne of God is not altogether wrong. It is simply a distortion of a tendency of divine origin. God "created man in his own image" to be with him. Humanity has finally found the right direction towards the throne of God through Jesus Christ, the "second Adam". This is exactly the main point of the Christian message, that culminates in the feast of the Ascension.

The final destination of humanity is precisely deification—to be made divine (what in Eastern theology we call *theosis*). But this is only possible in Christ who "emptied" himself, taking the form of a servant... (Phil. 2:7-11).

1. This basic theological message is transmitted by today's Feast of the Ascension. In accordance with the christological conscience and the worshipping subconsciousness of the ancient united church, we see in the Ascension the consummation, the end of all the other decisive aspects of the course of the life of Christ.

The first descent of the Logos of God from heaven to earth began with the Annunciation. The ascent of the same Logos of God from earth to heaven is fulfilled through the Ascension. The Annunciation was the introduction to the incarnation, whilst the Ascension is the conclusion of it. In the Annunciation, he descended from heaven to earth without flesh, whilst now he is

---

*The Right Rev. Professor Dr. Anastasios (Yannoulatos), Greece, Bishop of Androussa, presented these thoughts at an ecumenical service of worship for celebration of the Ascension on the occasion of the Australian Week of Prayer for Christian Unity and the WCC's World Conference on Mission and Evangelism, St. Patrick's Cathedral, May 15, 1980. This contribution was omitted by mistake in the first printing of this book.

ascending from earth to Heaven, carrying human nature with him. Forty days after his birth, he was taken to the temple and as the "first-born" was dedicated to God, according to the Law. Forty days after his resurrection from the dead, which is a rebirth, he ascends to the celestial Temple as the "first-born of the dead" in order to present his human nature, holy and pure, which is the "first-fruit" of our nature, to God his Father.

The basic key to the theological understanding of the message of the Feast of the Ascension remains the biblical concept of Christ as the "second Adam" and as "the first-born" of creation. The whole divine plan in Christ not only brings reconciliation between God and man, but reunites those things which the sin of the first Adam had separated: the human and the heavenly. It gives the divine glory again to humanity. Just as the fall of Adam opened for humanity the way to Hades, in a similar manner the ascension of the "second Adam", Jesus Christ, opened the way for our entrance into Heaven, where the presence and the will of God reign (Heb. 10:19-20). With his incarnation, Christ became the "first-born among many brethren" (Rom. 8:29). His presence and work have cosmic dimensions. He is "the first-born of all creation" (Col. 1:15), the "beginning, the first-born from the dead, that in everything he might be pre-eminent". "For in him all the fullness of God was pleased to dwell, and through him to reconcile to himself all things, whether on earth or in heaven" (Col. 1:18-20).

The central aim of the redemptive mission of our Lord was not to add several ethical principles or to clarify various aspects of the Old Testament, but to regenerate "all things"; to raise up the fallen, to make incorruptible and to glorify the condemned, to deify human nature. This is precisely the heart of the Gospel message, that Jesus Christ did not simply assume flesh, dwell among us, preach the kingdom of God in word and power, suffer for us and be resurrected, but that he himself has opened the kingdom to humanity. He transfigured human nature which he himself assumed, our nature, and finally he elevated it with the glorified body of his divine human Person to heaven where God is absolutely present, above and beyond our comprehension, and yet so close to us.

Old classical language, bound within a static concept about "time" and "space", "up" and "down", threatens to place us within a compartment of false and dangerous dilemmas regarding the presence of Christ in heaven and at the same time with us. Nevertheless, the contemporary advances of the sciences emphasize that space is not static, that the universe is in motion, that space is continually developing. Space and time are interrelated.

The assuming of human nature by Christ and its elevation have been ontologically completed by the first-born Brother, our Lord. It is precisely this event which constitutes the summit of glory for human nature. But for us, for all people, it remains an *enormous potential*, still underdeveloped. Everyone, as a free person, is called to accept this possibility freely, to activate it through the power of the Holy Spirit, who brings into us the kingdom of God, who brings us to "the bosom of God".

2. All these things, while at first sight appearing to be theoretical, bear, like all the dogmas of the Church, a direct relation to the concrete and practical problems of our life in the same way that the mathematical equations offer a solution for the most practical problems of physics.

a) This view of the significance and elevation of the human body emphasizes exactly the enormous value of the material world and of the human being as a psychosomatic unity. It is the human body which Christ sanctifies, transforms, resurrects and elevates to Heaven. The transfigured body of the God-Man Jesus Christ which, before his resurrection, worked, walked, served, was crucified and bore "the print of the nails". The Christian revelation does not speak about a liberation of the soul and spirit from the prison of the body like other philosophical or religious systems. It is opposed to any vague idealism. It is opposed to any atheistic humanism. It preaches the resurrection and elevation of the whole human nature. After the presentation to the Father, the "first-fruits" of the new humanity reached the height of its development. *Humanity and the world acquire an indescribable dignity and significance.*

Those who take an authentic interest in human beings, in the recovery of their freedom, justice and dignity, find themselves in harmony with the great purpose of the elevation of human being which was realized by the resurrected and ascended Christ. In order to be truly human one must be "Christlike". Jesus Christ remains always the measure of the fullness. Captives — as we often are — to a post-Augustinian theological tendency to crush ourselves down, it is necessary to recover reverence in humanity and to realize the tremendous potentialities of human nature, the unimaginable horizons which were opened for it by the Ascended Jesus.

b) Likewise, missionary work in his name is not simply the proclamation of some moralistic sermon or the calling to a "spiritual salvation" of only a few people, but an invitation *to a process of transfiguration of the whole cosmos,* to the activation of the human potentiality for the elevation and the ascension of the whole humanity to "the throne of God", to participation in the life of love in the Blessed Holy Trinity.

Through the mission of the church, we are not simply called to know Christ, to gather around him or to submit ourselves to Christ's will; but we are invited to participate in Christ's glory, to be "glorified with him" (Rom. 8:17), to become acquainted with the infinite opportunities which were given to the human race through the Incarnation and Resurrection of Christ, to participate in the "fullness of life". that we may have "life and have it abundantly" (John 10:10). Our participation in this life and in this glory will reach its consummation in the eschaton, in the *Parousia.* "When Christ, who is our life, appears, then you also will appear with him in glory" (Col. 3:3-4). This participation in his glory radiates continually toward the whole world, to the whole of creation. Thus the kingdom of God which already has begun and consummation of which we are awaiting, is experienced with an astonishingly dynamic hope.

c) After the Ascension, the disciples "returned to Jerusalem with great joy" (Luke 24:52), full of certainty, strength, vision, hope. "This Jesus," said the angels, "who was taken from you into heaven, will come in the same way as you saw him go into heaven" (Acts 1:11) — "this same Jesus" in his divine human nature. There is a *deep joy springing from a dynamic understanding of the coming of the kingdom,* from the certainty that we know the most crucial message in human history.

There is a solid joy in the new power that Christ has promised: "You shall receive power when the Holy Spirit has come upon you" (Acts 1:8). There is joy because of the decisive role that has been bestowed on us as "sons of the kingdom" to collaborate "as co-workers of God" "to the end of the earth" (Acts 1:8).

Bringing the kingdom to new frontiers is not a human activity. It is the Holy Spirit that is continuing the mission of Christ through his "Christ-like" disciples in time and in space bringing the kingdom "within us", making the kingdom present and active in the church.

But mainly this great joy is diffused within our life as we view the tremendous potentialities which the Ascension of our Lord opened in the life of humanity and the whole world. And it is activated even in our difficult hours when we follow Christ in his way to the field of harvest, along the streets of the spiritual Jerusalem, to the mystical mountain of the Transfiguration, in his clash with the powerful religious or political leaders of his time, on his way to Golgotha, because we know that the same road ends in the Resurrection, in the Ascension, in the "bosom of the Father". *This joy is not closed,* individual; it is preserved in the church, it is the doxology of the community of the believers, the dynamic proclamation of the new potentialities of humanity.

In the last years, many proclamations have been made about human rights. Viewing people and our mission in the light of the Ascension, we come to realize more and more that our Christian mission is a proclamation about and a *struggle for the highest human right*— to become that for which we are created, to become, through grace, "Christ-like", "God-like" to realize our true nature. All other human rights are derived from this. In this they all find their fulfillment. Any thought which ignores the basic high right of the human person results in disorientation, and makes one indifferent towards the basic element of human existance: one's divine origin and one's divine destination. Our highest missionary obligation is summarized in the proclamation and in the living of the event that every person has the right but also the obligation to activate the infinite potentialities which are offered to each human being in Christ through the Holy Spirit; so that we can proceed to the fulfillment of human existance, to the "divine glory", to the "end" which the Ascension of our Lord reveals in a blissful and bold manner, overcoming any classical, static human thinking.

Greetings received from the Zimbabwe churches

From the Zimbabwe Christian Council Delegation to the World Council of Churches' Conference on World Mission and Evangelism, Melbourne, Australia, 12-25 May 1980.

We, the delegation from the Zimbabwe Christian Council, are delighted to be here as the first representatives to be sent out under the banner of the true name of our nation—ZIMBABWE.

We wish to greet you on behalf of the churches that have suffered isolation and have longed to identify themselves fully with their Christian brethren throughout the world for a long time.

We have just emerged from a situation of political domination of over six million indigenous blacks by a quarter of a million settler-whites. The subjugation of the blacks was a direct result of their defeat in the initial wars of colonization, as their weapons were no match for the more sophistication armament of the latter. A series of efforts aimed at maintaining white supremacy included subtle manœuvres which led the black rulers of the day to sign treaties which stripped them of their land rights.

One piece of legislature after the other saw the increased dehumanization of the black people, while the effects of social and religious deculturation were accelerated by economic deprivation.

The Christian Church for too long preached the Gospel in terms which demanded of its followers to aim for happiness and reward in the world to come (after death), and the turning of the other cheek when one is struck. The churches also maintained the status quo by their compliance with the provisions of social segregation in their own practices.

After about half a century, the wave of nationalism led to an ever intensifying struggle by the blacks to regain control of their country. From 1965 to the beginning of 1980, the country witnessed one of the most protracted and vicious wars of liberation. It was a struggle which demanded a high degree of self-sacrifice, and resulted in a lot of suffering for our people. Thousands were killed; countless numbers were maimed, and there are large numbers who were left displaced, dispossessed, and homeless. In the midst of this conflict, the churches in Zimbabwe were awakened and rose to identify their role as sufferers with the people.

Our hard-won victory was realized not only because of our own determination; we were sustained and reinforced by the co-operation and support—material, moral, and spiritual—accorded us by this Council and its member churches.

The 18th of April 1980 was indeed a great day for us. Your solidarity with us at the attainment of our independence was visibly and tangibly demonstrated by the Rev. Phillip Potter's letter of congratulation, admonition, encouragement, and assurance of our fuller participation within the world church body, which he wrote in his capacity as General Secretary of WCC. We wish to seize this golden opportunity to thank you in person for this great message sent on your behalf. Our pain and grief during the liberation struggle you empathized as your own; now we acknowledge as yours also the joy and excitement of the present.

We go forward in the full awareness that great challenges await us in the process of settlement, reconstruction, rehabilitation, and reconciliation in our beloved land and society. This is the time when we as the Church are challenged to proclaim and practice the Gospel according to its relevance to the total reality of the situation.

As long as the struggle for human liberation continues in this world, we shall not find full comfort in our own political independence. We shall endeavour to act in obedience to the call and command of Christ, the eternal Lord of Victory.

Letter to the Australian churches

May 24, 1980

To: The Australian Churches
The Australian Council of Churches

Dear Brothers and Sisters in Christ:

At the end of the World Conference on Mission and Evangelism we want to send you our warmest greetings in Jesus Christ and to convey our profound sense of gratitude for the hospitality you have given to us in your homes, your churches, your country. Through long months many of you have given generously of your time and energy to prepare for our arrival. We are deeply moved by this mark of ecumenical generosity.

We have participated also in common events with Christians in Melbourne, and specially in your simultaneous celebration of a Festival of Faith. In this way the evangelistic concern of the Conference received concrete expression in your desire to share the gospel of Jesus Christ with your fellow citizens.

We also had the immense privilege of participating during a weekend in the life of many of your congregations. About four hundred delegates were impressed by the warmth of your fellowship but especially for your serious search for the kingdom of God. We fell in love with your churches and your country. You will remain in our prayers.

You will find enclosed a statement of concern on the plight of aboriginal Australians. We are sure that this problem is very close to your heart and that from your passionate involvement with this issue we all will receive challenge and inspiration to face similar situations in our respective countries.

We remain together in our common passion to announce the Good News of the coming kingdom of God.

Once again, many thanks.

Fraternally,

Soritua Nababan   Emilio Castro
Moderator   Director

Enclosure

Action in solidarity with the Aborigines of Australia

Our deliberations on the Kingdom of God theme at the Conference on World Mission and Evangelism have compelled us to accept that the Gospel of Jesus Christ is Good News to the Poor, and that this message is to be proclaimed in both Word and Action.

On the occasion of the Conference we have had a personal encounter with the poor of Australia in the Aboriginal people of the land. We have heard the voice of the voiceless and we are challenged by the cry of the poor of Australia to demonstrate our obedience to the demands of the Kingdom of God.

The Aboriginal Australians have brought to our attention the way in which the Aboriginal people have been robbed of their own land and spiritual heritage and have experienced racial and cultural genocide, and then been denied any fair share in the fruits of the society constructed with their resources.

We are concerned about the continued oppression and suffering of the Aboriginal people and the blatant racism in Australia which is a denial of the kingdom of God.

Whilst we recognize the attempts made by some sectors of the Australian churches to support Aboriginal Australians in their struggles, we are particularly concerned by reports of Church co-operation in maintaining and condoning racist and oppressive policies of governments in Australia, failure to support action against second-class citizenship for Aboriginal Australians and reluctance to give adequate financial assistance to communities, organizations and projects controlled by the Aboriginal people.

The issues that have been raised by the Aboriginal Australians include:

1) Aboriginal Australians must be the ones who define what the issues are that need to be addressed in relation to their own people.
2) Aboriginal Australians should be assisted to print and circulate information concerning their situation, instead of relying on White interpretations.
3) Aboriginal Australians need to control their own institutions and the funds given to them.
4) The rights of Aboriginal Australians to their own land and sacred sites and their right to determine its use should be protected.
5) Aboriginal Australians have the fundamental right to accede to education at all levels, preferably in the form of crash programs which will enable them to attain national education standards; this education should insist on the cultural identity and values of the Aboriginal people.
6) Aboriginal Australians should share fully in the fruits of the Australian economy and not have the highest unemployment rate.

7) Aboriginal Australians need adequate housing.

8) Adequate health care should be available to Aboriginal Australians.

9) The Australian Federal Government has failed to use its powers, granted by overwhelming public vote in a referendum in 1967 to override discriminatory State Legislation, especially the Queensland Act.

While recognizing that in many of our own churches and countries we face similar situations of injustice, we call upon the churches and church organizations of Australia to acknowledge their past—and in some cases, continuing—complicity in this discrimination; to support Aboriginal Australians, their communities and their organizations.

In particular we urge the churches to adopt the following recommendations made by the Australian Council of Churches' Conference on Racism:

1. that the churches return some of their land and property to Aboriginal groups as a sign of their commitment to land rights and a stimulus to government action;

2. that the churches refuse to participate in the bicentennial celebrations of European settlement in 1988, unless adequate land rights legislation is adopted in every state prior to that date;

3. that the churches call upon the Federal Government to adopt an immediate policy of full recognition of the rights of Aboriginals to the ownership of their traditional land, and of just compensation for all land taken from them;

4. that the World Council of Churches call upon the International Commission of Jurists to come to Australia to investigate the denigration of the rule of law;

5. that the Australian Council of Churches invite the World Council of Churches to send an international team to visit Australia and acquaint itself fully with the Aboriginal situation, thus building international solidarity with them in the struggle; and

6. that the churches take immediate steps to prevent multinational corporations from exploiting Aboriginal land.

Further action should include the use of the influence and votes of church members, changing the policies and structures of mission organizations and giving the control of projects to Aboriginal Australians. In support of these the church will need to educate and challenge its leaders and members concerning discrimination, and support the Aboriginal Australians with direct action, including joining Aboriginal demonstrations against the oppressive system.

Call

We call on this conference on World Mission and Evangelism (WCC):
— to expose the plight of the Aboriginal people in Australia as a matter for concern and action for the Universal Church;
— to support the claim of the Aboriginal Australians to full personhood, to the right to land and to a full power-sharing in Australia;
— to urge Australian churches to action for justice.

Letter to the President of South Korea

Voted by conference plenary

The Honorable Choi Kyu-Hah
President, Republic of Korea
Seoul, Korea

The World Council of Churches' World Conference on Mission and Evangelism is following with great concern and anxiety the events in your country. We regret so many deaths and commend the bereaved families to God's consolation. We ask you to do your utmost to find a rapid, peaceful solution to the present situation, providing freedom for all political prisoners and speeding the return to a democratic constitution.

May God bless your country and people and lead it towards national reconciliation and full democratic processes.

Respectfully,

Soritua Nababan, Moderator
Emilio Castro, Secretary

May 24, 1980

Declaration on the situation of El Salvador and Latin America

Voted by conference plenary

"The Church which advocates God's rights, God's law and individual human dignity, cannot remain silent when confronted by so much abomination. We want the Government to realize that reforms serve no purpose if they are stained with so much blood. In the name of God, then, and in the name of this suffering people, whose laments reach the sky, louder every day, I implore, I beg, I order in the name of God: stop the repression."

These words are part of the last sermon preached by Archbishop Oscar Arnulfo Romero, who was treasherously murdered for uniting, in the name of
God, the outcries and defence of the people of El Salvador. He defended the
people who have organized themselves to fight against an unjust order that perpetuates misery and hunger, and who suffers the utmost consequences of a violent repression by a military dictatorship that pretends to silence the cry for liberation in the name of the order of a "Christian society". We speak in the name of the 30 lives sacrificed daily in confrontations between the people and the military dictatorship.

We are aware that this dramatic situation is not unique to El Salvador. It is an open sore or a sign that reveals the reality of the countries that are under military dictatorships which are inspired by the doctrine of national security and who continue the bloodshed of the people and their leaders. This very week, in Guatemala, a Dutch priest and a Filipino priest joined the very long list of martyrs.

We are also aware that this would not have been possible without the support of the military intervention of the United States of America. In a letter to President Carter dated February 17th, 1980, Archbishop Romero expressed the following:

"I am quite worried by the news that the Government of the United States of America is analysing the means to accelerate the arms race in El Salvador by sending military equipment and advisors to 'train 3 salvadorian battalions in logistics, communications and intelligence'! If this information is correct, the contribution of your government, instead of helping to increase justice and peace in El Salvador, will undoubtedly increase injustice and repression against the people, who have been struggling for so long to obtain respect of their most fundamental rights."

After Mons. Romero's death the Congress of the United States of America approved the additional sum of 5.7 million dollars for military aid for the Government of El Salvador.

Therefore, we, Christians from all parts of the world attending the World Conference on Mission and Evangelism, united under the prayer "Your Kingdom Come" and taking upon ourselves the challenge of Archbishop Romero, martyr of the people and the Universal Church, express the following:

1. Our deepest solidarity with the suffering and demands of the people of El Salvador and of all the Latin American people.
2. That a letter be sent to the President of the United States of America, appealing to his Government to stop the support and military aid to military regimes, and to respect the right of the people of Latin America to seek a new social order that is more just and more human.
3. In the prospect of an armed struggle of civil strife in El Salvador, we demand the respect of the sanctuaries, the Geneva War treaties and the right to life.

We make Archbishop Romero's outcry our own:

"IN THE NAME OF GOD, STOP THE REPRESSION!"

Melbourne, May 24, 1980

Statement on South Africa: Uprooting of the Poor

Voted by conference plenary

South Africa is being carved up at immense cost in human suffering and with only negative returns financially, economically and socially.

Having embarked upon a giant redistribution of the population to make the map of South Africa conform with its ideology, the Government continues to push people around with scant regard for the pain caused and with total disregard for what the actual people involved have to endure.

The Pass Laws, the Group Area Acts and the Homeland Citizenship Act are essential elements of the Government's fundamental policy of separation, of apartheid.

With influx control and migratory labour systems, *Population uprooting and Relocation* is the most destructive of all the policies that make up apartheid.

By their very nature, removals generally entail shifting families from homes too close for white comfort—"Black uprooting from white South Africa".

Resettlement violates the fundamental territorial instincts of man. People's roots in the land are violently wrenched from the soil which has nurtured them and their parents and their grandparents.

There are insuperable practical difficulties in re-establishing agricultural self-sufficiency in the black "dumping grounds".

Two million people have already been removed from their homes and relocated in black areas in the Bantustans of South Africa.

Under the resettlement programmes, removing black communities from "white areas" to the Bantustans means that the responsibility for their welfare, for their housing, pensions, hospitals, schools, parks, sport facilities and even jobs, is being taken off the shoulders of the central government and foisted upon the Bantustans governments.

Resettlement, along with the restricted influx control and labour legislation governing "white industrial areas", keeps out the 2.5 million black unemployed and puts the responsibility on to the Bantustans. Thus the government effectively exports problems like unemployment, the housing and school shortages and inadequate social care. It is a case of out of sight, out of mind—the problem does not exist!

Under the Group Area Act, thousands of people have been put into racial ghetto's. Together with the old, redundant and superfluous they have been removed individually from so-called white areas, and the people who are pushed off farms by new owners join the wandering displaced who are endlessly and hopelessly on the move, seeking refuge and permanency. Many have been moved "twice". The first time was to "clear" white land and the second time to sort them into ethnic bundles.

The large scale of demographic engineering carried out in South Africa cannot easily be comprehended nor can the resulting destruction of families, community and society. Chaos, disorder, confusion and disintegration are marks of South Africa's black disaster.

Resettlement and rural disaster

In view of the national crisis in South Africa resulting from:
a) dispossession of land under which people are compulsorily removed and resettled in or near Bantustans;

b) the government policy of deepening the division between urban and rural people, and according privileges to a few at the expense of the many;

c) the policy of removing South African citizenship from the black people of the land;

d) economic and social policies which have reduced tens of thousands of people to unemployment, extreme poverty, hunger to the point of starvation and hopelessness, and have destroyed the fabric of both family and community life for the larger part of South Africa's people.

The World Conference on Mission and Evangelism requests the conference (WCC) in conjunction with national councils of churches:

1. to focus the attention of the Universal Church, governments, international Christian organizations and Christians throughout the world on the current rural disaster affecting blacks in South Africa;

2. to expose the plight of South Africa's rural poor;

3. to channel Christian aid to the victims of social injustice and population uprooting;

4. to support the claim of South Africa's rural poor to a full share in the privileges, and the common wealth of South Africa;

5. to challenge the South African Churches with their missionary responsibility to minister to the poor in situations of need and injustice:
   — resistance and protest against uprooting of the poor
   — supportive Action and Aid.

Statement on South Africa: crisis in black education

Voted by conference plenary

Thousands of Black South African students are presently engaged in boycotting classes as a demonstration against apartheid in education; against the oppressive nature of the current political system, and the destructive social structures existing in South Africa.

The student protests are backed by parents and supported by the whole community in acts of solidarity with them in the struggle.

The student grievances include:

1. Discrimination in budget allocation for education.

2. An educational policy promoting the racial supremacy of whites.

3. Shortage of adequate schooling facilities, of schools, and overcrowded classrooms. Lack of school materials and teaching facilities (the teachers are unqualified).

In view of the situation described above, we call the Conference (WCC) in conjunction with national councils of churches to act upon the following points:

a) to condemn police violence against students engaged in peaceful demonstrations against apartheid in education and the oppressive nature of the present political system in South Africa;

b) to pledge their full support, in an act of universal solidarity with the black people in their struggle for a just, participatory and sustainable society in South Africa.

Resolution

Voted by conference plenary

We wish to state that the mentioning of specific countries and situations in the resolutions of this conference is partly to be attributed to current events in those countries. We recognize, however, that there are other countries where foreign powers are intervening militarily, and governments which oppress, exploit, imprison and kill innocent people. We may be able to identify some of those countries and peoples. Others, however, we dare not identify for the simple reason that such a specific public identification by the Conference may endanger the position—even the lives—of many of our brothers and sisters, some of whom are participating in this Conference. We therefore confess our inability to be as prophetic as we ought to be, as that may, in some instances, entail imposing martyrdom on our fellow believers in those countries—something we dare not do from a safe distance. We know that many of them suffer under different regimes for their faith in Jesus Christ and urge that freedom of conscience be respected as well as other human rights. At the same time, we want to assure our unnamed brothers and sisters in many unnamed countries that we have not forgotten them; we identify strongly in their suffering for the kingdom of God.

The Vision of the Kingdom According to Women

Text presented to the conference

We have come to Melbourne, women and men, gathered around a prayer of Jesus: "Your Kingdom Come", and so we pray together. We have come to find inspiration and help in the fulfilling of our task of mission and evangelism as we discover new callings and new challenges. We find here a word of encouragement for each other and for others who are trying to find a way of living out their faith in the vision and lifestyle of the kingdom that both is here and is coming. We express joy in being here with the opportunity to meet our sisters and brothers from around the world and from our many churches.

Yet, as women within the church, we are concerned and deeply engaged in thinking and reflection about our full identity as the women-people of God in the fulfilling of our missionary task. We are still struggling to find our voice and to be heard. This statement is part of that struggle. It is offered in the hope that it will further our dialogue. It is an open invitation to everyone at the conference.

As women we see ourselves as accountable to God and responsible for society, for our sisters who are not here, as well as for others who are oppressed, including children and youth, workers, old people, the poor, the handicapped. In affirming aspects of traditionally-given women's roles, we will continue to care, offer tenderness and serve others. We believe this to be an exercise of power similar to that of Jesus' behaviour and attitudes in the New Testament. In expanding our role, we are interested not only in service, but in deciding what ministry most needs to be done and how.

Unrecognized and invisible ministry as ways of exercising gifts and power is and has been the experience of women for centuries. As committed Christians in the Church, we have been well "educated" into this "background" status. We believe that our experiences, though not lifted up, are of vital importance for the church. We believe that the moment has arrived in the coming of the kingdom, when these must be included in the church's theological reflection and action in much more visible ways than we have found them here in this meeting and find them in many of the churches and congregations from which we come.

As part of our calling today, we are being challenged from within to establish our own God-given identity. Many of our sisters and brothers have left or are leaving the institutional church because they despair of its readiness for this new exchange. In addition to this challenge, a new style of dialogue with men and other women is required. It means not only sharing in decisions, but also living out a visible partnership in church and society. It means women and men in theological and critical exchange regarding our teachings, proclamation, and evangelistic task. These questions have not only to do with mission, reaching out, but with the renewal of the Church itself, freeing it from its captivity to past patriarchal structures and preparing the way for the coming of a truly and fully shared community in the Body of Christ.

Today we women are more aware of the importance of our participation in the church. On all local levels we are the majority—attending worship, taking part in the life of the community as unpaid workers, committing our lives to Christ through teaching the young, caring for the children and the elderly, and carrying out many serving ministries. We see clearly that with the existing church structures there are many women at the grass roots level of the institutional church hierarchy and few or no women in partnership with men in leadership.

Women have been told by those in power how to serve the Lord and men. The "church fathers" have told the "church mothers" what to do and why. In the past, it would seem that women have accepted the institutional church structures and its teaching, feeling that it upheld something sacred, divinely created and destined by God. Now many faithful women see that these structures, attitudes, and styles are not God-made but man-made. Therefore, on many levels and in many places, women are joining together and are seeking new ways to find and express their own identity, to formulate the witness of the Gospel. Women look for new spirituality and the new lifestyles of the kingdom out of their own context and experience, finding their own definitions and ways in the coming of the kingdom. We are both making new assertions and searching for those who want to be partners with us in a new dialogue, becoming the women and men who are fashioned in the image of God (Gen. 1:27-28). We believe that if the church is serious about mission and evangelism, it cannot do without the full participation of women in every area of its life. We also believe that women will not be free to be bearers of the Good News until they receive it fully from the church itself.

Proclaiming, celebrating, and living the Good News of the kingdom of God is the heart of the Church's existence, and we believe that our faith and baptism make us inheritors of equal identity and partnership in the Church, the Body of Christ (Gal. 3:27-28). Churches as we have known and experienced them have failed to practice this community. Our churches need to admit this sin against God, God's creation and redemption. We need to be willing to repent in our churches today. We are in need of Jesus, our Christ, to teach us over again and in new ways not only that we are heirs but how we are heirs of the kingdom that is dynamic and that is coming. We cannot "prepare the way" unless we are willing to repent and begin with a fresh start.

When we look at the way that Jesus acted in encountering women, we see that each time a woman turns toward him, he welcomes, affirms, accepts, and responds to her way of grasping the faith. Jesus confirms his messiahship first to a woman (John 4:25-26). He makes women the first evangelists of the faith charged to carry the news of the Risen Christ to the frightened disciples (Luke 24:1-11).

Jesus talks not just with the acceptable "nice women" like Mary, but with women who are considered by society outcasts and despised, women such as the woman of Samaria (John 4:7ff), the Syro-Phoenician woman (Mark 7:24, Matt. 15:21ff) whom he commends for her faith, etc. He accepts the ministry of women. He considers women, along with men, worthy of being taught, an attitude unprecedented for that time, and he calls them not to limit their work to the "house". Mary, who accompanied Jesus like any other student learning from the great Teacher, is commended for taking the time to engage Jesus about the kingdom. She understood what "was needful". She had chosen "the good portion" which shall not be taken away (Luke 10:38-42).

One of the images of the kingdom that helps to bring the vision of the kingdom down into concrete terms is the parable of the Great Banquet. We remember this parable of the kingdom, the story of the head of the household who prepares a great feast and invites special guests. But the invited guests make excuses and do not come. Then the servants are told to go out and get the people from the streets—the poor, the crippled, and the outcasts. After the servants have done this they report back and the host is still not satisfied; the table is still not full. He send them out again with the command, "I want my table full". In making real the vision of the kingdom, women are also called to help complete the table, to make the feast one that is full, and fully inclusive. But in trying to do this, women experience many difficulties. The following testimonies address some of those age-old obstacles still with us. These perspectives emanate from particular contexts, but they can apply to other cultural situations as well.

An Asian Woman—"When questioned about the wastage of the costly ointment by the woman who washed the feet of Jesus, Jesus said, 'the poor you will always have with you, but you do not always have me'. She gives the most costly material gift. She recognizes and acknowledges Jesus as Messiah, the one to be anointed.

"She needed to be liberated from her oppressors. They disapproved of her action, but Jesus commended her. The attitude of some of the churches toward women has not changed much over the last 2000 years. Some churches still feel that there is a wastage of dedication in the involvement of women. Women are not worth educating theologically. They are not worthy to administer the Holy Sacrament, or not good enough to be involved in the parish ministry at leadership levels.

"Because of her initiative, Jesus affirmed the liberating action of the woman who anointed his feet and recognized her true identity. Now, it is time that the church become more like Jesus in its behaviour and attitudes and involve more women who are dedicated to the spiritual and material support of the kingdom of God."

An African Woman—"In the New Testament, there is a woman with an issue of blood who spent all the earnings that she had on doctors, but could not be healed. The particular woman, in addition to being a despised human being, had a problem which made her position even worse. She had a form of bleeding. Menstrual blood from the woman was considered evil and the woman was considered unclean. So we can imagine the plight of this woman and why she had spent all of her money on physicians, yet she could not be cured.

"I chose this example to bring out into the attitudes toward women in the church, especially some of our churches in Africa. Church leaders and catechists impress upon women that they should not participate in the Eucharist while they are in their menstrual period. Why? Because, they say that menstruation makes a woman unclean and that 'it is a state which is highly repulsive and dangerous to any spiritual agent'.

"If we are here to pray, 'Thy Kingdom Come', we as women must pray that the kingdom is one in which all people are accepted as they are, fashioned by God. Jesus healed the woman with the issue of blood. Jesus was not content to leave her in her unfortunate position.

"This woman knew her plight. She knew she had no right to go near such an important spiritual leader as Jesus, yet she took the initiative, the risk, taking the bold step and challenging the culture and the religion that prevented her from living fully as a human being. She is a model for women today. She is a reminder to us to continue to challenge all of the impediments which prevent us from being healed and expressing our wholeness.

"In Africa the initiative toward equal participation of women and men must first and foremost come from women themselves. We women will be wasting our time if we sit down and hope that men will be fighting our cause. We must persist and, by the grace of God, the change will come. There is tremendous opportunity for women to participate fully in the life of the church at all levels. We African women are greatly oppressed by our men, but in many cases we do not know this. We can still be ourselves and retain the culture that encourages our humanity. Therefore, let those of us who have the opportunity show the way to others and let us be a light to light the way for others."

A North American Woman—"The missionary task of the church is to fulfil the gifts of creation. As women, we are committed to our part in proclaiming the Good News. Our statements and actions are directed toward the vision of the kingdom of God, the hope for the wholeness of creation. We do not desire to dominate the existing power structure, or to oppress men and other women in turn. We do wish for mutual recognition. Yet often the story of the women at the tomb is repeated in the lives of women today when our contributions are still discounted. *Luke* 24:1-11 tells us the story of how women came to the tomb and found it empty and how they were given the unique responsibility to witness to the Good News and to be bearers of it to the others. Yet, as they returned to the disciples, their words of proclamation seemed to the disciples as 'nonsense' and they would not believe them. Still today the witness that we make as women is often viewed as idle chatter, with no substance in it.

"The word of God calls us to the wholeness of God's image, male and female. To claim this fulness of the freedom to which God calls us means the full recognition of our need of each other, and the affirmation of all our gifts and our responsibilities in the work of the kingdom. If there is disbelief, we can find ways to encounter truth. We can travel, as did the male disciples who ran with the women to discover the risen Christ."

When we turn to this conference, "Your Kingdom Come", and see the visibility of women, we may say that it is a sign towards a fuller community between men and women in the church in decision-making positions. Many of the participants are women, most of them are delegates, a few are advisors, but quite a high number of women are drafters and moderators within the sections and sub-sections. We are moving toward a new society. But the numbers of women also tell us something of how women are given opportunities. Why didn't we find more women advisors? This question leads us to other examples where it becomes clear that we are equal with men only on paper, but not in practice. Only one woman has given a presentation in plenary, while addresses have been delivered by eight men.

In addition, this conference on mission and evangelism has not mentioned women in the history of mission, neither in the background material nor in the main presentations. Questions like: What have women contributed in mission since Edinburgh 1910 and even before that? How do they participate today in the task of mission? These have not been addressed.

Two voices from eastern Europe express the consciousness of the history of women in mission in founding churches and spreading the Gospel.

"In the Russian Orthodox Church women have played a significant role in proclaiming the Gospel and in bringing Christian education to children and youth. The personal *example* of living out the faith was the most important within the church. Many women were canonized as saints. For instance, St. Olga, who had strongly supported and spread Christianity in Russia long before it became an official religion of the country. Such examples can be made not only in the Russian Orthodox Church but in all the Orthodox Churches of the world. Even now, we can say that the main apostolic mission in the bringing up of children in a Christian spirit lies mainly on women."

"The role of women was recognized as equal with men in the struggle of the Czech Reformation, 100 years before the world Reformation of Luther, Calvin, and Zwingli. Jan Huss said: 'Women know the Bible better than some bishops'. This spirit in our church is still reflected today when one-third of our pastors, some of them superintendants, are women. Women are still primary spreaders of the Gospel."

The testimony of this message witnessed to the fact that visions of the kingdom according to women are not new. We women continue to struggle and hope in full confidence that a new incorporation of women and men in the Church will be manifested. For us, a mark of the lifestyle of the kingdom is to claim our own voice, and with this basic right of identity, to be in dialogue:

"Your Kingdom Come!"

Drafting Committee Moderator:
Gro Haaversen Barth

Recommendations

Voted by conference plenary

1. That the issues of the equal partnership of women and men in the church should be included in all units of the WCC. Special attention is drawn to the programs of CWME itself.

2. That WCC pre-conferences should be sponsored so that women, young people and others may be prepared to participate more fully.

3. That future conferences should be conducted in such a way that women are included in the modes of expression, in worship, in giving major theological presentations in plenary, in the use of language, images and forms of communication.

4. That the WCC, its member churches, and responsible mission agencies make theological education and the leadership training of women a *first* priority, beginning now and for the next decade. This is a need, visible and expressed at this conference.

5. That the issue of women and mission be further explored in co-operation with the WCC "Community of Women and Men in the Church Study" and that further documentation be prepared for the international consultation of the Study, scheduled for July, 1981, in England.

6. That we leave this conference with a question: What can I do in my church community and organization to be a leaven for the New Community of women and men, to help "live the future of the kingdom now?".

Document from the South Pacific

Text presented to the conference

The churches' concern for preaching the gospel involves concern for social justice between people within a country and within nations

In presenting this document our hope is not to call on this Conference (WCC) for immediate action but to create an awareness and deeper understanding of the problems and struggles of the people of the South Pacific. It is through this awareness that we hope positive action will eventually take place.

Having listened to various addresses and statements on the theme of this Conference, Thy Kingdom Come, it is clear that a fundamental aspect of the Gospel is the liberation of people from oppression.

We have heard about the struggles of people to be free in Latin America, South Africa, Australia, the Middle East and many other places. We would like to bring to the awareness of this Conference the almost unknown struggles of the people of the South Pacific region. For too long we have been silent about this issue and for too long the people of the South Pacific have not been heard in Conferences like this. Now it is time for us to speak out.

What are the concerns of the people of the South Pacific? We are concerned about the future of the Pacific in the following areas:

1. Over the last 25 years the Pacific area has been threatened by the build-up, stockpiling and testing of nuclear weapons. This has been done without the permission or the support of the people of the South Pacific. We feel that

this is both a violation and exploitation of the rights of the Pacific community. We strongly oppose the following:

a) the continued nuclear testing that is being carried out by the French Government in Tahiti;

b) the proliferation of nuclear weapons by the United States Government in Hawaii and other parts of the Pacific;

c) the recent testing of the nuclear ballistic missiles by the Chinese Government;

d) the intended use of the Pacific as a dumping ground for nuclear waste by Japan and other governments;

e) the deployment of naval nuclear-powered ships and submarines by the super powers.

2. The Pacific area is still a place where colonialism and political and economic domination prevail. Many of the people of the Pacific area are denied their rights to self-determination, freedom and economic independence. We refer specifically to the following:

The struggle for political and economic independence by the people of New Caledonia, New Hebrides and Tahiti from French domination.

The struggle by other people of the Pacific to govern themselves and shape their own destiny.

We fear that increasingly the Pacific will be viewed by the world's powers and multinational corporations as one of the last resource areas for profit-making and political expansion at the expense of the people.

3. We are concerned that the Pacific region has been seen and used by many churches as a classroom for missions. We resent this strongly and wish to make it clear to the churches in this Conference that we do not want to be exploited by the churches through their missionary programmes. The proliferation of missionary activities in the Pacific by the established churches and the independent missionary organizations is increasingly seen by the Pacific people as a threat to their cultures, their communities and their lives.

4. We strongly oppose and deplore the discriminatory immigration policies of nations such as Australia and New Zealand in relation to the people of the Pacific islands who seek to enter these countries for purposes of study. Such policies are violations of the rights and dignity of human beings. Likewise we also express concern about the increasing forced migration of the people of the Pacific. This creates immense social and human problems for all the countries involved. It tends to break down cultural and family ties, uproots people and hence disrupts the stability of the Pacific communities.

We solicit the support of this Conference in the following:

1. To support us in our efforts to establish the Pacific area as a nuclear-free zone.

2. To assist the churches in the Pacific as they strive to free many of the Pacific communities from colonial domination and economic manipulation.
3. To help us correct the attitude of churches regarding missionary expansion in the Pacific.
4. To develop better realistic Christian communities which can minister to people and help them find their identity and meaning in life in a changing society.

Last but not least, we strongly recommend that the World Council of Churches establish a post in Geneva to represent the concerns of the people of the churches of the South Pacific. This position will no doubt enable the South Pacific Community to be recognized and to have input into the policies and deliberations of the WCC.

In conclusion, we the delegates of the churches of the Pacific want to preserve our rich heritage, identity and unique way of living. By many we are seen as a "drop in the vast ocean". We believe that God has given us the right to be what we are and who we are, and it is only in this Spirit that God's kingdom can be found in the Pacific.

List of Participants

Rev. MARY ABBOTT
Delegate
South Africa
United Congregational Church

Bishop CLIVE ABDULAH
Delegate
Trinidad
Anglican Church

Prof. WILLIAM ADAMS
Advisor
Canada
Anglican Church

Fr. Dr. THEODOR AERTS
Fraternal delegate WCFBA
Belgium/Papua New Guinea
Roman Catholic Church

Rev. HOVHANNES AHARONIAN
Delegate
Lebanon
Armenian Evangelical Church

Mrs. LYDIA AHARONIAN
Guest
Lebanon
Armenian Evangelical Church

Archbishop SHAHE AJAMIAN
Delegate
Jerusalem
Armenian Apostolic Church

Mrs. JUDY ALLISON
Host church New Zealand
New Zealand
Presbyterian Church

Rev. DANIEL VON ALLMEN
Advisor
Switzerland
Reformed Church

Ms. EUNICE ALVES
Delegate
Portugal
Presbyterian Church

Prof. D. S. AMALORPAVADASS
Observer RC
India
Roman Catholic Church

Father AMBROSIUS OF VALAMO
Delegate
Finland
Orthodox Church of Finland

Bishop AMBROSSY
Delegate
Georgian SSR
Georgian Orthodox Church

Dr. ELIZABETH AMOAH
Delegate
Ghana
Methodist Church

Bishop Dr. YANNOULATOS ANASTASIOS
Delegate
Greece
Greek Orthodox Church

Dr. GERALD H. ANDERSON
Fraternal delegate IAMS
USA
United Methodist Church

Rev. CHARLES A. ANSA
Delegate
Ghana
Presbyterian Church

Bishop ANTONIE of Bucarest
Delegate
Roumania
Orthodox Church

Metrop. ANTHONY of Leningrad
and Novgorod
Delegate
USSR
Orthodox Church

Very Rev. ANANIA ARABAJIAN
Delegate
Armenian SSR
Orthodox Church

Father C. AREVALO
Observer RC
Philippines
Roman Catholic Church

Père CYRILLE ARGENTI
Delegate
France
Ecumenical Patriarchate

Rev. MORTIMER ARIAS
Delegate
Bolivia
Methodist Church

Oberkirchenrat WALTER ARNOLD
Fraternal delegate YMCA
FRG
Lutheran Church

Rev. GALUEFA ASETA
Host church Pacific
Western Samoa

Rev. MERVIN ASSUR
Delegate
South Africa
Ev. Lutheran Church

Metrop. ATHANASIUS
Delegate
India
Mar Thoma Syrian Church

Rev. DICK AVI
Delegate
Papua New Guinea
United Church

Rev. ELI KOFI AYIVI
Delegate
Togo
Eglise Evangélique

Fr. TISSA BALASURIYA
Advisor
Sri Lanka
Roman Catholic Church

Very Rev. AGHAN BALIOZIAN
Host church Australia
Syria/Australia
Armenian Apostolic Church

Bishop YORAMU BAMUNOBA
Delegate
Uganda
Church of Uganda

Rev. BEDFORD BANDA
Delegate
Zambia
African Methodist Episcopal Church

Rev. RAJENDRA NATH BAROI
Delegate
Bangladesh
Baptist Church

Rev. CANON S. BARRINGTON-WARD
Delegate
Great Britain
Anglican Church

Pastor RICHARD BARTLEY
Advisor
USA
Lutheran Church in America

Mrs. ETHEL BASKERAN
Delegate
India
Church of South India

Dr. JOSEPH BASS
Delegate
USA
Progressive Baptist Convention

Prof. JOAQUIM BEATO
Delegate
Brazil

Mr. BENA-SILU
Delegate
Zaire
Kimbanguist Church

Rev. JAMES BERGQUIST
Advisor
USA
American Lutheran Church

Rev. INDERJIT SINGH BHOGAL
Delegate
Great Britain
Methodist Church

Rev. Mrs. VRENI BIBER
Delegate
Switzerland
Reformed Church

Mr. NICODEMUS BILLEAM
Host church Pacific
Fiji

Rev. WALTHER BINDEMANN
Fraternal delegate WSCF
GDR

Ms. TELMA DE SOUZA BIRCHAL
Delegate
Brazil
Methodist Church

Rev. DONALD BLACK
Delegate
USA
United Presbyterian Church

Rev. Dr. HEINZ BLAUERT
Delegate
GDR
Evangelische Kirche der Union

Ms. JOAN BLOODWORTH
Delegate
Great Britain
Anglican Church

Mrs. NINA BOBROVA
Delegate
USSR
Orthodox Church

▉░░░ ░░░░░░░░ ░░░ ░░░ ░░░░░░░ ░░▉░░░░
Advisor
Netherlands
Reformed Churches in the Netherlands

Mr. ALAN BOESAK
Advisor
South Africa
Dutch Reformed Churches

Prof. PLUTARCO BONILLA ACOSTA
Advisor
Costa Rica
Ev. Methodist Church

Ms. HALINA BORTNOWSKA
Observer RC
Poland
Roman Catholic Church

Prof. Dr. DAVID BOSCH
Delegate
South Africa
Dutch Reformed Church

Rev. LESLIE BOSETO
Delegate
Papua New Guinea
United Church

Fr. MEL BRADY
Advisor RC
USA/Italy
Roman Catholic Church

Ms. ELIZABETH BRITTEN
Host church Australia
Australia
Anglican Church

Rev. ATZE VAN DEN BROEK
Advisor
Netherlands/Ghana
Reformed Church of the Netherlands

Rev. FREDERICK H. BRONKEMA
Fraternal delegate EDCS
USA
United Presbyterian Church

Rev. JOHN P. BROWN
Host church Australia
Australia
Uniting Church

░░░ ░░░░░░░░ ░░ ░░░░░░░
Delegate
Canada
United Church of Canada

Mrs. DORA BROWNE
Delegate
Barbados
Anglican Church

Rev. HELMUT BURGER
Delegate
Brazil
Lutheran Church

Dr. JOHN E. BUTEYN
Delegate
USA
Reformed Church in America

Rt. Rev. Dr. MANAS BUTHELEZI
Delegate
South Africa
Lutheran Church

Canon ROBERT BUTTERSS
Delegate
Australia
Anglican Church

Rev. PAUL GERHARDT BUTTLER
Delegate
FRG
Lutheran Church

Rev. ROGER CABEZAS GARITA
Delegate
Costa Rica
Pentecostal Church

Rev. EDWARD CALEB
Host church Pacific
Fiji
Methodist Church

Dr. EMIDIO CAMPI
Fraternal delegate WSCF
Italy/Switzerland
Waldensian Church

Rev. LYMELL CARTER
Delegate
USA
Christian Methodist Episcopal Church

Mrs. GLADYS CASTRO
Guest
Uruguay/Switzerland
Methodist Church

Ms. CAPTAIN TRINIDAD CENDANA
Delegate
Philippines
Salvation Army

Bishop FRANK CERVENY
Delegate
USA
Episcopal Church

Rev. NELSON CHARLES
Delegate
Sierra Leone
Methodist Church

Bishop ENRIQUE CHAVEZ CAMPOS
Delegate
Chile
Pentecostal Church

Rev. M. CHITTLEBOROUGH
Host church Australia
Australia
Anglican Church

Mrs. WANJIKU CHIURI
Advisor
Kenya
Presbyterian Church

Rev. CHI SONG CHO
Advisor
Korea
Presbyterian Church

Mrs. HILARY CHRISTIE-JOHNSTON
Guest
Australia
Uniting Church

Fr. MILTIADES CHRYSSAVGIS
Delegate
Greece/Australia
Greek Orthodox Church

Dr. Ms. CHAE OK CHUN
Fraternal delegate WEF
Korea
Methodist Church

Ms. JOYCE CLAGUE
Advisor
Australia

Mrs. KATHLEEN P. CLARK
Delegate
Fiji
Roman Catholic Church

Rev. PHILIP CLEMENTS-JEWERY
Delegate
Great Britain
Baptist Church

Rev. WANDA EILEEN COFFIN
Delegate
USA
Society of Friends

Canon ALAN COLE
Host church Australia
Australia
Anglican Church

Rev. Dr. DAVID COLES
Host church New Zealand
New Zealand
Anglican Church

Ms. VICTORIA CORPUZ-TAULI
Advisor
Philippines
Episcopal Church

Prof. ORLANDO COSTAS
Advisor
Puerto Rico/USA
American Baptist Churches

Rev. WILLIAM CREEVEY
Delegate
USA
United Presbyterian Church

Rev. JOSHUA DAIMOI
Delegate
Papua New Guinea

Mr. DEVAPITCHAI DAVID
Delegate
Malaysia
Anglican Church

Rev. NOEL ANTHONY DAVIES
Delegate
Great Britain
Union of Welsh Independents

Rev. EDLWIN PAUL
Delegate
Jamaica
Anglican Church

Sr. JOAN DELANEY
Advisor
USA/Italy
Roman Catholic Church

Bishop GRAHAM DELBRIDGE
Special guest
Australia
Anglican Church

Pastor CARLOS DELMONTE
Delegate
Uruguay
Waldensian Church

His Eminence KUNTIMA DIANGIENDA
Delegate
Zaire
Kimbanguist Church

Mrs. MVETE DIANGIENDA
Delegate
Zaire
Kimbanguist Church

Fr. IGNACIO DIAZ DE LEON
Observer RC
Mexico
Roman Catholic Church

Br. PARMANANDA DIVARKAR
Advisor
India/Italy
Roman Catholic Church

Mr. JOHN DOOM
Host church Pacific
Tahiti
Evangelical Church

Mr. IRAN DOS SANTOS-FERRAZ
Delegate
Brazil
Igreja Episcopal

Dr. FRANCIS M. DUBOSE
Advisor
USA
Baptist Church

Rev. ROLAND DUMARTHEREY
Delegate
Switzerland
Reformed Church

Rev. DENIS DUTTON
Delegate
Malaysia
Methodist Church

Dr. Ms. ANEZKA EBERTOVA
Delegate
Czechoslovakia
Czech. Hussite Church

Mr. LARRY EKIN
Delegate
USA
United Methodist Church

Mr. WAHETRA ELEHMAEA
Host church Pacific
New Caledonia

Mr. WILLIAM ELLINGTON
Delegate
USA

Pastor EMMANUEL ELOUTI
Delegate
Cameroon
Evangelical Church

Ms. JULIA ESQUIVEL
Advisor
Guatemala

Mrs. BARBARA FAHLBERG
Delegate
GDR

Mr. TOFIGA FALANI
Host church Pacific
Tuvalu

Prof. HORTENSIA FERREIRA COLOMBINO
Delegate
Paraguay
Disciples of Christ

Rev. JOAN ELIZABETH FEWSTER
Delegate
Australia
Churches of Christ

Rev. Dr. ULRICH FICK
Fraternal delegate UBS
FRG
Lutheran Church

Rev. Dr. ED FILE
Advisor
Canada
United Church

Bishop PATELISIO FINAU
Observer RC
Tonga
Roman Catholic Church

Rev. Dr. BJÖRN FJÄRSTEDT
Delegate
Sweden
Lutheran Church

Sr. PAUL FRANCIS
Host church Pacific
Fiji

Rev. PAUL FUETER
Advisor
Switzerland/Belgium
Moravian Church

Mr. RAYMOND WAI-MAN FUNG
Advisor
Hong Kong
Baptist Church

Rev. ISAIAS FUNZAMO
Delegate
Mozambique
Presbyterian Church

Rev. DUMITRU GAINA
Delegate
Roumania/Australia
Roumanian Orthodox Church

Fr. THEOPHAN GALINSKI
Advisor
USSR

Rev. ERIC GARDNER
Delegate
Northern Ireland
Presbyterian Church

Prof. JOSÉ GARRIDO CATALA
Delegate
Cuba
Methodist Church

Rt. Rev. JOHN G. GATU
Advisor
Kenya
Presbyterian Church

Rev. Dr. RON GERHARDY
Host church Australia
Australia

Bishop GIBRAN
Delegate
Australia

Mr. ALBERTO GONZALEZ
Advisor
Puerto Rico

Mrs. DAISY LEELA GOPAL RATNAM
Delegate
India
Church of South India

Dr. JERALD D. GORT
Advisor
USA/Netherlands
Gereformeerde Kerken

Mrs. ELEANOR GREGORY
Advisor
USA
United Presbyterian Church

Ms. DARSHINI GUNASEKERA
Delegate
Sri Lanka
Methodist Church

Archpriest Nikolai Gundyayev
Delegate
USSR
Russian Orthodox Church

Ms. Maria Fatima Gwata
Delegate
Zimbabwe
Assemblies of God

Dr. J. Harry Haines
Delegate
USA
United Methodist Church

Rev. Andrew Hake
Advisor
Great Britain
Anglican Church

Dr. William W. Hannah
Delegate
USA
Disciples of Christ

Rev. Dr. Alan W. Harde
USA

Rev. George Harding
Delegate
Sierra Leone
Anglican Church

Dr. Raimo Harjula
Delegate
Finland
Lutheran Church

Rev. William K. Harman
Fraternal delegate LWF
USA/Switzerland
Lutheran Church in America

Mr. George St. Hill
Delegate
India
Methodist Church

Mrs. Ane Hjerrild
Advisor
Denmark
Lutheran Church

Diakon Friedrich Hoffmann
Fraternal delegate LCWE
GDR
Evangelische Kirche der Union

Prof. Dr. Åge Holter
Delegate
Norway
Lutheran Church

Rev. Marianne Hornburg
Host church New Zealand
New Zealand
Anglican Church

Rev. Ching-Fen Hsiao
Delegate
Taiwan
Presbyterian Church

Rev. Alpo Hukka
Delegate
Finland
Lutheran Church

Sr. Colette Humbert
Advisor
France
Roman Catholic Church

Ms. Monica Humble
Delegate
Great Britain
Methodist Church

Ms. Sonja Ingebritsen
Delegate
USA
Lutheran Church in America

Mr. Samuel M. Isaac
Advisor
India/Thailand
Church of South India

Ms. Enitan Isaacs
Delegate
Nigeria/Great Britain
Anglican Church

Metrop. Zakka Severius Iwas
Delegate
Iraq
Syrian Orthodox Church

Mr. Alfred Jack
Host church Pacific
Fiji

Mr. Sol Jacob
Advisor
South Africa
Methodist Church

Rev. MANFRED JAHNEL
Advisor
FRG
Evangelical Lutheran Church

Rev. SHEM JIMMY
Delegate
Eastern Caroline Island

Rev. CHARLES JOE
Delegate
New Zealand
Baptist Church

Mrs. MARCEY JOEL
Host church Pacific
Eastern Caroline Island
United Church of Christ

Mr. ALEXANDER D. JOHN
Fraternal delegate CPC
Australia

Rev. Dr. TRACEY JR. JONES
Advisor
USA
United Methodist Church

Rev. MORRIS JORDAN
Host church Australia
Australia

Rev. JEAN-PIERRE JORNOD
Advisor
Switzerland
Protestant Church

Rev. GIBIEL ADAM KACHAJE
Delegate
Malawi
Presbyterian Church

Mr. SHADRACH KAJIRELO
Delegate
Tanzania

Dr. SAMUEL KAMALESON
Advisor
India/USA
Methodist Church

Ms. MELE KAMOTO
Host church Pacific
Tonga

Prof. Dr. ERNST KÄSEMANN
Advisor
FRG
Evang.-Lutheran Church

Mrs. MARGARETHA KÄSEMANN
Guest
FRG
Evang.-Lutheran Church

Archbishop KAREKIN KAZANJIAN
Host church Australia
Australia
Armenian Apostolic Church

Rev. Dr. HYUNG TAE KIM
Delegate
Korea
Presbyterian Church

Rev. Dr. KWAN SUK KIM
Advisor
Korea
Presbyterian Church

Mr. KABIRU KINYANJUI
Delegate
Kenya

Rev. GRIGORIJ KOMENDANT
Delegate
USSR
Baptist Church

Prof. KOSUKE KOYAMA
Advisor
Japan/USA
United Church of Christ

Mr. JENS KRISTIAN KRARUP
Delegate
Denmark
Lutheran Church

Rev. RENÉ KRÜGER GRAF
Delegate
Argentina
Iglesia Evangélica del Rio de la Plata

Bishop LASZLO KÜRTI
Delegate
Hungary
Reformed Church

Rev. CHIREVO VICTOR KWENDA
Delegate
Zimbabwe
Methodist Church

Rev. NAI WANG KWOK
Delegate
Hong Kong
Church of Christ in China

Bishop VICTOR E. LABBE DIAZ
Delegate
Chile
Iglesia Misiones Pentecostales Libres

Ms. MARY LAKE
Delegate
USA
Disciples of Christ

Mr. JOHN LAVENDER
Guest
Australia

Sr. CARMEL LEBLANC
Advisor RC
Canada/Papua New Guinea
Roman Catholic Church

Rev. ANDRE LEENHARDT
Advisor
France
Reformed Church

Rev. Dr. GARTH LEGGE
Delegate
Canada
United Church

Rev. Dr. MARTIN LEHMANN-HABECK
Advisor
FRG
United Lutheran-Reformed Church

Mr. GÜNTER LETSCH
Advisor
FRG
Württembergische Landeskirche

Father JOÃO LIBANIO
Advisor
Brazil
Roman Catholic Church

Dr. JAN VAN LIN
Advisor
Netherlands
Roman Catholic Church

Rev. GERHARD LINN
Advisor
GDR
Ev. Kirche in Berlin-Brandenburg

Archbishop THOMAS F. LITTLE
Observer RC
Australia
Roman Catholic Church

Rev. HERMAN LUBEN
Advisor
USA
Reformed Church in America

Ms. TIUR MALINA LUBIS
Delegate
Indonesia
Lutheran Church

Mr. ARMANDO LUZA SALAZAR
Delegate
Peru
Methodist Church

Rev. DAVID LYON
Delegate
Great Britain
Church of Scotland

Mrs. Lt. FLORENCE MACDONALD
Host church Australia
Australia
Salvation Army

Rev. GARRY MACDOWALL
Delegate
Canada
Anglican Church

Rev. ALWYN MACONACHIE
Delegate
Northern Ireland
Church of Ireland

Archbishop MAKARY
Delegate
USSR
Russian Orthodox Church

Rev. F. J. MAKAMBWE
Advisor
Zambia

Fr. TADROUS YACOUB MALATY
Delegate
Egypt
Coptic Orthodox Church

Bishop ANTONIOUS MARKOS
Delegate
Egypt/Kenya
Coptic Orthodox Church

Mr. NEVILLE MARSH
Host church Australia
Australia
Uniting Church

Deaconess UNA MATAWALU
Host church Pacific
Fiji

Mr. PATRICK MATSIKENYIRI
Advisor
Zimbabwe
United Methodist Church

Rev. JACQUES MAURY
Delegate
France
Protestant Church

Rev. FRANÇOIS MBEA
Delegate
Cameroon
Presbyterian Church

Rev. JOHN WESLEY MCCARTHY
Fraternal delegate CPC
Australia
Uniting Church

Rev. PATRICIA MCCLURG
Delegate
USA
Presbyterian Church in USA

Rev. JOHN MCINTYRE
Host church Australia
Australia
Anglican Church

Rev. BARBARA MCNEEL
Advisor
USA
American Baptist Church

Mr. URSINUS ELIAS MEDELLU
Delegate
Indonesia
Protestant Church

Monsignor BASIL MEEKING
Observer RC
Vatican City
Roman Catholic Church

Rev. HECTOR MENDEZ
Delegate
Cuba
Presbyterian Reformed Church

Rev. DIETRICH MENDT
Delegate
GDR
Lutheran Church

Mrs. EMILY MENKE
Host church Pacific
Fiji

Rev. LAVERNE MERCADO
Delegate
Philippines
United Methodist Church

Ms. LOIS C. MILLER
Delegate
USA
United Methodist Church

Dr. BELLE MILLER MCMASTER
Delegate
USA
Presbyterian Church

Mr. RADU C. MIRON
Delegate
FRG
Ecumenical Patriarchate

Mrs. ETHEL MITCHELL
Host church Australia
Australia

Mr. TARIK MITRI
Delegate
Lebanon
Orthodox Church of Antioch

Rev. STANLEY MOGOBA
Delegate
South Africa
Methodist Church

Mr. ESTO MOLLEL
Advisor
Tanzania

Rev. ALIFALETI MONE
Host church Pacific
Tonga

Sr. MARY MOTTE
Advisor RC
USA/Italy
Roman Catholic Church

Mr. JOHN MOYER
Advisor
USA

Rev. JOSIA MUFETI
Delegate
Namibia
Ev. Lutheran Ovambokavango Church

Dr. DIRK CORNELIS MULDER
Advisor
Netherlands
Reformed Churches in the Netherlands

Fr. KARL MÜLLER
Observer RC
FRG/Italy
Roman Catholic Church

Mr. MOSES MURRAY
Delegate
Papua New Guinea
Roman Catholic Church

Bishop GERALD MUSTON
Host church Australia
Australia

Dr. SORITUA NABABAN
Delegate
Indonesia
Lutheran Church

Mr. ALAN NAFUKI
Host church Pacific
Fiji

Ms. MAUD NAHAS
Delegate
Lebanon

Rev. JOHN MASAAKI NAKAJIMA
Delegate
Japan
United Church of Christ

Mrs. NOEMI NAVARRO
Delegate
Philippines
United Church of Christ

Rev. MICHAEL NAZIR-ALI
Delegate
Pakistan
Church of Pakistan

Rev. Dr. JACOB NDLOVU
Delegate
Zimbabwe
Methodist Church

Ms. NOMMSO NGODWANE
Delegate
South Africa

Mr. GRANT STEWART NICHOL
Host church Australia
Australia
Uniting Church

Mr. BRUCE NICHOLLS
Fraternal delegate WEF
New Zealand
Baptist Church

Fr. AUGUSTIN NIKITIN
Advisor
USSR
Russian Orthodox Church

Rev. NYANSAKO-NI NKU
Delegate
Cameroon
Presbyterian Church

Dr. WILLIAM J. NOTTINGHAM
Advisor
USA
Disciples of Christ

Ms. DINAH NSEIR
Delegate
Lebanon
National Evangelical Church

Bishop BENJAMIN NWANKITI
Delegate
Nigeria
Anglican Church

Ms. DAISY OBI
Delegate
Nigeria
Anglican Church

Ms. MARIA ELIZABETH O'DONOGHUE
Observer RC
New Zealand
Roman Catholic Church

Bishop HENRY OKULLU
Advisor
Kenya
Anglican Church

Fr. MICHAEL OLEKSA
Delegate
USA
Orthodox Church in America

Rev. DUANE ALLAN OLSON
Advisor
USA
American Lutheran Church

Rev. GOTTFRIED OSEI-MENSAH
Fraternal delegate LCWE
Kenya
Baptist Church

Metropolitan GEEVARGHESE OSTHATHIOS
Delegate
India
Orthodox Church of India

Rev. JAMES OTTERNESS
Advisor
USA
American Lutheran Church

Ms. ELISABETH OTTMUELLER
Delegate
FRG
Evang. Church

Mr. ANIVALDO PADILHA
Fraternal delegate FIM
Brazil/Switzerland
Methodist Church

Mr. WASHINGTON PADILLA
Advisor
Ecuador
Lutheran Church

Bishop FEDERICO PAGURA
Delegate
Argentina
Methodist Church

Rev. Dr. DAUD PALILU
Delegate
Indonesia
Indonesian Christian Church

Rev. HYUNG KYU PARK
Advisor
Korea
Presbyterian Church

Rev. JAY BONG PARK
Delegate
Korea
Presbyterian Church

Rt. Rev. CYRIL PAUL
Delegate
Trinidad
Presbyterian Church

Mr. STEPHEN PAYTON
Host church New Zealand
New Zealand
Baptist Church

Ms. SHANTI PEIRIS
Delegate
Sri Lanka
Methodist Church

Ms. DOMINGA PEREZ RODRIGUEZ
Delegate
Puerto Rico
Episcopalian Church

Rev. WALTER PERSSON
Delegate
Sweden
Mission Covenant Church of Sweden

Rev. RUBIN PHILLIP
Delegate
South Africa
Anglican Church

Ms. OUTI PIIROINEN
Delegate
Finland

Dr. CLARK H. PINNOCK
Advisor
Canada
Baptist Church

Rev. TARA PITOMAKI
Delegate
Cook Islands
Christian Church

Mr. SAMUEL PONRAJ
Delegate
India
Church of South India

Rev. MAURICE PONT
Delegate
France
Reformed Church

Very Rev. ALEXANDER POPOV
Delegate
Bulgaria/Australia
Bulgarian Eastern Orthodox Church

Metropolitan DIONYSIOS PSIAHAS
Special guest
New Zealand
Orthodox Church

Mr. DAVID PURNELL
Host church Australia
Australia
Religious Society of Friends

Rev. NORMAN PRITCHARD
Special guest
Australia

Mr. JUAN QUEVEDO
Delegate
Cuba

Mr. MANUEL QUINTERO PEREZ
Advisor
Cuba/Mexico
Presbyterian Church

Rev. NOËL RABEMANANTSOA
Delegate
Madagascar
Lutheran Church

Rev. Ms. YVETTE RABEMILA
Delegate
Madagascar
Church of Jesus Christ

Rev. VICTOR RAKOTOARIMANANA
Delegate
Madagascar/France
Reformed Church

Rev. RICHARD RAKOTONDRAIBE
Fraternal delegate AACC
Madagascar/Togo
United Church of Jesus Christ

Rev. KENNETH RALPH
Advisor
Australia

Rev. JEAN RAMONI
Delegate
Switzerland
Reformed Church

Ms. J. RASOLO RAHELIARISOA
Delegate
Madagascar
Church of Jesus Christ

Mr. SERGEY RASSKAZOVSKY
Advisor
USSR
Orthodox Church

Bishop PEDRO RATERTA
Delegate
Philippines
United Church of Christ

Bishop JOHN ROBERT REID
Fraternal delegate LCWE
Australia
Anglican Church

Fr. JOHN REILLY
Observer RC
Australia
Roman Catholic Church

Präses Dr. HEINRICH REISS
Delegate
FRG

Dr. BENTON RHOADES
Advisor
USA

Ms. RUBY RHOADES
Delegate
USA
Church of the Brethren

Mr. JULIAN RIKLON
Host church Pacific
Marshall Islands

Dr. NEGAIL RILEY
Advisor
USA
Methodist Church

Mr. DENIS WAWERU RIMUI
Delegate
Kenya
Presbyterian Church

Rev. JUAN MARCOS RIVERA
Delegate
Puerto Rico
Disciples of Christ

Dr. WILLIAM ROBERTS
Advisor
Australia

Ms. MARIA ROCCHIETTI
Delegate
Uruguay
Methodist Church

Deaconess MARGARET RODGERS
Host church Australia
Australia
Anglican Church

Rev. SEBASTIAN RODRIGUEZ-GOMEZ
Delegate
Spain
Evangelical Church

Rev. SIGRID ROEMELT
Delegate
FRG

Ms. WENDY ROSE
Fraternal delegate YWCA
Australia
Anglican Church

Lt. Col. ARTHUR ROTHWELL
Delegate
Australia
Salvation Army

Mr. K. RRURRAMBO
Host church Australia
Australia

Lic. JERJES RUIZ CASTRO
Delegate
Nicaragua
Baptist Church

Mr. ABRAHAM SAHETAPY ENGEL
Delegate
Indonesia

Rev. GEORGE W. SAILS
Fraternal delegate WM
Great Britain
Methodist Church

Ms. LETICIA SALONGA
Delegate
Philippines
Alpha & Omega Church Iemelip

Ms. VIVIENNE SAMBUBA
Delegate
Papua New Guinea
Anglican Church

Ms. DORINDA SAMPATH
Advisor
Trinidad
Presbyterian Church

Rev. CARLOS SANCHEZ
Delegate
El Salvador

Rev. PETER SANDNER
Delegate
FRG
Evangelical Church

Mr. PRITAM B. SANTRAM
Delegate
India
Church of North India

Mr. JOSÉ SARACCO
Delegate
Argentina
Pentecostal Church

Rev. HERBERT SCHEKATZ
Fraternal delegate EUKUMINDO
FRG

Prof. JAMES SCHERER
Advisor
USA
Lutheran Church in America

Prof. RUDOLF SCHNACKENBURG
Observer RC
FRG
Roman Catholic Church

Ms. MARIA SCHNEIDER
Fraternal delegate EYCE
GDR
Lutheran Church

Rev. JÖRG SCHNELLBACH
Delegate
FRG
Evangelical Church

Rev. ECKHARD SCHÜLZGEN
Advisor
GDR
Evangelical Church Berlin-Brandenburg

Mr. WALDRON SCOTT
Fraternal delegate WEF
USA
United Presbyterian Church

Mr. JUAN SEPULVEDA GONZALEZ
Delegate
Chile
Pentecostal Church

Rev. TSUTOMU SHOJI
Delegate
Japan
United Church of Christ

Rev. SOHAN LALL SIDDIQ
Delegate
Pakistan
Church of Pakistan

Rev. CARLOS SINTADO
Advisor
Argentina
Methodist Church

Fr. TATAU SIOPE
Delegate
Tonga
Roman Catholic Church

Rev. CALVIN SIPAYUNG
Delegate
Indonesia
Protestant Christian Church

Fr. DRAGONIZ SIPOVAC
Delegate
USSR
Russian Orthodox Church

Ms. JEAN SKUSE
Special guest
Australia

Rev. DONALD SMITH
Host church Australia
Australia
Churches of Christ

Sr. GABRIEL SMYTH
Observer RC
Australia
Roman Catholic Church

Mrs. SRI SETIJATI SOEDITO
Observer RC
Indonesia
Roman Catholic Church

Archpriest GEBRE S. SOLOMON
Delegate
Ethiopia
Ethiopian Orthodox Church

Rev. KNUD SØRENSEN
Delegate
Denmark
Evangelical Lutheran Church

Rev. PABLO SOSA
Advisor
Argentina
Methodist Church

Rev. ONELL SOTO
Advisor
Cuba/USA
Episcopal Church

Dr ARNE SOVIK
Fraternal delegate LWF
USA/Switzerland
American Lutheran Church

Rev. HOWARD E. SPRAGG
Advisor
USA
United Church of Christ

Rev. CHRISTA SPRINGE
Advisor
FRG
Evangelical Church

Rev. REINER STAHL
Delegate
FRG
United Methodist Church

DEAN GUNNAR STÅLSETT
Advisor
Norway
Lutheran Church

Prof. KRISTER STENDHAL
Advisor
USA
Lutheran Church in America

Rev. Ms. BARBARA STEPHENS
Delegate
New Zealand
Ass. Churches of Christ

Dr. EUGENE STOCKWELL
Delegate
USA
United Methodist Church

Mr. ALEXEI STOIAN
Delegate *Baptist*
USSR

Dr. DAVID STOWE
Delegate
USA
United Church of Christ

Fr. TOM STRANSKY
Observer RC
USA
Roman Catholic Church

Archbishop STYLIANOS
Delegate
Australia
Greek Orthodox Church

Mr. FESTUS F. SURUMA
Delegate
Solomon Islands

Archpriest Prof. JAROSLAV ŠUVARSKÝ
Delegate
Czechoslovakia
Orthodox Church

Rev. KIREE TABAI
Host church Pacific
Fiji

Ms. MELE TAGOA'I KEILANI
Delegate
Samoa
Congregational Christian Church

Mr. TOSHIHIRO TAKAMI
Delegate
Japan
United Church of Christ

Rev. P. TALAGI
Host church Pacific
Niue Island

Rev. EDWIN TAYLOR
Delegate
Bahamas
Methodist Church

Bishop JOHN V. TAYLOR
Advisor
Great Britain
Anglican Church

Ms. SHARMEN TAYLOR
Delegate
USA
United Presbyterian Church

Ms. YVETTE TEMAURI
Delegate
Tahiti

Mr. RUUNGUKHO TERHUJA
Delegate
India
Baptist Church

Rev. KLAUS TESCHNER
Delegate
FRG
Protestant Church

Dir. U KYAW THAN
Advisor
Burma

Rev. MICHAEL THAWLEY
Host church New Zealand
New Zealand
Presbyterian Church

Mr. AARON THOAHLANE
Delegate
Lesotho
Evangelical Church

Rev. Dr. ROBERT THOMAS
Delegate
USA
Christian Church (Disciples)

Ms. PHYLLIS THOMPSON
Delegate
Great Britain
New Testament Church of God

Rev. BERNARD THOROGOOD
Delegate
Great Britain
United Reformed Church

Rev. Dr. PAUL A. TOASPERN
Delegate
GDR
Evangelical Church

Ms. CATHY TODD
Guest
USA/Switzerland
United Presbyterian Church

Bishop RAMON TORRELLA
Observer RC
Spain/Italy
Roman Catholic Church

Mr. JOSÉ TORRES PEREZ
Delegate
Nicaragua
Primera Iglesia Bautista

Archimandrite SOTIRIOS TRAMBAS
Delegate
Greece/Korea
Ecumenical Patriarchate

Prof. SAUL TRINIDAD CULLIGOS
Advisor
Peru/Costa Rica
Evangelical Church of Peru

Rev. W. GEOFFREY TUCKER
Delegate
New Zealand
Methodist Church

Rev. TUN MEH
Delegate
Burma
Baptist Church

Mr. U TUN ZIN
Delegate
Burma
Methodist Church

Rev. MICHEL TWAGIRAYESU
Fraternal delegate EPR
Rwanda
Presbyterian Church

Rev. REIN JAN VAN DER VEEN
Delegate
Netherlands
Reformed Church in the Netherlands

Rev. Mrs. JOKE VAN DER VELDEN
Delegate
Netherlands
Dutch Reformed Church

Rev. GUSTAVO VELASCO GUEVARA
Delegate
Mexico
Methodist Church

Mr. FRANS VERSTRAELEN
Fraternal delegate IAMS
Netherlands

Mr. JÜRGEN VOGELS
Delegate
FRG
Protestant Church

Rev. ANTHON VOS
Advisor
Netherlands
Reformed Church

Rev. PER-ÅKE WAHLSTRÖM
Delegate
Sweden
Swedish Baptist Church

Dr. ALAN WALKER
Fraternal delegate WM
Australia
Methodist Church

Rev. GEORGE WAN TIAN SOO
Delegate
Malaysia/Singapore
Methodist Church

Rev. NELSO WEINGÄRTNER
Delegate
Brazil
Lutheran Church

Rev. H. JEAN WETE
Delegate
New Caledonia
Evangelical Church

Ms. MARY E. WHALE
Delegate
Canada
Presbyterian Church

Mr. JOSEF PURNAMA WIDYATMADJA
Advisor
Indonesia
Reformed Church

Mr. AISAKE WILIAME
Delegate
Fiji

Rev. JAMES WILKIE
Advisor
Great Britain
Church of Scotland

Fr. CHRISTOPHER WILLCOCK
Advisor
Australia/France
Roman Catholic Church

Deacon TADESSE WOLDEGEBREAL
Delegate
Ethiopia/FRG
Ethiopian Orthodox Church

Brother WOLFGANG
Advisor
FRG/France
Taizé Communauté

Rev. SAMRIT WONGSANG
Delegate
Thailand
Church of Christ

Dr. KIM HAO YAP
Delegate
Malaysia/Singapore
Methodist Church

Prof. JOHN YODER
Advisor
USA
Mennonite Church

Rev. EUN PYO YONG
Delegate
Korea
Methodist Church

Rt. Rev. DAVID YOUNG
Delegate
Great Britain
Anglican Church

Rev. Dr. GEORGE YOUNGER
Advisor
USA
American Baptist Churches

Rev. GERMAN ZIJLSTRA
Delegate
Argentina
Reformed Church

WCC Staff and Co-opted Staff

Rev. IAN ALLSOP
Australia
Churches of Christ

Mrs. CAROLE ANDERSON
Australia
Uniting Church

Rev. CLIVE AYRE
Australia

Ms. NITA BARROW
WCC/Christian Medical Commission
Barbados
Methodist Church

Rev. JEAN-JACQUES BAUSWEIN
WCC/Press Section
France
Evangelical Church of the Augsburg
Confession in Alsace and Lorraine

Rev. ARNOLD BITTLINGER
FRG/Switzerland
Reformed Church

Pastor ALAIN BLANCY
WCC/Ecumenical Institute Bossey
FRG/France
French Reformed Church

Rev. JOHN BLUCK
WCC/Press Section
New Zealand
Anglican Church

Prof. ION BRIA
CWME
Roumania
Roumanian Orthodox Church

Rev. GORDON BROWN
Australia

Rev. THÉODORE BUSS
Interpreter
Switzerland
Reformed Church

Ms. CECILIA CABRAL
CWME
Netherlands
Roman Catholic

Ms. GWEN CASHMORE
CWME
Great Britain
Anglican Church

Rev. EMILIO CASTRO
CWME
Uruguay
Methodist Church

Rev. HAMISH CHRISTIE-JOHNSTON
Australia
Uniting Church

Rev. GARY CLARKE
Australia

Rev. ALDO COMBA
Italy/Switzerland
Waldensian Church

Rev. MARTIN CONWAY
Translator
Great Britain
Anglican Church

Rev. FRANK CUTTRISS
Australia

Archbishop ROBERT DANN
Australia

Rev. DOUG DARGAVILLE
Australia

Mrs. ELISABETH DELMONTE
Interpreter
Uruguay
Waldensian Church

Pastor PIERRE DURAND
Translator
France
Reformed Church

Mrs. TOMOKO EVDOKIMOFF
WCC/Language Service
Japan
Orthodox Church

Mr. ROBERT FAERBER
Interpreter
France
Lutheran Church

Mr. JEAN FISCHER
WCC/CICARWS
Switzerland
Protestant Church

Rev. Dr. DOUGLAS FULLERTON
Australia
Uniting Church

Rev. DAVID GILL
Australia
Uniting Church

Mr. SERGUEI GORDEEV
Interpreter
USSR
Orthodox Church

Rev. ROBERT GRIBBEN
Australia

Dr. GERHARD HOFFMANN
FRG
United Church

Rev. PETER HOLDEN
Australia

Mr. DON HOLMES
Australia

Mr. LEON HOWELL
USA

Ms. SARA IRIZARRY
Interpreter
Puerto Rico

Rev. ROSS KINSLER
WCC/Programme on Theological
Education
USA
United Presbyterian Church

Mr. SAM KOBIA
CWME
Kenya
Methodist Church

Dr. JOHN W. ZVOMUNONDITA KUREWA
CWME
Zimbabwe
United Methodist Church

Mr. Ninos Lambrou
Australia

Ms. Pat Languiller
Australia

Dr. William Lazareth
WCC/Faith and Order
USA
Lutheran Church in America

Dr. Samuel Lee
Interpreter
Korea/FRG
Presbyterian Church in Korea

Mr. Hartwig Liebich
FRG

Mr. Porfirio Martinez-Laboy
Interpreter
Puerto Rico
Roman Catholic Church

Rev. Alan Matheson
WCC/Migration
Australia
Churches of Christ

Mr. Jacques Matthey
CWME
Switzerland
Protestant Church

Mr. Ezra Mbogori
CWME
Kenya
Methodist Church

Mrs. Frances McKechnie
Australia

Mrs. D. McMahon
Australia

Fr. Stelios Menis
Australia
Greek Orthodox Church

Mr. Peter Moss
WCC/Youth Department
Great Britain
Presbyterian Church in Ireland

Mr. Pontas Nasution
CWME
Indonesia
Lutheran Church

Rev. John W. Newbury
Great Britain
Methodist Church

Rev. George Ninan
India/Hong Kong
Church of North India

Ms. Zenaida Nosova
Interpreter
USSR
Russian Orthodox Church

Mr. Luis Enrique Odell
Translator
Spain
Methodist Church

Rev. Connie Parvey
WCC/Faith and Order
USA
Lutheran Church in America

Ms. Margaret Pater
WCC, interpreter
Great Britain/Switzerland
Methodist Church

Mr. Harvey Perkins
Australia/Singapore
Uniting Church in Australia

Dr. Philip Potter
WCC/General Secretariat
Dominica
Methodist Church

Ms. Dawn Ross
CWME
Canada
Presbyterian Church

Prof. Todor Sabev
WCC/General Secretariat
Bulgarian Orthodox Church

Rev. Eunice Santana de Velez (Ms.)
Translator
Puerto Rico

Schuldekan Ernst Schmidt
Translator
FRG
Evangelical Church

Ms. JEAN E. SCHMIDT
Finance
USA
Reformed Church in America

Ms. THELMA SKILLER
Australia

Ms. RUTH SOVIK
CWME
American Lutheran Church
USA

Mr. KOSON SRISANG
WCC/Churches' Participation in
Development
Thailand
Church of Christ

Rev. BERN STEVENS
Australia

Ms. JEAN STROMBERG
CWME
USA
Lutheran Church *Baptist*

Rev. ROBBINS STRONG
USA
United Church of Christ

Mr. LAWRIE STYLES
Australia

Dr. JOHN B. TAYLOR
WCC/Dialogue with people of living
faiths and ideologies
Great Britain
Methodist Church

Ms. BRIGITTE THALER
WCC/Conference secr.
FRG
Roman Catholic Church

Mr. T. K. THOMAS
India/Singapore
Mar Thoma Church

Rev. GEORGE TODD
CWME
USA
United Presbyterian Church

Ms. DENISE TOERNER
CWME
Switzerland
Reformed Church

Mr. WILLIAM VELEZ-SOTOMAYOR
Interpreter
Puerto Rico
Episcopalian Church

Mrs. MICHELINE VILLEBRUN
Interpreter
Switzerland/Australia
Reformed Church

Mr. MSTISLAV VOSKRESSENSKI
Interpreter
USSR
Orthodox Church

Mgr. BRIAN WALSH
Australia
Roman Catholic Church

Rev. DAVID WEBSTER
Australia

Ms. RENATE WIEDEMANN
Translator
FRG/Australia

Dr. THOMAS WIESER
Switzerland
Protestant Church

Rev. MARC-ANDRÉ WOLFF
Translator
France
Evangelical Church of the Augsburg
Confession in Alsace and Lorraine

Ms. ANN WYNDHAM-WHITE
CWME
Great Britain
Episcopalian Church

Rev. LOURDINO YUZON
Philippines/Singapore
United Church of Christ

Prof. NIKOLAI ZABOLOTSKI
WCC/Churches' Participation in
Development
USSR
Russian Orthodox Church

Ms. URSULA ZIERL
CWME, interpreter
FRG
Lutheran Church

Stewards

Mr. BENNY ACE
Indonesia

Mr. RICHARD AMOOTI MUTAZINDWA
Uganda
Anglican Church

Mr. ALISTAIR ARENDS
South Africa
United Congregational Church

Mr. BIBHUTI BALA
Bangladesh

Mr. MICHAEL BARNES
Australia
Uniting Church

Mr. MICHAEL BROWN
Australia
Uniting Church

Ms. KATHI BÜRKI
Switzerland
Reformed Church

Ms. ELIZABETH BURNARD
Australia
Uniting Church

Ms. MANDY CALDWELL
Australia

Rev. JOHN CLEGHORN
Australia

Ms. JENNY DARBYSHIRE
Australia
Uniting Church

Ms. IRENE DE VRIES
Australia
Uniting Church

Mr. CHARLIE DJORDILA
Australia

Ms. EDITH ENOGA
Papua New Guinea

Ms. CATHLEEN FLUTER
Canada
United Church

Ms. NOEMI FRIAS
Philippines
Roman Catholic Church

Mr. CHRIS GARDINER
Australia

Mr. STEPHEN GENTLE
USA

Mr. MICHAEL GLASER
FRG
Lutheran Church

Ms. GUNILLA GUNNER
Sweden
Covenant Church of Sweden

Ms. GRO HAAVERSEN-BARTH
Norway
Lutheran Church

Rev. BARANIKE KIRATA
Fiji

Ms. KRISTINA KIRSCHNER
FRG
Lutheran Church

Rev. WILLIAM KLOSSNER
USA
Congregational United Church
of Christ

Mr. BONNY KYALIGONZA
Uganda
Roman Catholic Church

Ms. PATRICIA LLOYD
USA
United Presbyterian Church

Ms. ROSEMARY LLOYD
Australia
Uniting Church

Mr. GERALD MAHAI
Fiji

Mr. ERIC MCGILL
Australia
Uniting Church

Ms. LIB MCGREGOR SIMMONS
USA
Presbyterian Church

Ms. HEATHER MCMINN
Australia

Mr. DAVID MIRAWANA
Australia

Mr. JOBSON MISANG
Papua New Guinea
United Church

Mr. PAUL OROBAL MONDLE
Bangladesh
Church of Bangladesh

Mr. CAMERON NICHOL
Australia
Uniting Church

Ms. RUTH NICHOLSON
Australia
Uniting Church

Ms. RINSKE NIJENDIJK-CNOSSEN
Netherlands
Dutch Reformed Church

Ms. LESILA RAITIQA
Fiji

Mr. LUCIEN RANDRIAMAMPIONONA
Madagascar

Mr. GREG ROSS
Australia
Uniting Church

Ms. EVA SANDBORG
Sweden

Mr. HERMAN SHASTRI
Malaysia
Methodist Church

Mr. PHILIP SIDLE
USA
United Methodist Church

Ms. KARIN SPORRE
Sweden
Covenant Church of Sweden

Rev. RHODRI THOMAS
Great Britain
Congregational Church

Mr. ROBERT THORPE

Mr. GEORGE TUINUKUAFE
Fiji

Mr. RUUD WITTE
Netherlands

Press

Mr. EDUARD ABEL
Switzerland

Mr. COLIN ALCOCK
Australia

Mr. HARTMUT ALBRUSCHAT
FRG

Mr. C. R. AMBROSE
Australia

Dr. JOHN ANAND
India

Ms. M. ANDERMO-JOHANSSON
Sweden

Mr. ALAN AUSTIN
Australia

Mrs. PAT BAKER
Australia

Mr. ROBERT BARRETT
Australia

Mr. PETER BERGWERFF
Netherlands

Ms. B. BOLTON
Australia

Mr. G. BONAFEDE
FRG

Mr. SENZA MASA BONGEYE
Togo

Mr. F. C. BORLONGAN
Philippines

Mr. FRANS BOUWEN
Netherlands

Ms. PAULINE BROEKEMA
Netherlands

Mr. JAN J. VAN CAPELLEVEEN
Netherlands

Mr. JÉRÔME CARLOS
Senegal

Bishop PUI-YEUNG CHEUNG
Taiwan

Mr. L. H. WARREN CLARNETTE
Australia

Rev. J. COLEMAN
Australia

Ms. JUDITH COLLINS
Kenya

Mr. JACQUES COUSOUYAN
France

Rev. COLVILLE CROWE
Australia

Rev. A. DE GRAAF
Australia

Mr. FRANK LLOYD DENT
USA

Mr. OTTO DILGER
FRG

Mr. CAESAR D'MELLO
Philippines

Mr. COLOMBO DOMENICO
Italy

Mr. GOTTFRIED EDEL
FRG

Mr. JAN FILIUS
Netherlands

Mr. HANS-JOACHIM GIROCK
FRG

Mr. GEORGE W. GISH
Japan

Mr. ARTHUR GLASSER
USA

Mr. JAN GREVEN
Netherlands

Mrs. JOYCE GRIMMETT
Fiji

Mr. MICHAEL HANSEN
Australia

Mr. EDWARD W. HEARD
Australia

Mr. VOLKER HOCHGREBE
FRG

Mr. HARVEY HOEKSTRA
USA

Ms. RUTH IHLE
Australia

Mr. HANS-NORBERT JANOWSKI
FRG

Mr. PETER JESSE
Switzerland

Rev. WARD KAISER
USA

Mr. MICHAEL KELLY
Australia

Ms. HANNU KILPELAINEN
Australia

Mr. DAVID KINGDOM
Australia

Mr. HELGE KJØLLESDAL
Norway

Mr. ANDRIES G. KNEVEL
Netherlands

Rev. ATTILA KOMLOS
Hungary

Mr. BRUNO KROKER
USA

Mr. REINHARD KUSTER
Switzerland

Mr. CREIGHTON LACY
USA

Mr. ALBERT LONGCHAMP
Switzerland

Mr. GÜNTER LORENZ
GDR

Mr. JOHN MACKENZIE
Australia

Rev. ANGUS MACLEOD
New Zealand

Mr. BASEILA MBEKO
Zaire

Dr. CARL McINTYRE
USA

Ms. K. McLENNAN
Australia

McMASTER
USA

Mr. JOHN MILLHEIM
USA

Mr. DAVID MOL
Netherlands

Mr. W. D. MÜLLER-RÖMHELD
FRG

Ms. MBUYU NALUMANGO
Zambia

Mr. BRUCE C. NICHOLLS
India

Mr. JOHN NICHOLSON
Australia

Mr. KJELL OWE NILSSON
Sweden

Sr. HELEN O'BRIEN
Papua New Guinea

Mr. KARL ALFRED ODIN
FRG

Mr. ØIVIND ØSTANG
Norway

Mr. VYACHESLAV OVSYANNIKOV
USSR

Mr. DAVID PEEL
Australia

Mr. H. A. PFLASTERER
FRG

Rev. ROBERT PLANT
Canada

Rev. K. C. QUEK
Singapore

Mr. CECILINE RAUL
FRG

Mr. CORNISH R. ROGERS
USA

Mr. RUSSELL ROLLASON
Australia

Mr. JOHN RONNÅS
Sweden

Mr. OWEN SALTER
Australia

Mr. F. C. SCHILLING
FRG

A. SCHIPPER
Netherlands

Dr. Ms. VIOLA SCHMID
FRG

Mr. WILHELM SCHMIDT
FRG

Mr. GARRY SHEERAN
Australia

Mr. BONAR SIMORANGKIR
Indonesia

Fr. T. SOUTHERWOOD
Australia

Mr. BERNARD SPONG
South Africa

Mr. JOHN STAPERT
USA

Mr. DOUG TASKER
Australia

Prof. K. M. THARAKAN
India

Dr. NORMAN THOMAS
USA

Mr. PETER THOMAS
Australia

Mr. GREG THOMPSON
Australia

Dr. PETER TOON
Great Britain

Mr. ALFREDO TORRES PACHON
Columbia

Mr. BRUCE UPTON
Australia

Dr. J. VERMAAT
Netherlands

Mr. VINCENTE OSCAR VETRANO
Argentina

Rev. FRED WAINE
New Zealand

Fr. P. K. WALCOT
Papua New Guinea

Mr. B. WENHAM
Australia

Mr. ROGER WIIG
Australia

Ms. JOYCE WILLIAMS
Australia

Mr. HELMUT WINTER
FRG

Mr. RUUD F. WITTE
Netherlands

Bibliography of Conference materials published by CWME

Preparatory papers
— Invitation to Christians
— Bible Study texts, stimulating regional production
— Initial theological exploration of the kingdom theme
— History of the world conferences on mission.

Reflection of groups and individuals from many parts of the world on the theme and the sub-themes of the conference

No. 1 Donald Black, USA, Your Kingdom come: Mission and Power
— No. 2 A Melanesian Contribution:
    Leslie Boseto, The Kingdom of God and Stages in my Personal Experience
    Timo Ani, What does "Your Kingdom Come" mean to us in Melanesia?
    Albert ToBurua, "Your Kingdom Come" — A Protestant View
    Sr. Wendy Flannery, "Your Kingdom Come" — A Roman Catholic View
    Dick Avi, Seeking the Kingdom of God — Cargo Cult Perspective
— No. 3 Ronald J. Sider, USA, The Cross and Violence
— No. 4 Christian Conference of Asia, Singapore, booklet "Witnessing to the Kingdom" (articles by Samuel Rayan, Kosuke Koyama, Emerito Nacpil, Raymond Fung, Ruth Page, Tsutomu Shoji, George Ninan, Nicolaas Rose, B. J. Prashantham, Victor San Lone, Korea and Philippines)
— No. 5 Norwegian Study Group, Your Kingdom Come
— No. 6 Roman Catholic Church, Secretariat for Promoting Christian Unity, Your Kingdom Come
— No. 7 Metropolitan Geevarghese Mar Osthathios, India, Lessons from a Tea-Estate
— No. 8 Ametefe Nomenyo, Togo, A Voice from Africa
    Michel Bouttier, Togo, "Blessed are the Poor..."
— No. 9 The Netherlands Missionary Council, The Power and the Cross
— No. 10 Theological Commission of the Evangelical Missionary Agency, FRG, Our Missionary Task in the Federal Republic of Germany

— No. 11 Contributions from Latin America (pre-Melbourne conference)
     Philippines (Bicutan Political Detainees)
     FRG (Martin Lehmann-Habeck)
     Africa (Study Group)
— No. 12 Submitted stories on the Kingdom theme.

Conference Agenda, Your Kingdom Come

International Review of Mission
— July 1978   : Edinburgh to Melbourne
— January 1979: Australia
— April 1979   : Your Kingdom Come
— October 1979: The Kingdom of God and Human Struggles
— January 1980: The Kingdom and Power
— April 1980   : The Church Witnesses to the Kingdom
— July 1980   : Melbourne Conference Notes
— October 1980/
   January 1981: Melbourne Reports and Reflections

Music, Meditation, Prayers for Mission: a Risk Book Series publication on worship from Melbourne